HOW QUALITATIVE DATA ANALYSIS HAPPENS

How is qualitative data actually collected, analyzed, and accomplished? Real stories of *How Qualitative Data Analysis Happens: Moving Beyond "Themes Emerged"* offers an in-depth look into how qualitative social science researchers studying family issues and dynamics approach their data analyses. It moves beyond the usual vague statement of "themes emerged from the data" to show readers how researchers actively and consciously arrive at their themes and conclusions, revealing the complexity and time involved in making sense of thousands of pages of interview data, multiple data sources, and diverse types of data.

How Qualitative Data Analysis Happens focuses on a diversity of topics in family research across the life course. The various authors provide detailed narratives into how they analyzed their data from previous publications and what methodologies they used, ranging from arts-based research, autoethnography, community-based participatory research, ethnography, grounded theory, to narrative analysis.

Supplemental figures, images, and screenshots, which are referred to in the chapters, are included in an accompanying eResource, as well as links to the previously published work on which the chapters are based. This book is an invaluable resource for experienced and novice qualitative researchers throughout the social sciences.

Áine M. Humble is Professor in Family Studies and Gerontology at Mount Saint Vincent University, in Halifax, Nova Scotia, Canada.

M. Elise Radina is Professor in Family Science and Social Work at Miami University in Oxford, Ohio, USA.

HOW QUALITATIVE DATA ANALYSIS HAPPENS

Moving Beyond "Themes Emerged"

Edited by Áine M. Humble and M. Elise Radina

Routledge
Taylor & Francis Group

NEW YORK AND LONDON

First published 2019
by Routledge
52 Vanderbilt Avenue, New York, NY 10017

and by Routledge
2 Park Square, Milton Park, Abingdon, Oxon, OX14 4RN

Routledge is an imprint of the Taylor & Francis Group, an informa business

© 2019 Taylor & Francis

The right of Áine M. Humble, and M. Elise Radina to be identified as the authors of the editorial material, and of the authors for their individual chapters, has been asserted in accordance with sections 77 and 78 of the Copyright, Designs and Patents Act 1988.

Trademark notice: Product or corporate names may be trademarks or registered trademarks, and are used only for identification and explanation without intent to infringe.

Library of Congress Cataloging-in-Publication Data
A catalog record for this book has been requested

ISBN: 978-1-138-04465-4 (hbk)
ISBN: 978-1-138-04467-8 (pbk)
ISBN: 978-1-315-17164-7 (ebk)

Typeset in Bembo
by Apex CoVantage, LLC

Visit the eResource: www.routledge.com/9781138044678

CONTENTS

TABLES

FIGURES

ACKNOWLEDGMENTS

We would like to thank the entire team at Taylor & Francis for their support and assistance throughout this process. We are also grateful to Katie Guban, who provided us with administrative support during the process of compiling all the details of this book; and Dr. Katherine Kuvalanka for her careful reading and thoughtful feedback. Finally, we both know that work such as this takes time and energy. We are therefore grateful to our families, colleagues, and friends for their unwavering support to us both.

EDITORS

Áine M. Humble, PhD, CFLE
Professor
Department of Family Studies and Gerontology
Mount Saint Vincent University
Halifax, Nova Scotia, Canada

Áine Humble carries out primarily qualitative research in family studies and in gerontology. Her research interests focus on family dynamics related to family rituals and transitions, in particular the transition to marriage, and in recent years, she has studied same-sex couples and LGBT aging issues. Secondary research interests are older women and healthy aging, qualitative research methods, and computer-assisted qualitative data analysiS (CAQDAS) software programs. She has published her work in scholarly journals such as the *Canadian Journal on Aging*, *Family Relations*, *Journal of Family Theory & Review*, *Journal of GLBT Family Studies*, and the *Journal of Woman & Aging*. She has served on the Editorial Board for *Family Relations*, and she is an Editorial Assistant for *Forum Qualitative Sozialforschung/Forum: Qualitative Social Research*. Dr. Humble also provides introductory and advanced training on MAXQDA software through her consulting company, Fada Research Consulting, facilitating full-day training workshops since 2009 to academic and government audiences.

M. Elise Radina, PhD, CFLE
Professor and Chair
Department of Family Science and Social Work
Miami University
Oxford, Ohio

Elise Radina is a qualitative methodologist whose research focuses broadly on families and health. Specifically, her research primarily focuses on mid- and later-life women in family contexts (e.g., breast cancer survivorship, positive aging, breast cancer-related lymphedema). More recently she and her student research team have turned their attention to understanding the experiences of parents who are raising children with primary lymphedema. She has published over 40 peer-reviewed articles that have appeared in scholarly journals. In 2012, she co-edited a special issue of the *Journal of Family Theory & Review* on "Qualitative Methodology, Theory, and Research in Family Studies," and she serves on the *Journal of Family Theory & Review* Editorial Board.

CONTRIBUTORS

Katherine R. Allen, PhD
Professor
Department of Human Development and Family Science
Virginia Tech
Blacksburg, VA

Liciane Alves, BS
Graduate Student
George Mason University
Fairfax, VA

Mary M. Ball, PhD
Assistant Professor
Division of General Medicine and Geriatrics
Department of Medicine
Emory University School of Medicine
Atlanta, GA

H. Daniel Castellanos, DrPH
Director of Research and Evaluation
Partnership for the Homeless
New York City, NY

Andrea Doucet, PhD
Canada Research Chair in Gender, Work and Care
Professor
Sociology and Women's and Gender Studies
Brock University
St. Catherines, Ontario, Canada

Laura Golojuch, MS
Doctoral Candidate
Family Science Department
University of Maryland
College Park, MD

Rachael D. Goodman, PhD, LPC
Associate Professor
Counseling and Development Program
George Mason University
Fairfax, VA

John R. Hart, PhD, LGMFT
Scientific Research Consultant
Public Health and Research Services
Greenbelt, MD

Gwen Katheryn Healey, PhD
Executive and Scientific Director
Qaujigiartiit Health Research Center
Iqaluit, Nunavut

Tyler Jamison, PhD
Assistant Professor
Human Development and Family Studies Department
University of New Hampshire
Durham, NH

Candace L. Kemp, PhD
Associate Professor
The Gerontology Institute and Sociology Department
Georgia State University
Atlanta, GA

Wendy E. Lazo, BS
Research Assistant
George Mason University
Fairfax, VA

Bethany L. Letiecq, PhD
Associate Professor
Human Development and Family Science
George Mason University
Fairfax, VA

Marlene Marquez, MASW
Alexandria City Family Service Specialist
Alexandria, VA

Roberto C. Martinez, MEd
Research Assistant
George Mason University
Fairfax, VA

Evonne Miller, PhD
Associate Professor
Director, QUT Design Lab
Creative Industries Faculty, Queensland University of Technology
Brisbane, Queensland, Australia

Molly M. Perkins, PhD
Assistant Professor
Division of General Medicine and Geriatrics
Department of Medicine
Emory University School of Medicine
Atlanta, GA

Karen A. Roberto, PhD
University Distinguished Professor
Director, Institute for Society, Culture and Environment
Senior Fellow, Center for Gerontology
Virginia Tech
Blacksburg, VA

Paul C. Rosenblatt, PhD
Professor Emeritus
Family Social Science Department
University of Minnesota
Minneapolis, MN

Kevin Roy, PhD
Associate Professor
Family Science Department
University of Maryland
College Park, MD

Katherine E. Speirs, PhD
Extension Specialist and Assistant Professor
Norton School of Family and Consumer Sciences
University of Arizona
Tucson, AZ

Andrea Swenson, PhD
Assistant Professor
Human Development and Family Studies Department
University of Wisconsin-Stout
Menomonie, WI

Colleen K. Vesely, PhD
Assistant Professor
College of Education and Human Development
George Mason University
Fairfax, VA

Marcus B. Weaver-Hightower, PhD
Professor
Educational Foundations and Research
University of North Dakota
Grand Forks, ND

Elizabeth Wieling, PhD
Associate Professor
Family Social Science Department
University of Minnesota
Minneapolis, MN

Anisa Zvonkovic, PhD
Dean
College of Health and Human Performance
East Carolina University
Greenville, NC

INTRODUCTION: REAL STORIES OF HOW THIS VOLUME HAPPENED

M. Elise Radina and Áine M. Humble

This edited volume offers an in-depth look into how qualitative social science researchers studying family issues and dynamics approach their data analyses. Numerous scholars have pointed out that far too often, little detail is provided about how data analysis actually occurs. For example, Richards and Morse (2013) note that "how abstracting is done is far too often presented as a mystery. A constant theme in the literature is that the theory 'emerges' from the data, but we have never had the privilege of seeing such an aspiration" (p. 120). Similarly, Dickie (2003) notes:

> Just as the account of the findings needs to tell a story, so does the account of the process itself. This account needs to go far beyond the use of terms such as "open coding," "triangulation of data sources," and "line by line reading." Writing a separate data analysis section in a qualitative study can too easily result in a cursory text composed more of labels than descriptions.
>
> *(p. 50)*

What is left are vague representations of qualitative analysis processes that offer little to the reader about the realities of what they look like. This limited glimpse can lead to misunderstandings and misconceptions about the nature of the methodology (e.g., its [often inevitable] complex messiness, decision-making of the researcher and/or research team, how techniques are executed perhaps differently by various researchers, attention to rigor).

Our primary aim with this edited volume is to shed light on the usually hidden nature of these processes that are all too often, and by necessity, stricken from published work. A central reason for this missing information is that researchers are typically not provided with room to describe how they carried out their analysis in scholarly journals articles, the typical outlet for publishing their research. Peer-reviewed journal articles have word count or page number limits. The methods section in a journal article is usually about seven pages long in a 35-page article (Goldberg & Allen, 2015) and consists of many critical topics in addition to data analysis (e.g., data collection methods, interview questions, the researcher's positionality, and ethical issues). However, just because there are such limitations placed on researchers, readers new to qualitative research should not mistake lack of detail for a lack of complexity in analysis from which much can be learned. Indeed, there is a considerable amount to discuss about one's methods, and in particular, the data analysis. One outcome of this edited volume, we hope, is to draw attention to the limitations of space placed on qualitative research in journal articles. Another outcome is to encourage qualitative researchers to be more explicit and clear with the space they do have about what their processes actually entailed.

With those related, broader outcomes in mind, in this edited book we aim to move beyond the common practice of merely providing citations for terms such as "open coding" and "the constant comparative process" as sufficient explanation of methodological processes. To this end, our goal here was to provide qualitative researchers the space and encouragement to move beyond jargon and vague phrases such as "themes emerged from the data." We encouraged our authors to become vulnerable by providing detail about their data analysis and showing readers how they actively and consciously arrived at their themes (Richards & Morse, 2013), or what Richards (2014) refers to as "*making* data" (not to be confused with "*making up* data," which a graduate student in one of Áine's classes once thought it meant!). This book offers *behind the scenes* narratives from researchers that show the complexity and messiness that comes with attempting to make sense of thousands of pages of transcribed interview data, multiple data sources, and/or diverse types of data (e.g., observations, interviews, photos, and diary entries). In doing so, we respond to Sharp, Zvonkovic, Humble, and Radina's (2014) call to expand and improve the terrain of qualitative family studies research—by "having more qualitative research available for consumption in publication and expanding the types of paradigmatic framing, research designs, and qualitative analyses" (p. 154).

Intended Audience

This book serves as a resource for both novice and experienced qualitative researchers who are seeking specific examples of how to carry out qualitative data analysis. This book may also be useful as a supplemental textbook for graduate-level research methods courses not only in Family Science but also in a variety of social science disciplines studying family relationships and dynamics across the lifespan (e.g., sociology, gerontology, psychology, nursing, anthropology, and social work). This book builds on what students may be learning in research methods courses and moves their understanding to a new level. In our experience of teaching qualitative methods, students are often desperate for examples and detailed recipes for how to conduct qualitative research (Radina & Sharp, under review). In this book, readers can engage with the researchers through the researchers' accounts of their processes and reflections on their craft. This occurs through the narratives presented in the first section of the book along with the supplemental materials (e.g., examples of handwritten coding) provided by the authors and located at the book's eResource. Instructors may want to assign some or all of the original pieces of work for which the chapter authors are describing their data analysis. For example, students could be provided with an example of Miller's co-authored article, "'You could scream the place down': Five poems on the experience of aged care" that appeared in *Qualitative Inquiry* (Miller, Donoghue, & Holland-Batt, 2015), for which the data analysis process is described in Chapter 2. Students are able to engage with our contributors in a second way through reading their dialogues in the book's second section.

There is yet so much to learn about qualitative methods, and those who are immersed in this research design will know that their learning is always a work in progress. This book, therefore, may also benefit experienced researchers by introducing them to new ways (to them) or innovative ways of analyzing family-related data, whether by, for example, creating a poem (Chapter 2) or purposely choosing certain words or creating certain types of sentences (Chapter 1) to have maximum impact on the reader. Additionally, this book may provide advanced scholars with ideas for mentoring their students in qualitative data analysis.

Book Structure Overview

There are two sections. Thirteen chapters comprise the first section, which is called "Stories." These chapters document *behind the scenes* details for recently published work (e.g., in the last five years or so). A supplemental eResource provides figures for 12 of these chapters, as well as links to the journal articles for which the analysis is described in 11 of the chapters (excluding one chapter that focuses on data analysis for a book, and another based on a conference presentation). The second section ("Dialogues") consists of four short, dialogue chapters where we brought small groups of authors together from the first section and asked them to engage in a brief conversation with each other around common themes in their chapters. Next, we describe both of these sections in more detail.

"Stories" Section

Similar to others who have given advice about qualitative research (e.g., Goldberg & Allen, 2015), the intent of the chapters in Stories is not to provide a "step-by-step formula" (p. 3) in carrying out data analysis, but to provide readers with a variety of stories about how data analysis actually occurs. In an effort to be mindful that there is not just one right way to analyze qualitative data (i.e., one recipe), we identified chapter authors for this book whose work represented varied approaches to how data can be analyzed.

We wanted to include a diversity of qualitative methodologies, such as grounded theory, phenomenology, autoethnography, and arts-based inquiry. Naturally, this resulted in a variety of approaches to data analysis. We sought to include a range of researchers' experience (i.e., doctoral students to emeriti faculty). We also intentionally included research that used a variety of qualitative data analysis software programs, including some research that did *not* use such software. We knew that we wanted at least one chapter that involved a large team of researchers. Finally, when choosing chapter authors, we made sure that the topics related to families and relationships reflected a life course perspective (e.g., ranging from parents with young children to families with aging parents) and also represented diverse racial/ethnic/cultural backgrounds and sexual orientations.

To identify authors whose recent work met all of the previously mentioned goals, we read widely and searched through databases to find primarily journal articles, and as we progressed, we kept track of this information in a matrix (Word document). We were familiar with the work of some of the authors before compiling this book—in some cases we had ideas about scholars who we, having read their work and noting their ability to be reflexive about their processes (e.g., Rosenblatt, 2012), would be appropriate people to approach. We had the pleasure of meeting others for the first time during this process. We especially enjoyed our process of *discovering* and working with those authors who were new to us. Overall, we feel that we were successful in meeting these multi-faceted diversity goals. We note, however, that it was impossible to include every methodology, data analysis technique, and family type in the book. Table I.1 shows an additional component of our diversity: the variety of publications on which each chapter in the first section is based.

The chapters that make up the Stories section include a combination of narrative, demonstration, and/or story telling of the data analysis processes in which the researchers engaged. We asked our contributors to share the stories of how they navigated the often complex process of analyzing qualitative data. We prompted them to specifically focus on telling the stories that scholars never read about in typical journal articles. We asked them to provide detailed descriptions along with their own reflections on questions such as: If they worked in a team, how did they build consensus, how long did it take, was it simple? How exactly did their team reach agreement? If they reported intercoder agreement or reliability, how was that reached? How did they go about doing that? If they used a software program, how did they use it? If they decided against using it or decided not to use certain parts of it, what was their reason for doing so (note: we did not assume that an analysis carried out with a qualitative software program or an analysis using all of a program's functions made one's analysis "better"—see Humble, 2012).

Qualitative analysis often produces visuals of processes (e.g., a screenshot of coding from a software program, hand-written notes in the margins of transcripts,

TABLE I.1 Chapters and Primary Study Publication Sources

Chapter/Author	Publication Source
Chapter 1: Weaver-Hightower	*Journal of Contemporary Ethnography* (2012)
Chapter 2: Miller	*Qualitative Inquiry* (2015)
Chapter 3: Healey	*International Journal of Circumpolar Health* (2014)
Chapter 4: Rosenblatt & Weiling	Book: *Knowing and Not Knowing in Intimate Relationships* (2013)
Chapter 5: Allen & Roberto	*The Gerontologist* (2013)
Chapter 6: Doucet	*Journal of Marriage and Family* (2015) and Book: *Do Men Mother?* (2006- 1st edition, 2018- 2nd edition)
Chapter 7: Roy, Hart, & Golojuch	*New Directions in Child and Adolescent Development* (2014)
Chapter 8: Vesely, Letiecq, Goodman, Marquez, Alves, Lazo, & Martinez	NCFR conference presentation (2017)
Chapter 9: Speirs, Vesely, & Roy	*Child and Youth Services Review* (2015)
Chapter 10: Jamison	*Journal of Family and Economic Issues* (2017)
Chapter 11: Kemp, Ball, & Perkins	*The Journals of Gerontology, Series B* (2018)
Chapter 12: Zvonkovic & Swenson	*Journal of Marriage and Family* (2018)
Chapter 13: Castellanos	*Journal of Homosexuality* (2016)

research memos, color images of highlighted/color coded sections of data, images of whiteboards after group discussion and analysis). Therefore, we also specifically requested that authors provide and discuss such visuals. The majority of these visuals are located on the book's eResource, and represent a variety of images, such as photographs of whiteboard scribblings (Chapters 7 and 8) to summarize team meetings; photographs of hard copies of transcripts or project notes with different colored highlighting in the margins (e.g., Chapters 5, 6, 10, 11, and 12); photographs (Chapters 1 and 3); genogram diagrams (Chapter 5); various matrices and tables (e.g., Chapters 9 and 12); and screenshots of qualitative data analysis software (e.g., Chapters 1, 3, 7, 9, 11, and 13).

Finally, we also invited the authors of each chapter to share with us between two to four key works that influenced their approach to data analysis. These key works are included in a box at the end of each chapter. Thirty-one key works are listed in total.

"Dialogues" Section

This section consists of four shorter chapters, each focusing on a theme that cut across multiple chapters from the contributors in the Stories section. We determined the topics for these Dialogue while reading, reviewing, and providing feedback to authors as they completed their Stories chapters. The structure of these chapters is conversational in nature; we were inspired by a similar type of writing that appeared in Morse's (1994) *Critical Issues in Qualitative Research Methods.*

As we read the drafts of the chapters in the Stories section, we each kept track of possible Dialogues topics in separate tables on Google Docs. In these tables we noted what we thought were possible main topics being mentioned in each chapter. Then we looked for commonalities across the chapters, doing this separately and then comparing our notes. In our discussions with each other (face-to-face, via email, via phone/video calls), we decided on four topics that were common across several chapters: (a) reflexivity/attention to social location in qualitative research, (b) engaging in arts-based research, (c) utilizing data displays, and (d) using qualitative data analysis software. Determining who to assign to the different dialogues was based not only on who fit into a particular theme but also based on a desire to balance out the number of contributors in each chapter in an effort to keep dialogues manageable (i.e., wanting at least three people per chapter and no more than five). Thus, a person might have fit into two categories, but if one of those categories already had four contributors and the other one had two, they were assigned to the latter category. At the same time, it was not possible to include all authors in the Dialogues as some chapters included a large number of authors or we had already five authors for a Dialogue. After determining who best to group together around those themes, we sent emails to the groups to introduce authors to one another.

Roughly a month later we sent detailed instructions to each group. Included were specific questions we asked the groups to answer as a way of structuring their conversations. We provided the groups with two different options for completing their conversations: (a) Google Docs where group members could work either synchronously or asynchronously on a collaborative document, and (b) email through which group members could send messages back and forth to each other. To keep these more informal and conversational, and not further burden our authors with more work, we imposed a word count limit and gave them a one month window to complete their conversations. During this process, several of these authors shared with us and each other how much they enjoyed this opportunity to learn from each other, reflect on their own work, and engage in intellectually stimulating conversations with one another. With the exception of Chapter 17, authorship is alphabetical, reflecting the equal contributions of all authors in these dialogues.

Unique Contributions

This book provides readers with the unique opportunity to be seemingly in the moment with the researchers getting their own hands vicariously dirty with the data. As Cuthbert, Arunachalam, and Licina (2012) and DeLyser (2008) argue, the teaching and learning of qualitative research methods requires the use of hands-on activities almost more so than more traditional learning that relies on the use of targeted readings on techniques. Similarly, Breuer and Schreier (2007) suggest that learning how to conduct qualitative research should be very much viewed as "learning a 'craft' . . . [that] ultimately requires students to cooperate in carrying out related activities" (p. 5). This book is offered from this perspective. Although the actual apprenticeship of learning a craft at the foot of a master is beyond the scope or ability of any book, this volume provides an intimate approximation of this experience for the reader.

In the Dialogue chapters readers are witnesses to the contributors' interactions with each other. In answering our questions, they responded to each other and sometimes posed questions to their colleagues, which we were delighted to see. We are not aware of any recently published books that offer this kind of conversation. A greater level of insight into arts-based research, reflexivity, data display, and qualitative data analysis software is achieved by this seldom seen, and sometimes seldom experienced, interactive exercise.

The narratives and dialogues we have collected and curated here are further enhanced by the supplemental materials available on the book's eResource.

An Inside Look at Our Process

Pulling this book together and working with the chapter authors was both an exciting and rewarding experience. We feel privileged to have been given an insider's view into their work and to have been able to engage with them to help them really bring their data analysis processes alive for our readers. In this final section, we share five observations from our own experiences editing this book.

First, we were encouraged and often excited to see that several authors specifically addressed the need for more detailed and explicit discussion of qualitative data analysis processes. Jamison (Chapter 10) argues that authors, "rarely report the idiosyncratic aspects of our data analysis processes (e.g., using highlighters rather than coding software) in favor of simply stating that we engaged in 'open coding'" (p. 152). In other words, authors all too often resort to using appropriate jargon in reporting on their analysis with little detail given to what their analysis actually entailed. Like Jamison, Weaver-Hightower (Chapter 1) addresses how qualitative analysis is far from a linear, clear process. He writes,

> I hope that qualitative researchers learn to tell that important secret we share, that our analyses, like our lives, are often messy, partial, influenced, and time- and culture-bound. . . . So, enough! It's time to tell secrets.
>
> *(p. 15)*

Similarly, Allen and Roberto (Chapter 5) explain how "writing this chapter together, which provides the freedom of transparency and disclosure, is [was] a welcome and liberating experience, rare in academic work" (p. 78).

Second, we were struck by the importance of talking about one's research with other people and of the different ways in which research can be discussed. For example, regular team meetings are an important part of talking through ideas, but important insights also came from informal conversations, such as those that occur when driving home from doing an interview and scribbling down one's insights before they are forgotten (Chapter 7). Talking through ideas with colleagues helps individuals gain clarity and insight into their ideas. Research is not a solitary activity, and even if a study only includes one researcher (i.e., no collaborators), it can be beneficial for that person to seek out colleagues with whom to hash out ideas. Such dialogue may even occur with reviewers, as it did for Weaver-Hightower (Chapter 1), Allen and Roberto (Chapter 5), and Jamison (Chapter 10). In fact, we actively encouraged this kind of conversation in the Dialogues section. As these chapters began to unfold, it became clear that we had underestimated the amount of space these authors would need for their Dialogues. Both the fact that most of the Dialogues exceeded our word count limit and that the authors were so engaged with each other during this process speaks to our earlier claim that there was, and possibly remains, a need for qualitative researchers to share, discuss, and debate their craft with each other. As editors, we too found being able to engage in dialogue with each other as we identified potential authors and the topics for the Dialogues section to be an important part of our research and writing processes.

The key works list identified by all the authors at the end of their chapters is the focus of our third observation. In looking at the complete list of all the key works, we noticed four things. First, and not surprisingly, there was a wide variety of resources listed, which we were pleased to see. Second, only three resources were mentioned in more than one chapter. Moreover, these three resources (two books and one journal article) all dealt with grounded theory, which speaks to the influential role that it continues to play in family science qualitative research. Finally, we noticed that two thirds of the key works were books or book chapters ($n = 21$). We find this particularly noteworthy for two reasons. First, it is a reminder for both novice and experienced qualitative researchers to read widely and not limit their learning of qualitative methodologies to the brief description that appear in journal articles. Second, this pattern further supports our argument that most journal articles do not provide the level of detail needed for researchers to get the guidance they need to conduct quality qualitative research. That being said, we note that some journals created by fields outside family science do provide this kind of information (e.g., *Forum Qualitative Sozialforchung/Forum: Qualitative Social Research, International Journal of Qualitative Methods, Qualitative Health Research, Qualitative Inquiry*).

Not surprisingly, there were challenges in putting together this book, and our fourth observation relates to a *learning curve* that happened for all our contributors in terms of understanding the level of detail we were looking for. Similar to giving interview participants cues as to what level of detail in their answers is being sought (Rubin & Rubin, 2005), we often had to probe authors for more information. We often found ourselves asking for *specific examples* as it was vital that we gave readers as deep an insight into the specific experiences of our contributors as possible. We would ask, "What do you mean by that? Can you give a specific example? What does that look like?" Questions such as these were our attempts at trying to uncover what is often hidden. For example, if an author said there were some challenges in collaborating with someone, we asked for specific examples of how this was a challenge and how it was resolved or not resolved. If an author said they started using a software program but then moved away from it, we asked them to include a reason for this decision. Additionally, we often asked authors for examples of images, whether it was screenshots from a computer program or images of a transcript with handwritten notes on the side. We feel strongly that having such visual examples of how the analysis actually happened is essential to helping readers gain the experience of *being in the room* with the researchers.

As qualitative researchers, we are often not pushed to describe our data analysis or *show our work*, so to speak, unless it is a thesis or dissertation. Moreover, academic journal articles have socialized us into giving sound bites rather than detailed lectures about our data analysis experiences. Moreover, in some cases it might feel like second nature to those of us who have been conducting qualitative research for many years. We recognize the inherent challenges that the broader research context places on us in terms of thinking about how we describe our qualitative research.

Our final observation is about the phrase "themes emerged." We choose the title of our book deliberately (Moving beyond "themes emerged") to build on as Richards' (2014) work in which she talks about how data is *made* and Dickie's (2003) observation that codes do not magically emerge from data analysis, but rather, they "were more likely to 'emerge' from the researcher's mind" (p. 51). We then found ourselves struck that we occasionally had to remind contributors not to use the phrase "themes emerged." We prompted authors to be more specific and demystify their process, and we also encouraged them to choose a different word or to rephrase the sentence in a way that made their active engagement with the material more obvious. This phrase is so ingrained in our scholarly vernacular, and indeed, we also had to train *ourselves* to not overlook this phrase in our review of the chapters. Based on the insights we gained here, and the way in which we were able to encourage our authors to tell us a detailed story, we encourage other authors to try to avoid this phrase, even in journal articles.

Conclusion

Earlier in this introduction, we commented that a main reason qualitative researchers do not provide much detail about their analysis is due to journal article limitations. We also identified that qualitative researchers are often not asked to talk about how they came to their findings. However, there may also be a certain vulnerability implicit in providing detail about one's data analysis. Years ago, Doucet, one of our contributors, wrote about this very issue, stating:

> Data analysis is our most vulnerable spot. It is the area of our research where we are most open to criticism. Writing about data analysis is exposing ourselves for scrutiny. Perhaps it is for these reasons that data analysis fails to receive the attention and detail it deserves.
>
> *(Mauthner & Doucet, 1998, p. 6)*

Certainly, we found that our authors, and we ourselves in discussing our own processes as part of our time together writing this book, were in many ways forced to make the implicit—and sometimes the difficult, painful, and messy—explicit and clear. And so, we thank our contributors for their vulnerability in sharing their stories and thoughts with us, and we also thank them for their patience with us in responding to our multiple requests for "more detail" and "specific examples" (insert smiley face here!). Our goal has been to demystify the research process by providing these researchers' narratives—to pull back the curtains on how "themes emerge." We hope we have achieved that.

References

Breuer, F., & Schreier, M. (2007). Issues in learning about and teaching qualitative research methods and methodology in the social sciences. *Forum Qualitative Sozialforschung/Forum: Qualitative Social Research*, 8(1). Retrieved from www.qualitative-research.net/index.php/fqs/article/ view/216/477

Cuthbert, D., Arunachalam, D., & Licina, D. (2012). "It feels more important than other classes I have done": An "authentic" undergraduate research experience in sociology. *Studies in Higher Education*, 37(2), 129–142.

DeLyser, D. (2008). Teaching qualitative research. *Journal of Geography in Higher Education*, 32, 233–244.

Dickie, V. A. (2003). Data analysis in qualitative research: A plea for sharing the magic and the effort. *The American Journal of Occupational Therapy*, 57, 49–56.

Goldberg, A. E., & Allen, K. R. (2015). Communicating qualitative research: Some practical guideposts for scholars. *Journal of Marriage and Family*, 77, 3–22.

Humble, A. M. (2012). Qualitative data analysis software: A call for understanding, detail, intentionality, and thoughtfulness. *Journal of Family Theory & Review*, 4, 122–137.

Mauthner, N. S., & Doucet, A. (1998). Reflections on a voice-centred relational method of data analysis: Analysing maternal and domestic voices. In J. Ribbens & R. Edwards (Eds.), *Feminist dilemmas in qualitative research: Private lives and public texts* (pp. 119–114). London: Sage.

Miller, E., Donoghue, G., & Holland-Batt, S. (2015). "You could scream the place down": Five poems on the experience of aged care. *Qualitative Inquiry*, 21, 410–417.

Morse, J. M. (Ed.). (1994). *Critical issues in qualitative research methods.* Thousand Oaks, CA: Sage.

Radina, M. E., & Sharp, E. A. (under review). Student and faculty experiences of qualitative research methods courses in family science. *Family Science Review*.

Richards, L. (2014). *Handling qualitative data: A practical guide* (3rd ed.). Thousand Oaks, CA: Sage.

Richards, L., & Morse, J. M. (2013). *Readme first for a user's guide to qualitative methods* (3rd ed.). Thousand Oaks, CA: Sage.

Rosenblatt, P. C. (2012). One interviewer versus several: Modernist and postmodernist perspectives in qualitative family interviewing. *Journal of Family Theory & Review, 4,* 96–104.

Rubin, H. R., & Rubin, I. S. (2005). *Qualitative interviewing: The art of hearing data* (2nd ed.). Thousand Oaks, CA: Sage.

Sharp, E. A., Zvonkovic, A., Humble, A. M., & Radina, E. (2014). Cultivating the family studies terrain: A synthesis of qualitative conceptual articles. *Journal of Family Theory & Review, 6,* 139–168.

SECTION I
Stories

1

ANALYZING SELF AND OTHER IN AUTOETHNOGRAPHY

Telling Secrets About One's Stillborn Child

Marcus B. Weaver-Hightower

How Do You Tell a Secret? Not *why?* or *how do you summon the courage to?* tell a secret, but *how*—mechanically, structurally, with effectiveness.

How do you convey a secret experience you know—because you've *been there* and *done that*—to someone who doesn't know it? Every qualitative researcher faces this primary task. How do I tell my reader what my participant felt, believed, or did? What quotations tell that story? What themes? How do I get my readers to understand another way of being human? To know what it looked or felt like? Autoethnographers are no different than, say, grounded theorists in this regard; they just focus on their own experience *in addition to* the experiences of others.

I have a secret experience. My daughter Matilda was stillborn in 2006. She is my wife's and my first child.

Our stillbirth experience, according to a helpful statistical chart (MacDorman, Kirmeyer, & Wilson, 2012), connects me to the parents of 25,971 *other* stillborn children (Matilda makes 25,972) in the United States in 2006 alone. In almost every way, I do not know these parents. In one very important way, though, I do.

I've told that secret already in an article called "Waltzing Matilda: An Autoethnography of a Father's Stillbirth" (Weaver-Hightower, 2012). I suppose, then, for those who have read the article, the secret is out. It has transmogrified into a revelation. I won't rehearse the whole secret again. (I'll wait here if you want to go read the article first.) Rather, in this chapter, I answer my opening question. This story, as the title of this book promises, pulls aside the curtain of *themes emerged*. This is *how* I came to understand my secret well enough to tell it.

***

Autoethnography, much like creative or arts-based research forms, relies on analysis processes perhaps even more elusive and ephemeral than those in traditional qualitative research, such as grounded theory (e.g., Charmaz, 2006; Glaser & Strauss, 1967) or phenomenology (e.g., Moustakas, 1994). The paper trail in autoethnography evades auditing because so much happens within analysts' heads.

As antidote to such analytical lacunae in autoethnography, this chapter goes beyond simple labels and shorthand (Dickie, 2003) to uncover challenges of data analysis about the self and researchers' close social networks. "Waltzing Matilda" provides a powerful example, I suggest, because I used numerous analytical approaches—drawing comics, analyzing photos, policy analysis, gender theory, discourse analysis, and medical literature—to assemble a multifaceted understanding of the larger, usually hidden experience of stillbirth.

This chapter is a kind of autoethnography about making an autoethnography, and it adds to the larger collection by consciously *using* the self as data rather than hiding the self behind third-person pronouns, statistics, and (feigned?) methodological confidence. Autoethnographic analysis instead *necessitates* total honesty, self-critique, and vulnerability—all the things our masculinized disciplines demand we hide in order to be *scientists*.

Collecting

In autoethnography, data collection and data analysis intermingle. (It does in all research, even quantitative.) Just distinguishing an event *as data* represents analysis. In autoethnography one must, within the flow of thousands of events and interactions, either in the moment or as memory, recognize one's own experiences as relevant data.

Understanding how humans learn ways of thinking and behaving when they set out to do or become something has defined my intellectual career. How does one learn to be *a boy*, especially a *real, appropriate, masculine* boy (Weaver-Hightower, 2008)? How does one learn to be a groom (Weaver-Hightower, 2002)? How does one learn to be a father—or, at least, an almost-father to a dead child? What I counted as data for "Waltzing Matilda" were those people and things I encountered that were *trying to teach me*.

I tried to stay aware of cultural artifacts I came across that provoked a feeling. I would collect mail from companies that kept me on their mailing lists even after Matilda was dead and would no longer need their diapers, formula, or insurance products. I read books, whether explicitly about grief or about fathering that did not admit to grief. I pondered objects related to Matilda and why they were so meaningful (this eventually became a section in the article on "Things"). I stared at photos of Matilda and of us, trying to capture exactly what it was I was saying to myself and feeling.

The analysis that led to "Waltzing Matilda" started almost immediately after her death and continued as each new datum appeared, happened, or arrived.

The disembodied researcher persona I wear so comfortably surfaced very soon into the experience of losing Matilda, a coping mechanism providing distance between myself and the simmering horrors of it all. I could engage my cool, interested ethnographer's brain and tamp down the emotional brain that seemed raging, muddled, sometimes out of control. Analyzing became balm.

Others' Stories

Literature, both literary and scientific, played a central role in the analytical construction of "Waltzing Matilda." Reading or hearing "other self-narrators" (Chang, 2008, pp. 100–102) with similar experiences provided critical analytical tools. These let me know that my thoughts and experiences weren't unusual. *Yes, I experienced that,* I would say. I quoted from C. S. Lewis' (1996/1961) memoir of his wife's death, for instance, because his articulation of spiritual doubt resonated with me.

Or, at times, the contrasts would be instructive. For example, McCracken's (2008) memoir of stillbirth was ripe with stark, emotionally potent metaphors that I quoted. Yet, we had contrasts. She never saw her stillborn son, a choice different from mine, which provoked my pondering about the importance of the body, *seeing* the body, *touching* the body, *knowing* the look of death. Insights from this reflecting appear in my thematic section called "My Daughter's Body." (As I write this, I worry that such a section affronts my fellow parents of stillborns, like McCracken, who chose not to look.)

I also found the scientific literature—medical and psychological discourses— to hold tremendous value for analyzing my own experience. Some participants in empirical studies had it so much worse than me. Some had nightmarishly cruel relatives. Their relationships fell apart (e.g., Vance, Boyle, Najman, & Thearle, 2002). They descended into addiction or pain seeking (Aho, Tarkka, Åstedt-Kurki, & Kaunonen, 2006). Discovering these dynamics in the literature led me to consider reasons why I did not experience some of the worst possibilities. Did the strength of my relationships protect me? Was it my race or income? Did my background in gender studies afford me identity flexibility beyond just stoic masculinity? Such introspection directly impacted the analysis, such as discussion of the "politics of crying" (Weaver-Hightower, 2012, pp. 483–484). No other act is as gender-regulated, by self or others, as crying. I *might* have discussed crying without seeing it in the literature, but having seen it so often made discussing crying mandatory.

I collected the scholarly and literary references, their abstracts, notes of my impressions, and detailed keywords in a database of references using EndNote software (see Figure 1.1). As I composed the autoethnography, certain keywords in

SEE FIGURE 1.1   at eResource—Screenshot of EndNote Library for "Waltzing Matilda."

the database became themes, points of reference for common experience. Layne's (2003) ethnographic work, for instance, introduced themes of *material culture*—things that I then began to notice in others' works. Having the detailed keywords in the database then allowed me to search for other writing about "things," "stuff," "pictures," "materials," "memories," "keepsakes," and other terms related to material culture. Grouped together in a search result, the matching works became themes that spoke to common experience.

Ultimately, common themes in the literature became a guiding influence, and I "often selected points specifically to reflect themes prevalent in the larger literatures" (Weaver-Hightower, 2012, p. 463). Other stillbirth narratives describe pregnancy events that quickly went from normal to horrific, they focus on hospital scenes, they discuss difficulties of asymmetrical grief between men and women, they lament feeling unprepared for the possibility of stillbirth, they challenge authors' religious beliefs, and they contemplate what could have been done differently (e.g., Conklin, 2006; Schwartz, 2006). By structuring my own story with these themes, I aligned my analysis with the experiences of others to whom I am connected. Although it feels strange to see yourself represented as coldly described themes—realizing *you* are the rat in the maze—it can also feel oddly comforting. I might not have the free will I initially assumed (for how else do I fit so many of the *typical reactions*), but these also let me know I'm not alone, not unusual—just human and grieving.

My autoethnographic analysis involved listening closely to my internal dialogue—what I said to myself. Much as Dickie (2003) describes, I had to try to catch insights made in the stream of consciousness while contemplating a topic, doing "activities that allow[ed] my mind to wander and puzzle over what I [was] finding" (p. 53).

Listening to oneself is harder than it sounds. In autoethnography one must be vulnerable, honest, and self-critical—acts that can be hard for humans. We want, instead, to be the heroes of our stories, always knowing the right answers and projecting confidence. For researchers, this can be doubly hard because admitting mistakes remains the easiest way to get an article rejected; admitting human frailty is like blood in the water to reviewers for whom scientificity is next to godliness. Lest I risk diluting insights with my impulse to appear as the confident, infallible hero, I had to listen closely and record quickly (sometimes a sticky note before going to bed, a jotting on my phone in the car, and—rarely—sitting in front of my computer), with fearless dispassion about how I would *look* to others for telling the truth.

I usually keep a *physical* file folder of data, even in our digital era. Paper-based ephemera remain a huge part of the world we learn in, so these scraps contain invaluable information. For this study, I kept a file that included ads, hospital documents, brochures, notes, and miscellanea. Storing files and notes, and moving them around from folder to folder, provided an easy, basic form of analysis for me. *What other ideas does this one belong with? What labels will I put on the folder and subfolders that will give me new insights into organization and themes?* (My "Waltzing

SEE FIGURE 1.2   eResource—Screenshot of *Junk Drawer File* for "Waltzing Matilda."

Matilda" electronic parent folder eventually contained subfolders called ARTI-CLES, COMIC, Interviews, IRB, EndNote Library, MISS Fndtn, and Share Initial Packet; about 60 files were loose in the parent folder, as well.)

I almost always work from what I call a *junk drawer note* (Figure 1.2), a Microsoft Word document where I stash theoretical and exemplar odds and ends—things I want to make sure to say. Sometimes I wrote polished, expansive notes, and sometimes I simply jotted a key phrase. Often I cut and paste from this junk drawer into the final manuscript, sorting the disparate ideas into the emerging structure. These rambling, unordered notes functioned much like the grounded theorist's *memos* (Glaser & Strauss, 1967), allowing me to work out ideas on the screen that need articulation and explaining. Frequently, whole chunks of this text made their way into the final draft with only minor changes.

Picturing Matilda

Autoethnography has been a fertile ground for experimenting with mixing representational genres. *Crystallization*, Richardson (1994) called it, where validity arises from multifaceted ways of knowing and representing (see also Ellingson, 2009). Poetry, for example, requires different means of encoding and decoding knowledge than does, say, a medical journal article. Ethnographic fieldnotes have different epistemological means than a memoir. Each genre provides its own knowledge structure for the writer and reader. Cobbling several together into a single manuscript positions writers and readers at varied standpoints from which to view and understand a phenomenon.

In developing "Waltzing Matilda," I used crystallization both behind the scenes and in the article itself. Each use—seen or not—provides a genre-based scaffolding for analysis, a cognitive structuring device. For example, how does encoding an experience in free verse poetry help one understand an experience? How about a limerick? A sonnet? How does creating a drama from ethnographic research (e.g., Saldaña, 2005) structure the analyst's thinking? In my case, I wondered how *translating* a story into the comics form—words and images in panels with speech balloons, etc.—creates analytically productive, cognitive affordances (Kuttner, Sousanis, & Weaver-Hightower, 2018).

This notion of creating a comic to represent experience first occurred to me in 2007 as I was trying to decide how to represent Matilda's death (see Figure 1.3). I needed a form that could help me *show* things that I didn't quite know how to *say*. I was a comic book fan in my youth and quite familiar with the form, but it struck me suddenly, long before I had tried much writing about Matilda, that I might attempt a graphic version to convey my story. Although I ultimately decided that comic pages were not (yet!) the right format for Matilda's story,

SEE FIGURE 1.3 at eResource—Page From a Draft Comics-Based Telling of Matilda's Story.

my efforts to narrate the tale in comics influenced my eventual prose telling. (I returned to the comics form for another father's stillbirth in Weaver-Hightower, 2017; see also Weaver-Hightower, 2013).

To make a comics page, one must choose the important moments, frame them using distance and angle, style the images, choose words that work well with the images, and make it flow around the page (McCloud, 2006). These are analytical decisions, much like choosing moments from interview transcripts or participant-observation events. Importantly, though, drawing can lead one into a *flow* that clears out the cache of language that often dominates thinking. It allows a different form of thinking—visualization—that can, in turn, inform language again later.

In Figure 1.3, my comic page gave me a way to visualize what caused Matilda's death—a *fetal-maternal hemorrhage*—not possible to see by other means. I had to investigate medical illustrations to make the images on the page, to imaginatively look inside the body, which helped me understand the probability that Matilda's death was a slow process—a drip, drip, drip and a weakening heartbeat. In notes for an early draft of the prose manuscript, I extended the heartbeat "THUMP!" sound effects from this page—my visual solution to show her death process by the thumps becoming smaller and smaller—into a list of sounds associated with our stillbirth experience. Although that full list did not make the final version, creating the comic provided the realization that sound details were a key analytical tool. The comic thus originated the lines "I asked the doctor to . . . check with the handheld Doppler, that device that had always so reliably found the thump-thump-thumps of Matilda's heart. But no thumps sounded, only the swishy, marine-like sounds of emptiness" (Weaver-Hightower, 2012, pp. 466–467). It was an image—converted as if through synesthesia from sound—that stuck with me from graphic narration to prose.

Writing Matilda

Some might misperceive autoethnography as quick and easy, as if "It's just telling stories about yourself." That's not true if you do it well. "Waltzing Matilda" was in production for five years. Because my personality drives me to research anything and everything (natural to the academic's life), "Waltzing Matilda" quickly became a project I knew I had to do, even just a few weeks into our stillbirth experience. I knew that understanding myself, and helping others understand the experience, would be a way to heal.

It took years before I could finally write down a full draft of "Waltzing Matilda." Over that time, I realized that a one-time analysis (a cross-sectional writing of an event, if you will) would have been dangerous. I could perhaps plot my arc of grief and my arc of analysis on correlated trajectories. If one day I was angry with the world for spinning on despite my despair, I wanted my autoethnography to be angry, to be *in the face* of readers. (It was not rational or nice, but it was how I felt.) On other days when I felt more accepting—to use Kübler-Ross's (1969) famous terms—I could be clinical, detached, forgiving. The autoethnographer perhaps must be *more* vigilant of this day-to-day emotional entanglement with the analysis, but I would venture that everyone who pursues qualitative research suffers this effect, even if they do not know or admit it.

Analysis in autoethnography often happens *during* the writing—*by writing* (Richardson, 1994). You can find out what you know by writing it, a kind of ouroboros of analysis and writing. As Richardson (1994) says of "evocative experimental forms" like autoethnography,

> evocative writing touches us where we live, in our bodies. Through it we can experience the self-reflexive and transformational process of self-creation. Trying out evocative forms, we relate differently to our material; we know it differently. We find ourselves attending to feelings, ambiguities, temporal sequences, blurred experiences, and so on; we struggle to find a textual place for ourselves and our doubts and uncertainties.
>
> *(p. 521)*

The *struggle* Richardson notes is an analytical one. It is the struggle I asked about at the outset: *How* do you tell a secret?

In my experience, the analysis-writing infinity loop included cognizance—in a sense of metacognition—of *how* I was writing. How did the ways I wrote show meaning? A perfect example was a tendency to say *she* or *her* when speaking of Matilda. As I was writing then—and now—I struggled to put Matilda into the story *by name*. Pronoun-ing Matilda perhaps demonstrated my acquiescence to the prohibition against naming or talking about stillborn babies. *She who must not be named.* Often others do not talk about Matilda by name, at least not as often as they use my living children's names. In turn, that discursive conduct invades my language, too. Seeing this, analytically, while writing led to more explicit and frequent use of Matilda's name.

Another subtle shift that happened through the writing was moving from describing fathers as *invisible* to fathers as *hidden*. In my first, abandoned draft (one of several versions), I wrote:

> I am six feet and two inches tall—not unimposing—but I am often invisible. . . . I am invisible in doctor's offices, where the nurses and doctors caring for my wife do not ask my name, do not ask how I am coping. I am largely invisible in the scientific literature. I am invisible in society and in the culture. I am a father whose baby has died.

Invisibility doesn't capture it correctly. I'm not *invisible*, but *hidden* or *overlooked*. The latter are more active, more purposeful. They take effort to accomplish. Invisibility denotes a characteristic of me, but *hiding* stillbirth was something others (and sometimes I) do. That small change of diction provoked the analytical breakthrough for my section on "The Sociopolitical Economy of Stillbirth," that "Yes, the average person finds it hard to bring up in polite conversation (the micro-level hiding of stillbirth), but much more is needed to keep stillbirth a little-known pregnancy outcome throughout an entire culture" (Weaver-Hightower, 2012, p. 477). It takes no less than the cooperative efforts of media, businesses, the baby advice industry (often including doctors), and the government. Of course, I realize no grand conspiracy operates behind the scenes, in some smoke-filled star chamber, but obscuring the death of 25,000 babies a year is no small feat.

During the writing of "Waltzing Matilda" I also struggled to contain *angry Marcus*. In early iterations, including notes relegated to the junk drawer, I just seemed mad. I *felt* mad, honestly. And I was taking it out on the reader, with challenging tones and presumptions that readers would have dismissive attitudes. Consider "You want valid data? Holding your dead baby, cold, heavy and lifeless in your arms is the most valid data you may ever see." I'm glad that line didn't make it to the manuscript. Yet it was also true at the time I wrote it.

Most importantly, *why was I so angry at the future reader who was nice enough to pick up my article and begin to read?* I had to interrogate my emotional drive toward anger in the writing, not solely to calm myself and avoid offending, but also to think about places where I could *constructively* (rather than alienatingly) present anger as a very real emotion of the stillbirth experience (again, language from Kübler-Ross, 1969). Anger has acceptability for men that other emotions do not. Was I using anger to hide other, more masculinity-threatening emotions? Such are the kinds of *analytical* decisions one makes in deciding how to tell secrets.

Setting Up and Tearing Down the *Montage*

A basic way that humans devised to communicate across their differences is comparison and contrast. I show you an apple, put it next to your orange, and—see!—they are different. In "Waltzing Matilda," I felt I could help readers relate to the stillbirth experience by having them compare it to what I think of as *the movie montage*, a kind of ideal progression of images about childbirth. Readers have likely seen the montage of *ideal pregnancy* countless times on film, or perhaps done it themselves. It goes something like this: extreme close up on pregnancy test with a pink plus; quick cut to happy embrace; transition to an ultrasound where the doctor points out a heartbeat and genitals; cut to setting up a crib (perhaps with frustration/hilarity); close up on the expectant mother holding up cute clothes during a baby shower; jump cut to water breaking at an inconvenient time; medium shot of huffing mom rolling in on a wheelchair to the hospital desk; pan over to same huffing mom, knees spread wide while a doctor works away, dad holding mom's hand; slow motion as the tightly bundled baby is handed to the exhausted but ecstatic parents. I basically lay this out in "Waltzing Matilda" to establish the known, and then it all comes crashing down, all the harder because of that identification readers have been doing with these representative scenes.

I particularly found contrast analytically and rhetorically productive in the section "My Daughter's Body." Holding Matilda's body was a kind of out-of-body experience for me, so to speak. Even knowing she was dead did not deter my utterly compulsive behaviors of touching her gently and swaddling her. I wanted to understand how my rational mind could so easily go absent. The answer came in the contrasts: she was dead but she was also a baby. Being a baby overwhelmed any other consideration, so everyone treated Matilda as a baby, carefully and lovingly. Being present but not feeling, being a baby but not alive: such contrasts are overwhelming to the mind, so we hold on to the hopeful one. I hoped my readers would hold on to their favoritism toward living babies, too, because it held the key to understanding the sorrow of it simply not being true. As I noted in the article itself, these *dualities*—"the body as beautiful and horrible, simultaneously saying hello and goodbye, giving birth but leaving with empty arms" (Weaver-Hightower, 2012, p. 470)—are defining characteristics of the stillbirth experience.

Rhetoric as Analysis

I want to keep this next part secret. It seems crass, manipulative, mercenary. Yet, I am an autoethnographer, so secrets must be revealed. I hope readers will pardon my purposeful manipulation of their emotions. Stillbirth, grief, and bereavement are emotional topics, though. How could I accomplish my goal to share *what it's like* without provoking reactions like sadness, shock, disgust, fear, or sympathy? I needed to manufacture emotional connection for understanding, through moments and scenes that touch or perhaps even assault.

Transferring the story from my mind onto the page required carefully crafting the language, a set of analytical decisions meant to break down and best share the content. (Of course, part of the content of an evocative autoethnography is a particular emotional resonance.) Thus, part of interpreting through writing was looking for creative nonfiction techniques that fit my intentions.

Many of my techniques were simply playing with sentences. Short sentences have impact. The essay starts simply with "My baby died" and ends with "I miss her." Digressions (appositive material) break down the fourth wall, as it were, between reader and writer. As Brecht (1964) imagined happened in Chinese theater, moments of the narrator stepping out of the narrative flow eases readers' exhaustion from complete, unceasing empathy—which a more straightforwardly written narrative might provoke.

I employed figures of speech frequently to convey my meanings and the emotional context. Dotted throughout, for example, are numerous words that can refer to birth used in alternative ways, such as *borne, stillness, breathe life*, and *expected*. I used verbs and nouns meant to kick the reader squarely in their assumptions, like using "father" for my role even outside of a biological context. I have Christmas "sleigh by." The three of us—Matilda, her mother, and me—"fall in love." I wished to see my daughter "completely naked."

Double entendres layer on meaning, as well. The title has them—"A Father's Stillbirth" referred to Matilda's actual stillbirth as well as my fatherhood's stillbirth; "Waltzing" refers to the song "Waltzing Matilda," which, if you know the Australianisms, means *to carry* while the Matilda of the song refers to a blanket tied up into a backpack and containing one's worldly possessions. I could not have known when we named her just how I would have to *carry* Matilda (and her few worldly possessions) the rest of my days.

Naturally, metaphors abounded. I am particularly pleased with the layering of metaphors in the second paragraph of the section, "The Long After," where "wound . . . sutured," "tear . . . knit . . . fabric" and "laundry" weave together a metaphor for how death slowly incorporates itself into a resumed life. The metaphor of a curator provided a productive "far-out comparison" (Strauss & Corbin, 1990, pp. 90–91) in the "Things" section; this image opened my eyes to many of the actual properties of the stillbirth experience, particularly parents' almost fussy curatorial behaviors around their child's artifacts.

I used gerunds (*losing, becoming, waltzing*) for activeness, which I learned from Charmaz (2006, p. 49) who, in turn, learned it from Glaser (1978). Questions posed rhetorically, if phrased just so, can seem desperate or angry ("Would my wife and I ever have a date again—or sex?" or "Whose baby dies?"). I used the orator's standby of repetition in key places ("The laundry must be done. Meals must be cooked" in the section "The Long After" and "I have learned . . ." in the "Not a Conclusion" section). And literary allusions were made to Eliot's (1922) *The Waste Land* ("a brown fog" on p. 471), Shakespeare's *Hamlet* ("pale cast" on p. 473 and "undiscovered country" on p. 486), and Judy Blume (1970) in my section heading, "Are You There God? It's Me, Marcus."

I also intentionally played with tone, register, and genre throughout "Waltzing Matilda." As discussed already, the article purposefully combines numerous genres—*crystallization*. I wanted to *do the voices* of each genre, discussing *sociopolitical economy* in my sociologist voice, *death rituals in many cultures* in my anthropologist voice, *depression* and *psychological distress* in my psychologist voice, *fetal-maternal hemorrhage* in my medical voice, and *horrible, beautiful, maddening* in my father voice. The diction changes with each voice as do the sentence structures and uses of literature.

All these writing conventions are, again, analytical decisions. In other words, the *how* of telling my secret was crucial, for telling it in these ways helped me understand the experience and hopefully aids others in their understanding, too—hopefully subtly rather than didactically.

Reviewing and Reanalyzing Matilda

The academic peer review process also aided analysis. Having that back and forth with reviewers forced me to think about how others viewed the situation and my representation of it. I typically take reviews quite personally and defensively, but probably never quite so much as in the reviews for "Waltzing Matilda." Luckily, I also always wait to respond to reviews until I have had time to talk myself down! (I know it had to be hard for reviewers, too; how does one diplomatically critique a story about not only a dead baby, but the *author's* dead baby?) Still, reviewers' commentary frequently sent me back to helpfully recast some explanations or expand certain avenues. Take my discussions of stillbirth support groups. In the original draft, I had very few references to my support group, but a reviewer picked up on underdeveloped references and how, if further explored, these might fill out the picture of fathers' actual supports.

In other cases, reviewer reactions forced me to clarify my own understanding, to ponder more deeply why some things were important and others were not. I especially think about one reviewer's questions about the ethical acceptability of using the photograph of Matilda (Figure 1.4). The reviewer suggested that, "surely Matilda, even though she never lived on this earth, has a right to be considered ethically in relation to the publication of her photograph." My first reaction was to angrily rebut that the reviewer simply didn't want to look at a dead child—another iteration of everyone urging us to hide her away.

I knew Matilda's photograph would be distressing for some people. Hell, I *wanted* seeing Matilda's photograph to be distressing. Not as an act of cultural ignorance or insensitivity (some cultures are distressed by viewing photographs of the dead), not as a cruelty to readers, and not as an insensitivity to our families or to Matilda (she is dead, which has specific spiritual meaning *to me* about how much she would care about such things). Rather, perhaps with a quantum of malice, the provocateur's handiest tool, I intentionally rattled social mores because— let's be real—some readers don't want to see her and don't want me to show her. I sympathize. I do. Yet that is the very problem, the core of my argument. Some readers' desires for me to hide her, to keep it to myself, or—worse—forget her so that social comfort can return, creates an unbearably painful oppression for me, my wife, and millions of others. Matilda's picture offered resistance. Besides, she's beautiful; I'm just as proud of her as I am my living children, and I want to show her off.

Even so, I felt I needed to try to better understand exactly what the reviewer's concerns were about using the photograph, for the reviewer was surely being more charitable than my initial reaction credited him or her with. The reviewer's comment forced me to really ponder and analyze why I felt so strongly that the

SEE FIGURE 1.4   at eResource—Photo of Matilda.

picture be included. Thus, I added a lengthy footnote that spoke to the ethics, and it ended up taking me in directions that underscored the importance of *things* and of *social acceptance* to the parents of stillborn children. It was a kind of analysis team—the reviewer and me—who created this insight.

Of course, I cannot ignore my most important reviewer, my wife. Though her name does not appear on the article's byline, I consider her a co-analyst. We have spent many years analyzing together the data of our everyday lives. Naturally we have discussed Matilda's death thousands of times. What-if scenarios, member checking, replaying events, discourse analysis, applying theory to experience: These are the analytical routines we share on long car rides, in quiet moments before we crawl out of bed, or while dinner simmers on the stove. She is my first and last reader, and nothing about Matilda goes out of the door without her feedback. Not approval *per se*, for our experiences are individual, too, and we are each the final arbiter of that. Indeed, our individual experiences deepen our collective experience, showing each other through our differences the complexity and variability of grief. At times my wife's and my interrater reliability (e.g., MacPhail, Khoza, Abler, & Ranganathan, 2016) might be low, but that turns out to be a strength rather than a weakness for the autoethnographer. No one could better teach me about Matilda and grief than my wife.

Conclusion

As I look across the analytical processes that led to "Waltzing Matilda," the distributed, wild, and hybrid nature of my analysis fascinates me. Analysis happened informally as well as formally. It happened simultaneously with collecting artifacts and living experiences. Analysis happened within my lifeworld and in reading about others' lifeworlds. It happened of my own volition, through dialogue with others, and as a reaction to peer review. Analysis happened in pictures and in prose, before writing as well as during and after.

Perhaps such feral diffusion of analytic processes particularly afflicts autoethnography. To be one's own subject demands constant analysis of experience, and *all* experience might count. I think, though, that *all* qualitative researchers experience this wild diffusion of analysis to some degree. We may not notice as it happens. We overlook our inspirations. Or we might not feel free in our disciplines or publishing venues to admit that our processes are anything but clean and seamless. We may spin fictions of systematic, stepwise progress through our studies, unadulterated by bias. In the end, though, these are just fictions.

To counter these inventions about our analyses, I hope that qualitative researchers learn to tell that important secret we share, that our analyses, like our lives, are often messy, partial, influenced, and time- and culture-bound. It's a powerful secret, yes, and a dangerous one, too. Qualitative researchers have much to lose from telling this secret wrong—to suggest that it is somehow a failing inherent to the methodology. If other forms (quantitative, positivist forms) of research refuse to admit their human-produced frailties, too—numbers are as arbitrary and biased as words, even if they appear to work predictably—divulging this secret could be doubly dangerous to qualitative methodology. So, enough! It's time to tell secrets.

KEY WORKS GUIDING MY DATA ANALYSIS

Chang, H. (2008). *Autoethnography as method.* Walnut Creek, CA: Left Coast Press.

Chang's systematic approach to autoethnography came along at a good time in the development of "Waltzing Matilda." It was the first textbook-like treatment that laid out step-by-step ideas for data collection and analysis specific to autoethnographies, and it helped me corral an untamed process.

McCracken, E. (2008). *An exact replica of a figment of my imagination: A memoir.* New York, NY: Little, Brown and Co.

McCracken masters the emotionally powerful sentence in this memoir. It has a rawness, an honesty that I admire and hoped to emulate. Even at her most unflattering—like making fun of a couple who came to her reading—McCracken charms readers with unflinchingly truthful detail.

Tillmann-Healy, L. M. (1996). A secret life in a culture of thinness: Reflections on body, food, and bulimia. In C. Ellis & A. P. Bochner (Eds.), *Composing ethnography: Alternative forms of qualitative writing* (pp. 76–108). Lanham, MD: AltaMira Press.

I came across Tillmann-Healy's remarkable autoethnography about her bulimia early in my graduate school days. I found her story revelatory in the emotional impact of its fragmentary structure—its *crystallization* (Richardson, 1994). The essay cycles from tiny memory to poem to academic literature, and it enchants the reader with deep humor and deep tragedy, always helping us viscerally feel the shame, fear, and anger at the heart of the story. It was a model for what I wanted "Waltzing Matilda" to achieve.

References

Aho, A. L., Tarkka, M-T., Åstedt-Kurki, P., & Kaunonen, M. (2006). Fathers' grief after the death of a child. *Issues in Mental Health Nursing, 27,* 647–663.

Blume, J. (1970). *Are you there God? It's me, Margaret.* New York, NY: Yearling.

Brecht, B. (1964). Alienation effects in Chinese acting. In J. Willett (Ed.), *Brecht on theatre: The development of an aesthetic* (pp. 91–99). New York, NY: Hill and Wang.

Chang, H. (2008). *Autoethnography as method.* Walnut Creek, CA: Left Coast Press.

Charmaz, K. (2006). *Constructing grounded theory: A practical guide through qualitative analysis.* London: Sage.

Conklin, M. (2006). Hieroglyph. *Water-Stone Review, 9,* 200–217.

Dickie, V. A. (2003). Data analysis in qualitative research: A plea for sharing the magic and the effort. *The American Journal of Occupational Therapy, 57,* 49–56.

Eliot, T. S. (1922). *The waste land.* New York, NY: Boni and Liveright.

Ellingson, L. L. (2009). *Engaging crystallization in qualitative research: An introduction.* Thousand Oaks, CA: Sage.

Glaser, B. G. (1978). *Theoretical sensitivity.* Mill Valley, CA: The Sociology Press.

Glaser, B. G., & Strauss, A. (1967). *The discovery of grounded theory: Strategies for qualitative research.* Chicago, IL: Aldine.

Kübler-Ross, E. (1969). *On death and dying.* New York, NY: Palgrave Macmillan.

Kuttner, P., Sousanis, N., & Weaver-Hightower, M. B. (2018). How to draw comics the scholarly way: Creating comics-based research in the academy. In P. Leavy (Ed.), *Handbook of arts-based research* (pp. 396–423). New York, NY: Guilford Press.

Layne, L. L. (2003). *Motherhood lost: A feminist account of pregnancy loss in America.* New York, NY: Routledge.

Lewis, C. S. (1996). *A grief observed.* San Francisco, CA: HarperSanFrancisco. (Original work published 1961).

MacDorman, M. F., Kirmeyer, S., & Wilson, E. C. (2012). Fetal and perinatal mortality, United States, 2006. *National Vital Statistics Reports, 60*(8). Retrieved from Centers for Disease Control and Prevention website www.cdc.gov/nchs/data/nvsr/nvsr60/nvsr60_08.pdf

MacPhail, C., Khoza, N., Abler, L., & Ranganathan, M. (2016). Process guidelines for establishing intercoder reliability in qualitative studies. *Qualitative Research, 16,* 198–212.

McCloud, S. (2006). *Making comics: Storytelling secrets of comics, manga, and graphic novels.* New York, NY: Harper.

McCracken, E. (2008). *An exact replica of a figment of my imagination: A memoir.* New York, NY: Little, Brown and Co.

Moustakas, C. (1994). *Phenomenological research methods.* Thousand Oaks, CA: Sage.

Richardson, L. (1994). Writing: A method of inquiry. In N. K. Denzin & Y. S. Lincoln (Eds.), *Handbook of qualitative research* (2nd ed., pp. 516–529). Thousand Oaks, CA: Sage.

Saldaña, J. (Ed.). (2005). *Ethnodrama: An anthology of reality theatre.* Walnut Creek, CA: AltaMira Press.

Schwartz, J. B. (2006, December). The waiting room. *Vogue, 196*(12), 134, 140, 142.

Strauss, A., & Corbin, J. (1990). *Basics of qualitative research: Grounded theory procedures and techniques.* Newbury Park, CA: Sage.

Tillmann-Healy, L. M. (1996). A secret life in a culture of thinness: Reflections on body, food, and bulimia. In C. Ellis & A. P. Bochner (Eds.), *Composing ethnography: Alternative forms of qualitative writing* (pp. 76–108). Walnut Creek, CA: AltaMira Press.

Vance, J. C., Boyle, F. M., Najman, J. M., & Thearle, M. J. (2002). Couple distress after sudden infant or perinatal death: A 30-month follow up. *Journal of Paediatrics and Child Health, 38,* 368–372.

Weaver-Hightower, M. B. (2002). The truth about grooms (Or, how to tell those tuxedoed men apart). In F. V. Tochon (Ed.), *The foreign self: Truth telling as educational inquiry* (pp. 201–217). Madison, WI: Atwood.

Weaver-Hightower, M. B. (2008). *The politics of policy in boys' education: Getting boys "right".* New York, NY: Palgrave Macmillan.

Weaver-Hightower, M. B. (2012). Waltzing Matilda: An autoethnography of a father's stillbirth. *Journal of Contemporary Ethnography, 41,* 462–491.

Weaver-Hightower, M. B. (2013). Sequential art for qualitative research: Making comics to make meaning of the social world. In C. Syma & R. Weiner (Eds.), *Graphic novels and comics in the classroom: Essays on the educational power of sequential art* (pp. 260–273). Jefferson, NC: McFarland & Co.

Weaver-Hightower, M. B. (2017). Losing Thomas & Ella: A father's story (a research comic). *Journal of Medical Humanities, 38,* 215–230.

2

CREATING RESEARCH POETRY

A Nursing Home Example

Evonne Miller

Forgotten (Poem 1)

Alot of people think of us
of older people
as something that should be
shoved,
in the corner,
forgotten.

when you are getting old
you don't want
to feel
forgotten.
you want to—

live life
to the fullest
live for today
don't worry about next week.
just sit back and enjoy it.
And thank God
I am still here
                    Florence, age 79

When your time is up (Poem 2)

SEE FIGURE 2.1   at eResource—When Your Time Is Up.

You could scream the place down[1] (Poem 3)

My family said
I was too old
to be on my own,
that I needed organizing.

You lose everything
you lose everything
to come in here.
You only have the barest minimum
There's not much here.

It is not nice, not nice at all.
It is not good for me.
I can't get out.
That's what you lose, when you come in.

All your independence is taken away from you.
I'm not able to do it myself.
That's very hard to take,
you get so frustrated at times
you could scream the place down

Joy, age 85

You're taken care of[1] (Poem 4)

You're taken care of.
I'm very satisfied
with my room.
I got me own furniture,
so why wouldn't I be?
It's just like my own home,
only I don't do no work.

I got me friends here,
I go to bingo,

I join in exercises,
I go for any walks,
I have a good family,
they take me places.
though I haven't been able
to find a nice man yet.

Ethel, age 80

These research poems, created from interviews with older residents in an Australian nursing home (Miller, Donoghue, & Holland-Batt, 2015), provide immersive, meaningful, and powerfully emotive insight into their day-to-day lived experience. They were created using an under-utilized research technique variously labeled found poetry, poetic inquiry, poetic transcription, transcript or research poems, in which words, phrases, and whole sentences from interview transcripts are edited and reframed (by participants and/or researchers) into poetry or poem-like prose (Butler-Kisber et al., 2002; Faulkner, 2009; Galvin & Prendergast, 2016). The first two poems *(Forgotten* and *When your time is up)* reflect socio-cultural stereotypes of aging but also acknowledge that death and dying is a normal part of growing older. The last two poems evocatively convey how residents can either resist (*You could scream the place down*) or enjoy life in aged care (*You're taken care of*). Additionally, the second poem (Figure 2.1) is an example of concrete research poetry (Meyer, 2017), with the poem embedded within a related visual image (in this example, an hourglass).

In this chapter, I endeavor to *make visible* the often hidden processes of creating a research poem. Drawing on interview transcripts from semi-longitudinal qualitative research tracking older Australians' lived experience in one nursing home (Donoghue, Miller, & Buys, 2017; Miller et al., 2015), I outline five iterative steps that underpin my approach: (a) immersion, (b) creation, (c) critical reflection, (d) ethics, and (e) engagement. These steps are based on my experience with research poetry, with my acronym ICCEE reflecting my processes and acting as a metaphor for the journey through research poetry. That is, although at first the path may seem challenging, full of slips and icy terrain, it becomes a more obtainable undertaking with the help of a guide (and a little grit). By systematically unpacking my process, this chapter aims to facilitate exploration, engagement, and experimentation. First, I briefly define and discuss poetic inquiry, outlining the origins, key texts, and debates. Then, I walk slowly through some practical examples from my 2015 article, consciously interrogating my thought processes, alterative options, and key decision points at each step.

This chapter draws on data from the Inside Aged Care project,[2] a semi-longitudinal qualitative research where over 100 people—residents (retirement village, residential aged care, nursing home, dementia and respite), their family and friends, and the aged care workforce (from nurses and carers through to cooks and administrators)—participated in repeated in-depth interviews, workshops, surveys, observations, and creative arts-based activities (photovoice and poetic inquiry) to better understand, communicate, and improve the experience of aged care. The poems in this chapter are from interviews with 20 older aged care residents (average age, 80 years), created primarily from reading and listening to these interview transcripts, as well as fieldnotes.

The Power of Poetry and Poetic Inquiry

Compared to normal prose, poetry is a special language. There is a refreshing authenticity and often confronting *vulnerable vibrancy* to it that uniquely reaches and resonates (Rajabali, 2014). Although poetry is typically free verse, the literary tradition of *found poetry* creates poems from language not originally intended to be poetry. Excerpt words, phrases, and sentences are taken from a source text, both traditional (e.g., newspaper articles, books, magazines, speeches) and non-traditional (e.g., graffiti, street signs, junk mail, product packaging, court transcripts, tweets), and placed together to create a poem. Poems can also be created from qualitative interview transcripts in a process variously labeled research poetry, transcript poems, poetic transcription, and poetic inquiry (Faulkner, 2007). Typically, a short first-person poem is created from a single interview transcript, although multiple transcripts can be used (see Breheny, 2012). A significant number of researchers (e.g., Butler-Kisber et al., 2002; Faulkner, 2009; Galvin & Prendergast, 2016; Leavy, 2009) have actively engaged with found poetry as a form of data collection, interpretation, analysis, and representation, with their publications providing an essential starting point (e.g., see Galvin & Prendergast, 2016).

The process of research poetry involves two deceptively simple steps. The first step is a non-linear deep dive into interview transcripts searching for key words, phrases, and sentences. This step is analogous to the initial data reduction phase in any qualitative data analysis process, centered on data immersion. In the second step, participants' words are arranged and rearranged to craft a poem (Sparkes & Douglas, 2007). This poem creation process merges "the tenets of qualitative research with the craft and rules of traditional poetry" (Leavy, 2009, p. 64), drawing on a range of poetic techniques such as rhythm, rhyme, sound, repetition, metaphor, emotion, imagery, synthesis, alliteration, pitch and tone, and humor. Research poetry is a form of both narrative and lyric poetry, telling a story of actual experiences (narrative) and condensing emotions (lyric) so the reader feels the "episodes, epiphanies, misfortunes, pleasures" (Faulkner, 2009, p. 24). Critically, although a poet has creative freedom with word choice, a research poet works with the existing elements in the interview transcript. Of course, the research poet can draw out the poetic elements in a transcript and deploy poetic tropes to ensure the research poem is moving and has poetic impact. But, the poet is constrained by participants' individual speaking and communication styles; thus, although some interviews and transcripts will be full of colorful, evocative imagery, engaging metaphors, precise details, and emotive memories perfect for a poetic approach, others will not (Breheny, 2012).

As a form of arts-based research, the unique artistic and aesthetic representation of research poetry means "listeners and readers tend to be moved by their simplicity and power" (Poindexter, 2002, p. 70). Research poetry is an experimental text form that challenges listeners, readers, and researchers. Not all will enjoy the process or find it within "their internal tool kits to work with data in this manner" (Sparkes & Douglas, 2007, p. 186). Some researchers, however, will enjoy the creative process and how the dramatic presentation vividly convey participants' stories and engages diverse audiences, facilitating experimentation with different aesthetic, analytic, and creative approaches (Leavy, 2009). Meyer (2017), for example, recently reflected on her experience with concrete research poetry, in which poetry is embedded within a visual image and the metaphoric structure demands aesthetic processing. Poem 2 is an example of concrete research poetry where the poetic text is placed within an hourglass shape to highlight how quickly time passes. To do this, I sat and reflected on the words in the poem and if there were any potential shapes that might highlight these key concepts; after some deep thought, I realized that the hourglass shape was the perfect visual metaphor. By using metaphors as visual containers and physical structures, the reader is forced to pause—our visual senses are activated, as we approach and read the poem differently. Of course, as well as engaging in experimentation, the research post must always reflect on the aesthetic quality of their poems. Researchers in this space *must* devote time and energy to learning the art of poetry (*ars poetica*), just as they would any other data analysis technique (Thiel, 2001). Some people are "tired of reading and listening to lousy poetry that masquerades as research and vice versa" (Faulkner, 2007, p. 220), but most individuals pragmatically advocate for what is termed good enough poetry that enables social science researchers to evolve from inferior to effective research poets (Lahman & Richard, 2014).

Before delving deeply into my ICCEE process for creating research poems, let me first make a note about my own research background. Despite a lifelong interest in creative writing, I have no formal training in poetry and I was originally trained in experimental social psychology. In early 2014, a colleague emailed me a paper that used poetic inquiry. Intrigued, I reached out to a poet at my university to discuss the process and potential collaborations. Since then, working with colleagues, I have used poetic inquiry to convey the lived experience of older people in aged care and during disasters in four journal publications (Miller, 2018; Miller & Brockie, 2015, 2018; Miller et al., 2015), six conference presentations, numerous industry/public events, and two large photographic exhibitions that included research poems. Having seen the power of poetic inquiry, it is now one of my preferred qualitative analysis techniques. Although Thiel (2001) describes the process of learning to write a good poem as "something we must often stumble upon on our own" (p. 11), in the following section I unpack and reflect on the five iterative steps that guide my process.

Unpacking the Process of Poetic Inquiry

Step 1: Immersion

As mentioned earlier, the first critical step is data immersion. Wiebe (2015) describes this as "reading and rereading until the text reveals its key messages" (p. 154). Although this process sounds quite mysterious, data immersion is common to all qualitative researchers and thus this first step could be likened to coding. During the immersion process, the aim is to identify and group all words, phrases, and descriptions that will bring the poem to life. As Molnar (2010) explains, this process takes time, patience, and "many hours of reading transcripts, listening repeatedly to recorded conversations, rewriting my guide and assembling possible participants' quotes, before sorting selections, judging their worthiness and finally putting their words on to paper" (p. 167).

I worked on my laptop, cutting, pasting and rearranging key phrases and words from throughout the transcript onto a separate blank Microsoft Word page, which I called my *poem-working document*. This was a messy document, up to five pages in length, where I played with different ways of arranging the words in the poem. Butler-Kisber (2010) reminds us that the poem creation is a search for the most engaging, telling, and provocative phrases that enable the reader to viscerally see, hear, taste, smell, and/or feel the experience. Thus, I cut and pasted the phrases that spoke to and emotionally engaged me—any words that made me smile, frown, feel empathy, sadness, or anger. Not all phrases were used in the final poem, only those that flowed and, in my opinion, worked poetically. At times, a phrase, word, or a memorable description immediately *jumped out* of the page and became the starting focal point. Poems 3 and 4 provide obvious examples of this—the phrases "scream the place down" (Poem 3) and "I haven't met a nice man—yet" (Poem 4) immediately resonated with me when reading and engaging with the transcript. And, whereas I am generally comfortable working digitally, a colleague is more analogue; she prints the transcripts, circling and highlighting salient quotes. Both of us listen to the interview audio recordings, actively re-engaging with participants' speaking style, mannerisms, and colloquialisms. For clues about poem themes, I also revisited my fieldnotes, looking at any notes, highlights, or reminders of critical ideas/words I might have scribbled during the interview.

The following transcript excerpts demonstrate this process. The specific phrases and words that jumped out to me were: my family decided that I was too old to be on my own; you could scream the place down; you lose practically everything to come in here; and it's not nice. These key phrases become the basis for Poem 3: *Scream the place down*, with the general theme of unhappiness about living in aged care becoming the conceptual guide and search frame within that interview transcript. The excerpt also illustrates how the most engaging phrases in that poem were picked from throughout (start and end) the hour-long interview. In looking at these transcript excerpts, I am reminded that I had to remember that there was no one clear right or wrong path forward, but to trust the process, be present, and dwell with the text—at some point, the essence of the poem would emerge (Walsh, 2006).

> FIRST FIVE MINUTES: *What made you come here?* Well my family decided that I was too old to be on my own and I needed organizing (laughs). *How did you feel about that (laughs)?* Not at all. Not at all, ok. . . (laughs). Because everything had to go by the board. You lose practically everything to come in here. This is all we have got left now. *Right . . . so, in terms of your furniture and your items*——Yeah, you lose everything. You only have the barest minimum. As you can see, there's not much here. It is not nice . . . at all.
>
> LAST 10 MINUTES *Do you feel sad, ever?* Sad? *Like tears/sad?* Yeah. *Strongly?* You get so frustrated at times, you could scream the place down. *Is there anything else that you would like to say that I haven't asked about?* I think I have said more than enough (laughs).

Step 2: Creativity and Careful Crafting

This second step is the creative poetic process. Like any skill, the ability to craft a research poem will develop slowly over time with practice. Just as a poet ponders and carefully selects each word in a poem, I had to identify the most powerful and salient words in the data. This thoughtful and labor-intensive process of aesthetic compression is poetry's signature (Cohen, 2009), with Poindexter (2002) describing the ruthless carving away of words as "diamond-cutting" (p. 709). Brevity is key and every words counts, as "hours may be compressed into a line, monumental life experiences compressed onto a page" (Sullivan, 2005, p. 28). At the same time, it is important to acknowledge that not all research topics, people, and interviews transcripts will suit a poetic approach (Butler-Kisber, 2010). Some topics are more emotive and some people naturally more descriptive, using multiple powerful metaphors that make the poem creation process significantly easier. Some interview transcripts will be easier to work with than others.

Indeed, while a poet has total creative freedom to alter "word choice, structure, syntax, form, point of view, metaphor" (Wormser & Cappella, 2004, p. 56), the research poet is constrained by their participants' words. What we can do, however, is apply the poetic techniques of sound, rhyme, imagery, and metaphors to our data. We can rearrange our participants' words poetically. We can condense or expand the poem, move lines, reorder stanzas, or begin at a different place, exploring and assessing how such changes alter the flow, feeling, and impact of the poem.

To date, in my poetic inquiry process, I have followed the first rule in Glesne's (1997) approach: only use the exact words participants used and do not add or alter any words. Other research poets are more flexible and will modify and make minor changes to words, thus enhancing the poetic quality of the final product but (in my mind) losing the participants' voice. Now might be the time to explore concrete poetry as an option, testing whether the visual cue of a metaphoric structure (such as the hourglass in Poem 2) might be possible. By engaging purposely, consciously, and repeatedly in an iterative process of revision, we are honing and developing our skills as poet. Look past the first draft of the poem, to "resee" and find the "real poem" by constantly asking "*What if? What if I change this to that? What if I take line four out? What if I add some more adjectives? What happens?*" [italics in original] (Wormser & Cappella, 2004, p. 56).

This iterative poetic process is illustrated in Table 2.1. I created Poem 5 "*Before I came in here*" over two years ago for a conference. Looking at it closely now (with the benefit of time, distance, and maturity), I realized I could rework focus and reduce the words. Less, in poetry, is more. Thus, alongside the excerpt from the transcript on the left and the original poem in the middle, I present a second poem also created from the same short interview transcript (Poem 6: "*Home*"). In this reworked version, I consciously shortened the length of the poem, to (hopefully) maximize the emotional impact. Additionally, in crafting this new poem, I worked through two key considerations or decision points.

Decision Point 1: Concept of "Home"—Title, Length, Ending, and Presentation

As I reengaged with this emotive poem (in which Elizabeth shares how she considered suicide living at home) I realized the idea of "home" could be the central focus. Wiggins (2011) describes this process as identifying "the essence of the data, the story the data were telling, that became clearer and clearer through my process of choosing some words and eliminating others" (p. 7). While revisiting the transcript, I was immediately drawn to the word *home* as a title and guiding concept. First, most people hold positive, idealized, and romanticized views of home (even, or especially, if childhood memories of home were not positive). As an adult, the concept of home takes on a special meaning—it is usually valued as a safe space and place of sanctuary, with a whole research literature exploring the concept, importance, and meaning of home. Thus, while my poem creation process is always driven by the data and words on the page, my familiarity with that literature made me believe a poem exploring the concept of home might be of interest to, and resonate with, other audiences.

Second, the implicit irony appealed to me. Most people do not want to leave their homes, preferring to *age in place* in their own homes. Yet, Elizabeth recalls

TABLE 2.1 Example of Poetic Analysis Process: "Before I Came in Here"

Transcript excerpt	Poem 5 (original)	Poem 6 (edited)
Where at home, I thought I was in for a nervous breakdown, I really did, and so did my family because I was left there all day on my own, you know, as I said I fell and I was on the floor there for about over a half an hour wondering how I was going to pull myself up. And, if I had to leave here, I– I'd just, I'd just go, go right down. Since I've been in here it's gave me more … reason to, to get up in the morning. To get up in the morning, and get dressed and… when I was home I couldn't care, I used to open my eyes in the morning and think 'Oh, I'm still here another day.' But since I've been here, I've got, you know, 'Oh, I've got crafts to do tomorrow,' sort of thing. So, yeah. *And what about- approaching stuff?* Yeah, because, as I said, when you come in here, you feel like a family. You know what I mean? A big family. Yeah well I have a good girl friend, um, NAME. If I ever– see, when I was home on my own, I will admit there was a lot of times when I thought 'take your pills NAME, and you'll be out of all this stress and all this worry.'	**Before I came in here** At home, I was left there All day on my own Honestly and truly, I'd open my eyes And think, oh I'm still here, Another day, Alone. I admit there were times when I thought take your pills, Elizabeth and you'll be out, of all this stress and all this worry But since I've been here I have reason to get up, to get up, get dressed. we don't sit alone very much I've got, you know, company which I never had at home you feel like a family and, if I had to leave here, I know, I'd just go right down	**Home** At home I was left. On my own all day - alone. I thought— oh, I'm still here, another day— alone. I thought— take your pills, Elizabeth and you'll be out - from stress, from worry. But since I've been here I have reason to get up, get dressed every morning. I've got, you know, company which I never had— at home

feeling isolated, alone, and suicidal at home, and being much happier in aged care. This is counter to our dominant cultural narrative where people desire to stay at home and out of aged care for as long as possible. Home was my guiding concept; it became the poem title, and I purposely started and ended the poem with the same phrase—"*at home.*" This repetition was a choice, designed to drive home (pun intended) the contrast between isolation in her own home and happiness in aged care. Compared to two years ago, I also was more confident in deleting lines, hopefully crafting a research poem with fewer words, less irrelevant details, and more impact. Third, in terms of visual structure, I briefly considered adopting the concrete poem approach and placing the poem inside a metaphorical shape (a house or pill bottle) but eventually decided not to.

Decision Point 2: "Free From Stress; Free From Worry"

In reworking Poem 5, I was tempted to add in the descriptive word "free" to the third stanza, so it read "free from stress; free from worry." I felt it added the precision and clarity that is sometimes missing in spoken language, and given the context of the full interview transcript, believe it was what Elizabeth meant. Eventually, I omitted the word "free" for two reasons. First, Elizabeth did not actually use the word "free" in her original interview. Glesne's (1997) approach is not to add new words. Second, although this decision was primarily driven by a commitment to remain true to the found poetry tradition, on reflection I realized I also preferred the interpretive openness when the word "free" was omitted. That said, I find balancing my researcher mindset with a more open, interruptive, and ambiguous aesthetics of poetry challenging; I want to explain a concept in detail, rather than let the idea "float" (as a poet would) more ambiguously. Indeed, Butler-Kisber (2010) reminds us that a beginner research poet will often produce "untreated" poems, retaining "virtually the same order, syntax and meaning as the original" source text (p. 84). This is true of one of my early research poems ("*Scream the place down*"), in which the transcript and poem are very similar to each other. As with any qualitative research technique, developing skills, voice, and expertise with research poetry is a never-ending developmental journey. In fact, looking at that excerpt from the transcript again now, I realize that a short poem focused on Elizabeth's fear and experience of time when she lay on the floor for half an hour after a fall might be a topic worth exploring in the future.

Step 3: Criticality

The third step is to critically assess quality. Less engaging poems feel "flat and contrived" (Butler-Kisber, 2010, p. 90), whereas successful poems drawing on metaphors and imagery allow "the heart to lead the mind rather than the reverse" (Butler-Kisber & Stewart, 2009, p. 3). Research poets must pay careful attention to detail, to reflect and ponder on titles, word choice, punctuation, emotion, sound, rhyme, grammar, and metaphor, as these choices combine to determine the impact of a poem. Faulkner's (2007) proposes six criteria to guide the evaluation of research poetry: (a) artistic concentration, (b) embodied experience, (c) discovery and/or surprise, (d) conditionality, (e) narrative truth, and (f) transformation. She describes these criteria as "written in pencil" (p. 230), meaning that they simply offer a flexible starting point to think about, discuss, and develop the craft of poetry. Table 2.2 illustrates how I applied these criteria to assess the poems in this chapter. I asked myself how well each poem met each criteria, critically reflecting on the aesthetic and research merit, as well as their ontological or educative authenticity (see also Sparkes & Douglas, 2007).

Step 4: Ethics

This step focuses on ethical issues: concepts and processes of ethical engagement, member checking, control, and ownership. First, research poets must balance poetic impulse with the ethical imperative to remain faithful to the spirit and voice of the transcript, thus ensuring that the transcript poem both functions as a poem and as testimony. That said, each interview captures feelings at just one moment in time and the views, emotions, and perspectives of participants are not static. Second, an ongoing commitment to reflexivity and ethics in practice is essential (see Donoghue & Miller, 2016). My colleagues and I always endeavor to engage participants, building in an explicit member checking, review/feedback, and poem approval process (see also Sparkes & Douglas, 2007).

In this research project, whenever possible, we printed, shared, and discussed each poem with each interested resident, who self-selected their own pseudonym, altered and adjusted lines, or requested additional poems to be written/co-written. (Sadly, sometimes residents had died before we were able to engage in this member-checking process or their health had declined so significantly that they no longer wished to participate in the research.) In one situation, a resident felt this poem accurately represented his experience of declining health, but his spouse asked for a more positive poem to be written. Respecting this wish, the project team also wrote an additional more positive poem that both husband and wife enjoyed. Similarly, after consenting to having her poem publicly exhibited, another resident withdrew her permission when she saw it displayed as she felt it was too negative and potentially identifying. Although such member checking is always desirable, I acknowledge that it is not always practically feasible when working with an older frail cohort or when the data (transcript or poem) is revisited by researchers months or years after the project ended. Additionally, given that researchers do not routinely return their more conventional qualitative data analyses and interpretation to participants for approval, my pragmatic view is that member checking of poems is a desirable but not compulsory process.

TABLE 2.2 Applying Faulkner's (2007) Six Ars Poetica Criteria to the Poems

Criteria	Example poem	Critical reflection
Artistic concentration (careful attention to poetic detail and feeling)	Poem 3: *You could scream the place down*	Starting with the memorable deployment of metaphor in the title, this poem utilizes multiple poetic approaches (sound, rhyme, word choice, enjambment) to engage the reader. Repetition of words and phrases, the rhetorical technique of anaphora (e.g., "You lose everything, you lose everything, to come in here"), is effective.
Embodied experience (makes reader feel)	Poem 1: *Forgotten*	The purposely evocative title immediately resonates with reader, consciously taps into shared cultural narratives and fears about "being forgotten"—in life and in a nursing home. Direct second-person address (you don't want to feel forgotten; you want to live life to the fullest) engages, as does the imagery ("shoved into a corner"). Implicit question to readers: are you living your life to the fullest?
Discovery/surprise (learn something new)	Poem 4: *You're taken care of*	The poem is a surprisingly engaging and detailed account of daily life in aged care. The speaker's unique voice—her vernacular syntax and colloquialisms (e.g., "I don't do no work," "I got me own furniture") evoke a memorable sense of personality. Her sense of humor is conveyed in the last two lines, as she jokes: "I haven't been able/to find a nice man yet." The end contrasts against the rhythm and body of the poem, surprising with humor and subtly challenging socio-cultural stereotypes by reminding us that older people in aged care remain interested in relationships.
Conditionality	All poems. Compare Poem 3: *Scream the place down* to Poem 4: *You're taken care of*	By presenting multiple poems that traverse both positive and negative experiences of aged care, the reader can believe the researcher is honestly and holistically sharing the range of unique individual, conditional experiences. Compare, for example, the positivity in *You're taken care of* against the anger in *Scream the place down*; different views of the same nursing home experience.
Narrative truth (facts as presented ring true)	Poem 2: *When your time is up*	Reader has very personal and visceral experience, due to both topic (universal fear of death) and use of concrete poetry (the metaphoric hourglass image). Poem is purposely short, providing an authentic and honestly intimate reflection on experience of time and death in aged care.
Transform (new insight, social change)	Poem 5: *Before I came in here* and Poem 6: *Home*	Poem provides rare insight into an older person feeling isolated and suicidal at home, but happier in communal aged care environment. The narrative challenges the dominant view of nursing homes and older people's desire to age in place.

Step 5: Engagement

There are two components to this final step: (a) engagement with the practice of poetry and (b) engagement with the public. First, research poets must engage with and study the craft of poetry. I began my engagement with the world of poetry by signing up to be emailed a daily poem (from the Poetry Foundation), reading books of poetry (I started with Maya Angelou, Dorianne Laux, Wyn Cooper, William Stafford), and attending local poetry readings. In what started with a conversation over coffee, I now collaborate with acclaimed Australian poet Sarah Holland-Batt, who is equally excited to experiment with research data.

The second step involves sharing the poems. Whether it is spoken or read aloud, poetry is oral—the cadence, tenor, and speed of a voice will bring a poem to life. Finding the courage to publicly share my research poem was often challenging, in part because I had to remove "the false mask of academic distance and expertise to reveal, poetically, human dimensions beneath" (Galvin & Prendergast, 2016, p. 104). I was petrified the first time I read a transcript poem in public. Thoughts that ran through my mind were: How could I (a non-poet) dare to engage with this artistic medium? What would the general public, my academic peers, and industry networks think? Would they laugh at my first attempt to engage with poetry, thinking it too was trite, too sentimental, simply not very good, or just not academically rigorous? I felt very much outside my comfort zone, partly because my original training in experimental psychology privileged the scientific method and also because many people are unfamiliar with and fear poetry (see also Lahman & Richard, 2014). Yet, I persevered and grew in poetic confidence. Now, having read transcript poems publicly dozens of times, I can predict what will almost certainly happen: the energy in the room will palpably change, becoming so intense and quiet that people can hear a pin drop. Depending on the degree of emotion in a poem and the personal relevance of the topic, audience members may close their eyes, silently cry, or wipe away a tear. The topics I write about (aging, death, aged care, disasters) are emotive, but it is the unique presentation of poetic inquiry that enables connections: for a shared special moment, people look up from their social media updates to engage fully with the authentic lived experience in the poem.

Reflections

In closing, I offer three final reflections about my experience with research poetry. First, it is important to engage with and learn from the craft of poetry, as well as the large existent body of literature on research poetry. As a novice research poet, this literature was a critical source of inspiration, support, and confidence. Second, I have realized that when I am designing a project where poetic analysis is a planned outcome, I need to remember to patiently listen and probe for descriptive, memorable words, metaphors, and analogies during the interviews, as these will help vividly bring each participant's story to life (Glenn, 2016). To that end, I recommend keeping fieldnotes of initial thoughts, reactions, and reflections, and making a note of any particularly engaging phrases or metaphors that might make a nice poem. Scribbled fieldnotes were often a critical starting point for my poem creation process; for instance, the phrase "scream the place down" in Poem 3 was an evocative phrase I noted in my fieldnotes during the interview. Finally, I needed to be brave and just start experimenting with poetic inquiry, remembering that messiness, mistakes, and imperfection were part of the learning process. In closing, by explicitly unpacking my personal path to poetic inquiry, the key decision points, processes, and my five ICCEE steps, my hope is that this chapter will encourage other qualitative researchers to experiment with research poetry.

KEY WORKS GUIDING MY DATA ANALYSIS

Faulkner, S. L. (2009). *Poetry as method: Reporting research through verse.* Walnut Creek, CA: Left Coast Press.

Written by one of the leading scholars in poetic inquiry, this thorough, accessible and beautifully crafted book forced me to think about form and function, and through practical exercises, taught me how to create and evaluate poetry.

Galvin, K. T., & Prendergast, M. (2016). *Poetic inquiry II: Seeing, understanding, caring.* Rotterdam, The Netherlands: Sense.

I frequently refer to and reread this excellent edited collection, which provides detailed and inspirational insight into "doing" poetic inquiry in the fields of healthcare and education.

Leavy, P. (2009). *Method meets art: Arts-based research practice.* New York, NY: Guilford Press.

A highly accessible introduction to arts-based research, I frequently recommend this book as a key foundational text. Adeptly named Method Meets Art, this book provides practical, in-depth, and engaging insight into the theoretical and methodological considerations of six arts-based approaches.

Acknowledgments

Aspects of this work were supported by Ballycara and the Australian Research Council's Linkage Projects funding scheme, under Grant LP130100036 to Evonne Miller, Laurie Buys, and Nicole Devlin. I would like to acknowledge and thank the project team, management, staff, and residents of the aged care facility who so enthusiastically and graciously contributed to this research. I also thank Geraldine

Donoghue and Sarah Holland-Batt for multiple engaging conversations about research poetry and their thoughtful suggestions on this chapter.

Notes

1. Evonne Miller, Geraldine Donoghue, Sarah Holland-Batt. *"You could scream the place down"*: Five poems on the experience of aged care. *Qualitative Inquiry, 21,* 410–417. Copyright © 2015 (Evonne Miller). Reprinted by permission of SAGE Publications. doi/abs/10.1177/1077800415572396.
2. For more information on this research, please visit the project website: https://inside agedcareproject.wordpress.com/

References

Breheny, M. (2012). "We've had our lives, we've had our lives": A poetic representation of ageing. *Creative Approaches to Research, 5*(2), 156–170.

Butler-Kisber, L. (2010). *Qualitative inquiry: Thematic, narrative and arts-informed perspectives.* Thousand Oaks, CA: Sage.

Butler-Kisber, L., Allnutt, S., Furlini, L., Kronish, N., Markus, P., Poldma, T., & Stewart, M. (2002). Insight and voice: Artful analysis in qualitative inquiry. *Arts and Learning Research, 19*(1), 127–165.

Butler-Kisber, L., & Stewart, M. (2009). The use of poetry clusters in poetic inquiry. In M. Prendergast, C. Leggo, & P. Sameshima (Eds.), *Poetic inquiry: Vibrant voices in the social sciences* (pp. 3–12). Rotterdam, The Netherlands: Sense.

Cohen, S. (2009). *Writing the life poetic: An invitation to read & write poetry.* Cincinnati, OH: Writer's Digest Books.

Donoghue, G., & Miller, E. (2016). 'I understand. I am a participant': Navigating the 'fuzzy' boundaries of visual methods in qualitative longitudinal research. In D. Warr, M. Guillemin, S. Cox, & J. Waycott (Eds.), *Ethics for visual research: Theory, methodology and practice* (pp. 129–140). New York, NY: Palgrave Macmillan.

Donoghue, G., Miller, E., & Buys, L. (2017). Using participatory visual methods in aged care: The methodological, logistical and ethical considerations for qualitative research practice. *Sage Research Methods Cases Part 2.* Retrieved from http://methods.sagepub.com/case/participatory-visual-methods-in-aged-care-qualitative-research-practice?fromsearch=true

Faulkner, S. L. (2007). Concern with craft: Using ars poetica as criteria for reading research poetry. *Qualitative Inquiry, 13,* 218–234.

Faulkner, S. L. (2009). *Poetry as method: Reporting research through verse.* Walnut Creek, CA: Left Coast Press.

Galvin, K. T., & Prendergast, M. (2016). *Poetic inquiry II: Seeing, understanding, caring.* Rotterdam, The Netherlands: Sense.

Glenn, L. (2016). Resonance and aesthetics: No place that does not see you. In K. T. Galvin & M. Prendergast (Eds.), *Poetic inquiry II—Seeing, understanding, caring: Using poetry as and for inquiry* (pp. 99–105). Rotterdam, The Netherlands: Sense.

Glesne, C. (1997). That rare feeling: Re-presenting research through poetic transcription. *Qualitative Inquiry, 3,* 202–221.

Lahman, M. K. E., & Richard, V. (2014). Appropriated poetry: Archival poetry in research. *Qualitative Inquiry, 20,* 344–355.

Leavy, P. (2009). *Method meets art: Arts-based research practice.* New York, NY: Guilford Press.

Meyer, M. (2017). Concrete research poetry: A visual representation of metaphor. *Art/Research International: A Transdisciplinary Journal, 2*(1), 32–57.

Miller, E. (2018). Breaking research boundaries: A poetic representation of life in an aged care facility. *Qualitative Research in Psychology, 15,* 381–394. doi:10.1080/14780887.2018.1430733

Miller, E., & Brockie, L. (2015). The disaster flood experience: Older people's poetic voices of resilience. *Journal of Aging Studies, 34,* 103–112.

Miller, E., & Brockie, L. (2018). Resilience and vulnerability: Older adults and the Brisbane floods. In P. Samui, D. Kim, & C. Ghosh (Eds.), *Integrating disaster science and management: Global case studies in mitigation and recovery* (pp. 379–391). Cambridge, MA: Elsevier.

Miller, E., Donoghue, G., & Holland-Batt, S. (2015). "You could scream the place down": Five poems on the experience of aged care. *Qualitative Inquiry, 21,* 410–417.

Molnar, T. (2010). Hospitality and the Hôte: Revealing responsibility through found poetry. *Learning Landscapes, 4*(1), 157–173.

Poindexter, C. C. (2002). Meaning from methods: Re-presenting narratives of an HIV affected caregiver. *Qualitative Social Work, 1,* 59–78.

Rajabali, A. (2014). On writing a poem: A phenomenological inquiry. *Creative Approaches to Research, 7*(2), 39–50.

Sparkes, A. C., & Douglas, K. (2007). Making the case for poetic representations: An example in action. *The Sport Psychologist, 21,* 170–190.

Sullivan, A. M. (2005). Lessons from the Anhinga trail: Poetry and teaching. *New Directions for Adult and Continuing Education, 107,* 23–32.

Thiel, D. (2001). *Writing your rhythm: Using nature, culture, form and myth.* Ashland, OR: Story Line Press.

Walsh, S. (2006). An Irigarayan framework and resymbolization in an arts-informed research process. *Qualitative Inquiry, 12,* 976–993.

Wiebe, S. (2015). Poetic inquiry: A fierce, tender, and mischievous relationship with lived experience. *Language and Literacy, 17*(3), 152–163.

Wiggins, J. (2011). Feeling it is how I understand it: Found poetry as analysis. *International Journal of Education & the Arts, 12*(3), 1–18.

Wormser, B., & Cappella, D. (2004). *Surge of language: Teaching poetry day by day.* Portsmouth, NH: Heinenmann.

3

APPLYING INDIGENOUS ANALYTICAL APPROACHES TO SEXUAL HEALTH RESEARCH

A Reflection on ᐅᓂᒃᑲᖅᑎᒌᓐᓂᖅ *Unikkaqatigiiniq* (Storytelling) and ᓴᓇᓂᖅ *Sananiq* (Crafting)

Gwen Katheryn Healey

Indigenous scholars have shifted the discourse away from simply negotiating respectful relationships with Indigenous communities to the development and implementation of methods that originate from Indigenous epistemology and worldviews (Battiste, 2002; Kovach, 2009; Wilson, 2008). In this chapter, I reflect on the experience from my dissertation of analyzing and interpreting stories from Inuit parents regarding sexual health and relationships among young people (Healey, 2014a, 2014b, 2016). In this project, I analyzed and interpreted stories through a story and text-based narrative technique that originates from the Inuit concept of ᐅᓂᒃᑲᖅᑎᒌᓐᓂᖅ *Unikkaaqatigiinniq*, and through an immersive analytical experience originating from the concept of ᓴᓇᓂᖅ *Sananiq*, which means to *craft* or make something.

This study was developed at the request of community members who participated in consultations conducted between 2006–2008 in Nunavut Territory, Canada. The request was prompted by high rates of sexually transmitted infections, (Chlamydia and Gonorrhea) and a high rate of teenage pregnancy in Nunavut communities compared to the overall Canadian population. The research project was designed and implemented in partnership with three independent community wellness or research centers in three regionally and geographically distinct Nunavut communities. I worked with community health and wellness centers in the participating communities to engage community members in the study and to offer the opportunity to be project partners if they so desired.

In three geographically, regionally, and historically distinct Nunavut communities, 20 interviews were conducted with Inuit parents who had at least one son or daughter between the ages of 13 and 19 years. Three of the parents were fathers and 17 were mothers. Parents were asked open-ended questions about what terms such as: *relationships* and *sexual health* mean to them, and whether they discussed these topics with their children.

In the analyses, four primary concepts crystallized in the analyses:

1. *Inuit family understandings of sexual health and relationships are linked to historical and contextual factors.* Parents defined sexual health in terms of their experience of child sexual abuse. They strongly associated their abuse experiences with the residential school and settlement period of northern history, during which many Inuit families were separated and family relationships were severed.
2. *Parent-adolescent communication pathways are important for transmitting knowledge about sexual health and relationships.* Parents emphasized family communication about sexual health and healthy romantic relationships as being a critical aspect of promoting wellness among youth. They felt ill equipped to engage in communication about this topic because of previous trauma. They discussed parent-adolescent relationships, the role of elders in the community and how they might be of support, as well as other possible supports to help families revitalize Inuit knowledge sharing pathways and conversations about sexual health and relationships.
3. *The impacts of childhood trauma and severed family relationships/attachments have had lasting and continuing impacts on sexual health discussions in families today.* Inuit society, which is founded on a kinship system of relationships, has been particularly impacted by severed family relationships/attachments, and parents noted the subsequent impacts on sexual health and relationships among today's adolescents.
4. *The kinship system is like a fabric that can be damaged and repaired.* In the case of Inuit communities, that kinship system, or fabric that links the community together, was damaged by the traumas of settlement and residential school. On-going intergenerational effects remain. This fabric is repaired through programs and initiatives that revitalize community relationships and the kinships system.

For more detail, see Healey (2014a, 2014b, 2016).

Crafting and storytelling are important aspects of life for Indigenous peoples the world over. They can be the root of a cathartic experience to convey the reality of loss, grief, and traumatic stress in Indigenous communities. Digital storytelling, restorying, sewing/beading, and crafting/art-making are all methods being promoted in Indigenous communities, and increasingly recognized for their value in academia. Crafting and storytelling are powerful and influential ways to challenge the mind and plant new thoughts, document history and experiences, and transform our understanding by "surprising our consciousness into a new way of seeing" (Dion Buffalo, 1990, p. 120). Such methods are an essential contribution to our understanding of the world and the knowledge that can help move our communities forward in achieving wellness.

For as long as Indigenous peoples have been the subject of research, tension has existed among many researchers and their research subjects on the interpretation, ownership, and protection of data (Alfred & Corntassel, 2005). In Canada, a number of protocols have been developed to help researchers and Indigenous communities enter into respectful negotiations about how research takes place with and for Indigenous peoples, such as the CIHR (Canadian Institutes for Health Research) Guidelines for the Ethical Conduct of Research with Aboriginal Peoples, and the Tri-Council Policy Statement II (CIHR, NSERC, & SSHRC, 2010).

In the following section, I discuss two analytical processes applied to understand and interpret the shared/collected stories for a study exploring the perspectives of Inuit parents on sexual health and relationships, their perceptions of their relationship with their children, and their perceptions of their role in, and comfort with providing sexual health knowledge and relationship guidance to their teenage children. First, I describe how stories were analyzed and interpreted through a text-based narrative technique that I used in writing my dissertation. Second, I describe a concurrent process of immersion in crafting a decorative beadwork piece for the front of my *amauti*, a traditional parka used for carrying babies and toddlers. Through these two concurrent processes, I was able to explore layered and meaningful interpretations of the parents' stories that contributed to my greater overall understanding of the health phenomena under study.

Indigenous Knowledge Theory

Indigenous knowledge and research epistemologies have been the focus of discussions in Western and Indigenous research education and learning theory (Kovach, 2009; Wilson, 2008). This literature contributes perspectives on the assumptions implicit in different research approaches and provides models for doing or interpreting research based on Indigenous worldviews. For example, Wilson (2008) describes the process of interviewing Indigenous colleagues and conveying a research process aligned with ceremony. Alfred (2004) uses the term *warrior scholarship* to convey the process Indigenous scholars can follow to ensure their communities' values are present in academic work by working to empower individuals and communities.

Questions that focus on what people perceive as important aspects of health, what variations exist, and what lived experiences mean to individuals and groups are ideally suited for qualitative methods (Crabtree & Miller, 2004). A qualitative approach also incorporates the fact that the phenomena under study are inextricably bound within the social order and the context in which people live. In qualitative research, researchers usually start with a problem or issue that emerges from a story or some experiential context (Borkan, 1999; Crabtree & Miller, 2004), which gives rise to research questions. This aspect of qualitative research is in harmony with Indigenous methods (Kovach, 2009). Indigenous ways of knowing are formulated on understandings of the world based on human interactions as well as interactions with the land, animal, and spirit worlds (Chilisa, 2012; Wilson, 2008). In what Battiste (2002) referred to as Eurocentric thought, Indigenous knowledge was often represented by the term *traditional knowledge*, which suggested a body of old data handed down generation to generation relatively unchanged. However, Indigenous knowledge is *not* static but dynamic, and embodies the following characteristics (Battiste, 2002; Grenier, 1998). Indigenous knowledge:

1. Is accumulative and represents generations of experiences, careful observations, and trial and error experiments and observations;
2. Is dynamic, with new knowledge continuously added and external knowledge adapted to suit local situations and understandings;
3. Is in the possession of all community members (i.e., elders, women, men, and children);
4. Will vary in quantity and quality according to factors such as age, gender, socioeconomic status, daily experiences, and roles and responsibilities in the home and the community;
5. Is stored in people's memories and activities and expressed in stories, songs, folklore, proverbs, dances, myths, cultural values, beliefs, rituals, cultural community, laws, local language, artifacts, forms of communication, and organization;
6. Embodies a web of relationships within a specific ecological context;
7. Contains linguistic categories, rules, and relationships unique to each knowledge system;
8. Has localized content and meaning;
9. Has established customs with respect to acquiring and sharing knowledge; and
10. Implies responsibilities for possessing various types of knowledge.

Knowledge is viewed as something people develop as they have experiences with each other and the world around them (Chilisa, 2012; Wilson, 2008). This definition of knowledge is similar in many ways to social constructionism in sociological theory (Burr, 2003). Ideas are shared, changed, and improved upon through the understanding derived from experience. Fundamentally, this knowledge is rooted in a relational epistemology—a foundation for knowing based on the formulation of relationships among the members of the community of knowers or knowledge holders (Thayer-Bacon, 2003).

Knowledge is perceived, collected, and shared in ways that are unique to these communities. Indigenous knowledge is rooted in the long inhabitation of a particular place that offers lessons for everyone's benefit, from educator to scientist (Barnhardt & Kawagley, 2005). Many of the core values, beliefs, and practices associated with these worldviews have survived and are beginning to be recognized as just as compelling for today's generations as they were for generations past. The recognition and intellectual activation of Indigenous knowledge today is an act of empowerment by Indigenous peoples (Battiste, 2002). For this reason, Indigenous knowledge and methods are of critical importance in public health, where many Indigenous communities in Canada and around the world report greater health disparities than their non-Indigenous counterparts (Young, 2003). These knowledge and methods are important for self-determination and decolonization. However, despite decades of research into Indigenous health inequities, few advances have been made in achieving a deeper understanding of the underlying issues. Applying evidence-based public health solutions to build on the strengths of Indigenous communities and mitigate the challenges are essential (Healey & Tagak Sr., 2014; Martin, 2012). Delving more deeply into our understanding of what can be achieved when we immerse ourselves in an Indigenous worldview is a part of that process.

The research study was conducted within an Indigenous knowledge framework with a focus on Inuit ways of knowing, specifically, the ᐱᓯᓇᖃᑎᒌᐃᓐᓂᖅ *Piliriqatigiinniq* Partnership Community Health Research Model (Healey & Tagak Sr., 2014). In this model, five Inuit concepts form the foundation for a research approach:

1. ᐱᓯᓇᖃᑎᒌᐃᓐᓂᖅ *Piliriqatigiinniq* (working together for the common good),
2. ᐱᑦᑎᐊᕐᓂᖅ *Pittiarniq* (being good or kind),
3. ᐃᓅᖃᑎᒌᑦᑎᐊᕐᓂᖅ *Inuuqatigiittiarniq* (being respectful of others),
4. ᐅᓂᒃᑳᖃᑎᒌᐃᓐᓂᖅ *Unikkaaqatigiinniq* (the philosophy of storytelling and/or the power and meaning of story), and
5. ᐃᖅᐊᐅᒪᖃᑎᒌᐃᓐᓂᖅ *Iqqaumaqatigiinniq* (ideas or thoughts potentially coming into one).

These theoretical aspects of the study are described in greater detail elsewhere (Healey & Tagak Sr., 2014).

Locating My Position

This research emerges from a lifelong pursuit to understand the ways in which young people in Nunavut can be supported to be and feel well. I was born and raised in Iqaluit, Nunavut. My ancestors are not Inuit. I was raised as a member of the community—a community that did not point out to me in any way that I was not Inuk. As a result, I did not grow up feeling that I was different. My husband and my children are Inuit. My worldview is embedded in Inuit ways of knowing and understanding. I love my community and where I come from. I recognize and acknowledge that I am on a learning journey as a researcher and academic, and that my understandings of Inuit philosophy and theoretical perspectives are far from being as developed as that of our Elders. I feel privileged to have been taught and mentored by elders of my community including Aalasi Joamie, Martha Tikivik, and the late Andrew Tagak, Sr.

My role, as the primary researcher for this project, was to meaningfully engage in methodologies that wove ethical approaches, participatory research, self-reflexivity, and a critique of my own social subjectivities. Indigenous research practices and worldviews, with particular emphasis on implementation in Inuit communities, were particularly important to me, because they reflect the worldview I was raised in as well as the worldview of the participants in my project. Recognizing my motivations for this research was important for the bracketing process and to help me to reflect on my interpretations of the findings.

Two Analytical Approaches

I begin by describing the first analytical approach, which was ᐅᓂᒃᑲᐊᖃᑎᒌᐃᓐᓂᖅ *Unikkaaqatigiiniq* (storytelling), and the narrative analysis of stories through immersion in text. I then describe the second approach, ᓴᓇᓂᖅ *Sananiq* (the art of crafting), and the analysis of data through the creation of a beadwork for my amauti.

> ᐅᓂᒃᑲᐊᖃᑎᒌᐃᓐᓂᖅ *Unikkaaqatigiinniq—Approach 1: Narrative Analysis of Stories Through Immersion in Text*

ᐅᓂᒃᑲᐊᖃᑎᒌᐃᓐᓂᖅ *Unikkaaqatigiinniq* is an Inuktitut word for the Inuit concept related to storytelling, the power of story, and the role of story in Inuit ways of knowing and learning. Kovach (2009) states that a defining characteristic of Indigenous methods is the inclusion of story and narrative by both the researcher and research participant. In an Indigenous context, story is methodologically congruent with tribal knowledge (Wilson, 2008). Inuit have a very strong oral history and oral culture. The telling of stories is a millennia-old tradition for the sharing of knowledge, values, morals, skills, histories, legends, and artistry. It is a critical aspect of Inuit way of life and ways of knowing, and allows respondents to share personal experiences without breaking cultural rules related to confidentiality, gossip, or humility. Inuit stories and storytelling are rich with metaphor, lessons, and knowledge about time and place. When a story is told, each listener may interpret the story differently depending on their life experiences, where they come from, and where they are in life. Stories are not always explained clearly. It is up to the listener to interpret and seek understanding in the meaning of the story. Indigenous scholars Kovach (2009) and Wilson (2008) have underscored the importance of *story* in a research setting. Understanding this approach for sharing knowledge allows for greater insight into the meaning of the stories. It is for this reason that the recognition of the power of story is particularly important in the context of Inuit communities.

In a relational epistemology, stories are shared not collected (Thayer-Bacon, 2003). Interviews are experienced as conversations conducted in a natural, comfortable setting. The researcher's willingness to listen, quietly and carefully, without interrupting the storyteller is vital. Listening and observation are important values in Inuit society, and are part of a learner's pathway to understanding (QHRC, 2014). During interviews, I asked open-ended questions about where participants were from, their families, and their perspectives on relationships among young people. As part of the exchange, I also told them about where I was from and my family. In return, they told me about their families, life experiences, and feelings about different events in the community. We talked about residential school, harvesting, family relations, relationships in the community, their observations of youth in the community, and feelings of love for children and grandchildren. In much the same way as we might have a conversation around a kitchen table, the dialogue resembles a conversation more than a formal interview. This process of data collection is congruent with Indigenous storytelling traditions. I listened with an open heart and an open mind, as is expected in Inuit culture.

Parents defined the term *sexual health* largely in relation to community and social context. They identified specific events in community history, then shared stories of personal experiences related to the events. Historical events most frequently discussed in the interviews included settlement and residential school. Settlement refers to the time period in the 1950s and 1960s when Inuit families were forced and/or coerced into abandoning seasonal nomadic camps for habitation in year-round settlements or communities. Parents shared specific experiences of childhood trauma, hardship, and sexual abuse related to these events, and often highlighted their desire to create a different path for their own children as a result of these experienced traumas.

Data were analyzed through a process of "immersion and crystallization" (Borkan, 1999, p. 179), which is analogous to the Inuit concept of ᐃᖅᑲᐅᒪᖃᑎᒌᓐᓂᖅ *Iqqaumaqatigiinniq*, "all knowing coming into one" (Healey & Tagak Sr, 2014, p. 1). The goal of data analysis is to find meaning and understanding in the stories, return to the research question, and examine the data in the context that was set at the beginning of the study. To accomplish this, often a multi-stage process is needed (Creswell, 2013). Thinking about, interpreting, and analyzing dialogue at the time of the conversation with a participant is part of the process, allowing for some understanding to develop in the immediate moment of the conversation.

The recordings of interviews/conversations were listened to and transcripts reread to ensure the transcripts were verbatim and to fill in missing words (Creswell, 2013). Then, to make the volumes of text easier to manage, I used software. Although I had been trained in NVivo, I found the newest version unwieldy and overcomplicated. It was difficult to organize text the way I wanted to and when I tried to use the visualization tools, I became frustrated with the different and confusing arrangements. In the end, I used HyperRESEARCH software, which was one of the few text-management software applications available at the

SEE FIGURE 3.1   at eResource—Screenshot of HyperRESEARCH Software and Coding Text.

time for the Apple operating system. HyperRESEARCH was very simple, with a code and retrieve function. I was able to organize transcripts by individual and by community, and I was able to select large amounts of text (i.e., a full story), and code it, or assign that story to one or more ideas (see Figure 3.1 for a screenshot of HyperRESEARCH software and coding text). For example, one parent told a story about knowledge from elders about how children follow in the footsteps of their parents and their parents in the footsteps of their grandparents, much like the way caribou will follow a single path through the snow. This was coded to "ancestors."

The text was coded with short words or phrases such as "grandparents," "violence," "lost generation," and "sexual assault," which began to feed into bigger concepts such as "words from elders," "adolescent development," "knowledge about sexual health," "community economics," "intergenerational relational knowledge," and "what happens when relationships are severed and the path can't be followed."

The following excerpt was assigned to a category of "explain sexual health to child," which then became part of a larger concept called "knowledge about sexual health."

> My son and I have a very open relationship. My 17-year-old one. Um, cause I was a single mother with him for 10 years. And um we tell each other everything . . . growing up with my parents, I thought that like you know it was so . . . they lied to me so much about stuff like that. (laughing) I just wanted to be honest with my son. Tell him the truth and . . . that way he doesn't get any misinformation from anyone. (Laughing) . . . I tell him you know to wear protection and be respectful of girls when they say no and um like never—never force yourself on anyone. And if you get any kind of um discomfort or anything he has to go see the nurse or . . . But he knows. (laughing)

In the analysis, codes that had only appeared once in the complete analysis were reviewed to determine if they belonged to a larger concept or if they were independent ideas of their own. Codes tied to only one reference and not linking with another concept or group of codes became less of a focus in the analysis. I spent time reviewing the concepts and, in particular, looked closely at concepts appearing more than once in more than one story. I looked for the meaning of those stories, not just a literal interpretation of the words of the participant, but the deeper meaning as a part of a collective narrative about sexual health and relationships among young people in Nunavut.

During this process very few patterns emerged. Separating segments of text and assigning them to a category felt disingenuous. I was reminded of a passage in the book *Research is Ceremony* in which the author describes the breakdown of relationships when we break things down into their smallest pieces (Wilson, 2008). This process severed the relationship between the learner and storyteller. I abandoned the coding exercises and instead reflected upon the interviews and stories in their entirety in comparison to the original research question and examined them in the context of the literature review, similar to the processes described by Kovach (2009).

Data analysis followed a rigorous, respectful, and mindful process that included comparing findings to the known literature (Creswell, 2013) and reflexivity and bracketing of my perspectives before and during the study (Mays & Pope, 2000). This included reflecting on my motivations, the emotions I felt when listening to the stories, and my experiences growing up in my community. The data collection and analysis process was iterative because I started to analyze the story as it was being told to me, which informed future interviews. Placing the ideas in the context of the literature, the experiences of others, and the experiences of the community is part of finding meaning and understanding. I would write bullet-point reflections down in my notebook, and then go back into the narratives that evening or the next day, and review the stories that stood out to me in relation to that topic.

Discussing these ideas with others, colleagues, collaborators, or participants was also a critical part of the analysis at this phase from a relational perspective (Kovach, 2009; Wilson, 2008). After I finished data collection and went more deeply into the analysis, I discussed early findings with local Nunavut-based advisors who included representatives from two community wellness centers (the Arviat Community Wellness Centre and a second center that will remain anonymous), the Chief Medical Officer of Health for Nunavut, a Community Health Representative, and a public health nurse. For these conversations, I presented the findings in person or over the telephone to each individual. We discussed the findings in the context of their life or work. They provided support and indicated that the findings better helped them interpret and take action on their work activities.

I also reviewed findings in person with three participants who wished to be recontacted. We met in a comfortable setting where I explained all the topic areas I felt were crystalized in the analysis and asked for their perspectives on whether these accurately captured the experiences they shared and that of others in the community. Their responses were overwhelmingly positive. One participant stated,

> You were able to explain very clearly what I was not able to say. I know in my heart that what you have found is here is true. This is what has happened in our community. You have given voice to that.

Most importantly, I honored the stories shared by parents by keeping their words intact as often as possible in the presentation of results without breaching confidentiality (Healey & Tagak Sr., 2014; Kovach, 2009).

Finally, part of my analysis process involved taking a break from the text and audio data and working on something physical. For example, I would break from the computer to exercise, walk, sew, bead, or cook. During these activities, my hands or body would be busy (see next section), which left my mind free to roam and think about the stories in different ways, possibly seeing different meanings crystalizing in different ways as described by Borkan (1999).

ᓴᓇᓂᖅ Sananiq/Crafting—Approach 2: Narrative Analysis of Stories Through Beadwork

Documenting my own story is part of preserving my research process and both grounding my study in Inuit knowledge and acknowledging the inherent relational philosophy of ᐃᓄᐅᖃᑎᒌᑦᑎᐊᕐᓂᖅ *Inuuqatigiittiarniq*. Here I explain how the stories and analysis that were part of crafting my dissertation, by chance, became part of my own parallel story involving the process of crafting a beaded centerpiece for my *amauti*.

Storytelling and crafting are strongly linked concepts in Inuit culture. McGrath (2011) stated,

> Craft culture is not just about sewing, it is about making things of all kinds. Epistemology is a theory or philosophy of knowledge, a way of looking at knowledge and understanding it as knowledge and knowing. What are the metaphors for knowledge, knowing, and skill, and how are those metaphors organized in Inuit culture? In my understanding the main one is sananiq—craft. Sananiq is primarily relational and social. Skills are observed, taught, acquired, refined and developed through relationships; so is knowledge. It is also practical in its essential relationality; people make things that are needed by others or themselves in the service of others. So is knowledge. What is available is used to make things, and if what is needed is not available, qanuqtuurniq (innovation) is a natural way to think. In sum, sananiq/craft for me, is a metaphor for thinking, thought and knowledge.
>
> *(McGrath, 2011, p. 283)*

My crafting story began in 2011 after I completed the data collection for the sexual health study and my second daughter was born. In an effort to get out of the house, I joined an evening sewing group for women who wished to learn more about beading for an *amauti*. Beads were introduced to Inuit by traders in the 19th century (Driscoll, 1984). Inuit in different Arctic regions incorporated foreign objects like beads, coins, and spoons, into clothing, jewelry, and tools in different ways (Driscoll, 1984). An *amauti* is a traditional Inuit women's parka with a pouch on the back in which the baby or toddler is carried. *Amautiit* (pl) are very common today and almost all Inuit, and some non-Inuit, mothers (and many fathers) have one in Nunavut and Nunavik. The sewing group was taught by an elder in the Inuktitut language to a small group of women. I knew all of the women in attendance through one aspect of my life or another. During our sewing sessions, I discovered a relationship between my daughter's namesake and one of my fellow sewers, and I enjoyed listening to stories about the person for whom she was named. This is one of the joys that we derive from sharing stories in our northern communities in an informal setting like a sewing group.

I had learned the basic principles of beading as a child in elementary school when elders would visit the school and work on projects with us related to sewing, carving, building, or cooking. We would rotate through a schedule, which would allow us to spend time with each elder on different days of the week and develop different skills. Beading was one of the projects I remembered, but it had been over 25 years since I had tried it. I appreciated the opportunity to revive the skill as an adult with a group of women in my community.

Rather unintentionally, I started planning and crafting my beading project for the front-piece of my *amauti* at the same time that I *crafted* my dissertation. I analyzed data and wrote about the findings of the study while picking up beads on the thread and placing them on the fabric. The beading was part of my reflexive process. This is important because the crafting of the dissertation and the crafting of the front of my *amauti* were intertwined. The processes were linked, and the stories of the people I interviewed were in my head as I sat at the computer and wrote, and while I sat at the table and beaded. In Figures 3.2 to 3.4, the progression of the beadwork is documented.

To bead in this fashion, the beads are sewn into the fabric in groups of four. Four beads are picked up on the needle, pushed down the thread into position next to the previous row, and anchored. The grouping of four beads is then anchored again, by two additional stiches that run perpendicular to the row. If a tear develops in a thread, the anchors keep the whole piece from unraveling. Instead of losing a series of beads, one might only lose one or two. To repair such a tear, the loose string can be reknotted underneath and replacement beads can be sewn into the gaps in the pattern. It may not look exactly the same, but it will be strong and beautiful nonetheless.

SEE FIGURE 3.2 at eResource—Finished Work.

SEE FIGURE 3.3 at eResource—Close-Up of Owl.

SEE FIGURE 3.4 at eResource—Owl Sewn On to My Amauti.

Sitting at the table and beading led me deeper into thought about fabric—the fabric of society. When something happens to fabric to tear it or damage it, what do we do with the fabric? Do we throw it out? No. Do we repair it? Yes, because torn fabric is still beautiful, useful, and valuable.

I began to see the contextual events of our Inuit communities, which were embedded in the stories of the people I interviewed, as tears in Inuit relational *fabric*. Settlement, residential school, and medical evacuations tore families apart and ripped the relational fabric. Kinship, extended family bonds, and attachments, were metaphorically the *anchor* stitches in the beadwork that had become severed through the separation and relocation of families during these historical events in our communities. Intergenerational trauma and the systemic perpetuation of colonial policies continue to feed the unraveling of the threads, much as environmental elements and trauma wear away at sewing threads. In this analogy, the threads must be reanchored. To find new anchors, our community members need support to heal from trauma. The holes can be filled with other colors and other beads, such as the innovations and initiatives of the people in our communities. Such initiatives grow out of revitalized relationships between individuals, among parents and children, within and between families, and in the greater community. With time, effort, and skill, repairs can be made to the fabric. It will look different, and that is okay. What is important is that the fabric retains its beauty, strength, and story. This process of reformation acknowledges the past but also builds toward the future, cultivating hope.

Beading led to me to a place where I could develop this deeper understanding and vision of relational fabric. While I was beading, I would write down or draw the ideas that would come to me on an iPad and revisit them later in the analysis of the narratives.

The stories shared in the study were also metaphorically woven into the beadwork. That is, as I was beading in the evenings I was also immersed in the stories, thinking, analyzing, and reading and rereading transcripts. As McGrath (2011) notes, *sananiq* is not about crafting and making an object, it is a metaphor for thinking, thought, and knowledge. My interpretations of the narratives become more developed as I placed beads on the needle and anchored them to the fabric. The combined processes furthered my understanding of the topic, context, and impact of the health issue on societal and relational levels. Thinking deeply about this perspective on *craft-knowing* was an important part of the research process and is part of the concept of *Unikkaaqatigiinniq* (the power and meaning of story) described in the *Piliriqatigiinniq* Community Health Research Model, the theory upon which this study was based.

Conclusion

This data analysis process involved two concurrent analytical approaches, each of which contributed meaning and understanding to the findings.

ᐅᓂᒃᑳᖅᑎᒋᐃᓐᓂᖅ *Unikkaaqatigiinniq* and ᓴᓇᓂᖅ *Sananiq* were not mutually exclusive analytical processes; they built on each other and fed into each other in different ways permitting layered interpretations of the phenomena I was seeking to understand. Additionally, our age, the lands we come from, our knowledge, and our individual and collective experiences will influence our interpretations at any given time. This does not compromise the validity of the analysis, because each interpretation is equally legitimate. Crafting and storytelling are important aspects of life for Indigenous peoples the world over (Battiste, 2002; Kovach, 2009; Wilson, 2008). Conveying the reality of loss, grief, and traumatic grief or stress in Indigenous communities through digital storytelling (Iseke & Moore, 2012), restorying (Corntassel, Chaw-win-is, & T'lakwadzi, 2009), sewing/beading (Hanson, 2016), or crafting/art-making (Lavallee, 2009; Pauktuutit, 2012) can be a cathartic part of a healing journey. Crafting and storytelling are powerful and offer ways to challenge the mind and plant new thoughts, document history and experiences, and transform our understanding by "surprising our consciousness into a new way of seeing" (Dion Buffalo, 1990, p. 120). Such methods are an essential contribution to our understanding of health and the knowledge that can help move our communities forward in achieving wellness.

KEY WORKS GUIDING MY DATA ANALYSIS

Borkan, J. (1999). Immersion/crystallization. In B. Crabtree & W. Miller (Eds.), *Doing qualitative research* (2nd ed., pp. 179–194). Thousand Oaks, CA: Sage.

> This book chapter articulates a process of meaning-making similar to the Inuit concept of *Iqqaumaqatigiiniiq*. I was drawn to the analytical process described by Borkan for this reason.

Kovach, M. (2009). *Indigenous methodologies: Characteristics, conversations, and contexts.* Toronto, ON: University of Toronto Press.

> This book provides an excellent overview of Indigenous methods and considerations in the research and academic world. One particularly helpful section discusses moral and ethical questions a researcher may face when analyzing stories in an Indigenous story-telling context. For example, when coding text, some researchers might code one statement or phrase to a particular topic. From an Indigenous story-telling perspective, it can be viewed as unethical to separate segments of a story from each other and code in this manner. Kovach describes considerations for researchers who seek to find balance in this process.

Qaujigiartiit Health Research Centre (QHRC; 2014). *Inunnguiniq parenting program curriculum manual.* Iqaluit, NU: Qaujigiartiit Health Research Centre.

Inunnguiniq is the Inuktitut term for raising a capable human being. It is a philosophy commonly applied to childrearing, but valid over the life course. Core principles of *Inunnguiniq* include showing compassion, skill-building, recognizing the strengths in others, helping each other, and fostering well-being in ourselves and families. This manual on the topic of *Inunnguinq* was developed with the input of more than 25 elders from across Nunavut. Their perspectives were very helpful during the analysis of stories about families and family relationships.

Wilson, S. (2008). *Research is ceremony: Indigenous research methods.* Blackpoint, Nova Scotia: Fernwood.

One of my favorite quotes from this book is "They did not give me the answer. They took me to a place where I found the answer myself" (p. 118). Wilson and his colleagues explore some of the different ways in which we can find meaning and understanding in a research context, incorporating narratives from other researchers to beautifully articulate the topics and methods that are discussed.

References

Alfred, T. (2004). Warrior scholarship: Seeing the university as the ground of contention. In D. A. Mihesuah & A. C. Wilson (Eds.), *Indigenizing the academy: Transforming scholarship and empowering communities* (pp. 88–99). Lincoln, NB: University of Nebraska Press.

Alfred, T., & Corntassel, J. (2005). Being Indigenous: Resurgences against contemporary colonialism. *Government and Opposition, 40,* 597–614.

Barnhardt, R., & Kawagley, A. O. (2005). Indigenous knowledge systems and Alaska Native ways of knowing. *Anthropology & Education Quarterly, 36,* 8–23.

Battiste, M. (2002). *Indigenous knowledge and pedagogy in First Nations education: A literature review with recommendations.* Ottawa, ON: Government of Canada, Department of Indian and Northern Affairs (INAC). Retrieved from www.afn.ca/uploads/files/education/24._2002_oct_marie_battiste_indigenousknowledgeandpedagogy_lit_review_for_min_working_group.pdf

Borkan, J. (1999). Immersion/crystallization. In B. Crabtree & W. Miller (Eds.), *Doing qualitative research* (2nd ed., pp. 179–194). Thousand Oaks, CA: Sage.

Burr, V. (2003). *Social constructionism* (2nd ed.). Hoboken, NJ: John Wiley & Sons.

Canadian Institutes of Health Research, National Science and Engineering Research Council, Social Sciences and Humanities Research Council, (CIHR, NSERC, & SSHRC). (2010). *Tri-council policy statement: Ethical conduct for research involving humans.*

Retrieved from www.pre.ethics.gc.ca/eng/policy-politique/initiatives/tcps2-eptc2/ Default/

Chilisa, B. (2012). Postcolonial indigenous research paradigms. In B. Chilisa (Ed.), *Indigenous research methodologies* (pp. 98–127). Thousand Oaks, CA: Sage.

Corntassel, J., Chaw-win-is, & T'lakwadzi. (2009). Indigenous storytelling, truth-telling, and community approaches to reconciliation. *English Studies in Canada (ESC), 35*(1), 137–159.

Crabtree, B., & Miller, W. (2004). Research methods: Qualitative. In R. Jones, N. Britten, L. Culpepper, D. A. Gass, R. Grol, D. Mant, & C. Silagy (Eds.), *Oxford textbook of primary medical care* (pp. 507–511). Oxford: Oxford University Press.

Creswell, J. W. (2013). *Qualitative inquiry and research design: Choosing among five approaches* (3rd ed.). Thousand Oaks, CA: Sage.

Dion Buffalo, Y. R. (1990). Seeds of thought, arrows of change: Native storytelling as metaphor. In T. A. Laidlaw, C. Malmo, & Associates (Eds.), *Healing voices: Feminist approaches to therapy with women* (pp. 118–142). San Francisco, CA: Jossey-Bass.

Driscoll, B. (1984). Sapangat—Inuit beadwork in the Canadian Arctic. *Expedition, 26*(2), 40–47.

Grenier, L. (1998). *Working with indigenous knowledge: A guide for researchers.* Ottawa, ON: International Development Research Centre. Retrieved from www.idrc.ca/en/book/working-Indigenous-knowledge-guide-researchers

Hanson, C. (2016). Stitching the stories together: Studies of intergenerational learning among Indigenous women. In L. Formenti & L. West (Eds.), *Stories that make a difference: Exploring the collective, social and political potential of narratives in adult education research* (pp. 78–84). Caprioli, Italy: Pensa Multimedia.

Healey, G. K. (2014a). Inuit family understandings of sexual health and relationships in Nunavut. *Canadian Journal of Public Health, 105*, e133–e137.

Healey, G. K. (2014b). Inuit parent perspectives on sexual health communication with adolescent children in Nunavut: "It's kinda hard for me to find the words". *International Journal of Circumpolar Health, 73*, 1–7.

Healey, G. K. (2016). Youth perspectives on sexually transmitted infections and sexual health in Northern Canada and implications for public health practice. *International Journal of Circumpolar Health, 75*, 1–6.

Healey, G. K., & Tagak, A., Sr. (2014). Piliriqatigiinniq 'working in a collaborative way for the common good': A perspective on the space where health research methodology and Inuit epistemology come together. *International Journal of Critical Indigenous Studies, 7*(1), 1–14.

Iseke, J., & Moore, S. (2012). Community-based Indigenous digital storytelling with elders and youth. *American Indian Culture and Research, 35*(4), 19–38.

Kovach, M. (2009). *Indigenous methodologies: Characteristics, conversations, and contexts.* Toronto, ON: University of Toronto Press.

Lavallee, L. F. (2009). Practical application of an Indigenous research framework and two qualitative Indigenous research methods: Sharing circles and Anishnaabe symbol-based reflection. *International Journal of Qualitative Methods, 8*(1), 21–40.

Martin, D. H. (2012). Two-eyed seeing: A framework for understanding Indigenous and non-Indigenous approaches to Indigenous health research. *Canadian Journal of Nursing Research, 44*(2), 20–42.

Mays, N., & Pope, C. (2000). Assessing quality in qualitative health research. *British Medical Journal, 320*(7226), 50–52.

McGrath, J. T. (2011). *Isumaksaqsiurutigijakka: Conversations with Aupilaarjuk towards a theory of Inuktitut knowledge renewal*. (Doctoral dissertation). Carleton University, Ottawa, ON.

Pauktuutit Inuit Women of Canada. (2012). *Nipiqaqtugut Sanaugatigut—truth and reconciliation commemoration virtual quilt project*. Retrieved from www.pauktuutit.ca/abuse-prevention/ residential-schools/trc-virtual-quilt-nipiqaqtugut-sanaugatigut/

Qaujigiartiit Health Research Centre (QHRC). (2014). *Inunnguiniq parenting program curriculum manual*. Iqaluit, NU: Qaujigiartiit Health Research Centre.

Thayer-Bacon, B. (2003). *Relational epistemologies*. New York, NY: Peter Lang.

Wilson, S. (2008). *Research is ceremony: Indigenous research methods*. Blackpoint, Nova Scotia: Fernwood.

Young, T. K. (2003). Review of research on Aboriginal populations in Canada: Relevance to their health needs. *British Medical Journal, 327*, 419–422.

4

THEMATIC AND PHENOMENOLOGICAL ANALYSIS IN RESEARCH ON INTIMATE RELATIONSHIPS

Paul C. Rosenblatt and Elizabeth Wieling

This chapter describes our analysis of phenomenological (lived experience) interviews with 37 adults for our book *Knowing and Not Knowing in Intimate Relationships* (Rosenblatt & Wieling, 2013). The interviews explored what people had to say about what they knew and did not know about a spouse or lover, what they wanted to know and did not want to know, what the other knew and did not know about them, and what they did not want the other to know about them. For example, many people said they wanted to be known well, but some said they did not want their partner to know about past lovers or the ways they were different from how they represented themselves to their partner in such areas as what they ate, how they managed money, or how much they were monogamous. Similarly, they might want to know a great deal about their partner but also not want to know much about their partner's past lovers, experiences and activities at work, or their partner's negative judgments about the clothing they wore. The interviews also explored how people went about knowing and not knowing about the other, how they tried to help the other learn about them and block the other from knowing certain things, and the reasons people gave for what they and their partner did or did not do about knowing and not knowing.

Our data analysis began months before we started interviewing with thinking through the focus of the study and what questions to ask. Coming to a focus and arriving at questions created a framework for data analysis, because it set preliminary boundaries around the data to be gathered and the topic areas for most intensive questioning and thus what the richest data to be analyzed were likely to be.

We interviewed every person together and processed the interviews analytically through the ways we questioned each interviewee and discussed each interview immediately afterward. After the first four interviews were transcribed, we independently did thematic analyses of the transcripts and then discussed our analyses. The discussion was reassuring in that we agreed a great deal about the material. We had some differences in emphasis, and discussing those differences was useful in removing what might have been problems later on in data analysis and writing. We also identified some ways to change or add to our interviewing and hence our subsequent data analysis. (Coding as a study progresses and using that coding to change interviewing is consistent with a grounded theory approach—e.g., Strauss & Corbin, 1998). In the process, we tentatively decided what we would focus on in subsequent interviews and in the data analysis when all data were collected.

As the study went forward, Paul transcribed most of the interviews, using Microsoft Word, and carefully checked the few interviews transcribed by volunteers. Thus, he knew each interview very well prior to formal data analysis. With the two us being experienced qualitative researchers, and given the phenomenological framework we worked with that focused on meanings and understandings interviewees gave to things, we felt justified in carrying out a final analysis in which Paul did a preliminary thematic data analysis of all 37 transcripts, which sorted material into the detailed preliminary book outline categories we had by then developed. Following that, Liz reviewed Paul's preliminary thematic analysis and book outline in terms of accuracy, clarity of understanding of each interview quote coded, and the possibility of missing important things. One luxury we had for assuring quality and trustworthiness of data analysis was that we knew we intended to present the material in book form, and with a book length report we could provide readers with far more interview quotes than in a journal article. Book readers would have many more interview quotes to use in judging the fidelity of our claims about themes.

Key Steps in the Data Analysis

What follow are our key steps in data analysis. We describe processes of grounding the study and ourselves, interviewing together as part of data analysis, discussing each interview immediately after carrying it out, and transcribing interviews and reviewing transcripts as a step in data analysis. We then discuss how we conducted preliminary thematic coding of the first four interviews, followed by formal thematic analysis when all the data had been gathered and transcribed.

Grounding the Study and Ourselves

We reviewed the literature well enough to have a good idea about where the hole was in the literature that we wanted our research to address. There was no in-depth qualitative study of knowing and not knowing in long-term intimate relationships that was like what we wanted to do. Understanding this gap set up parameters in the thematic coding that we would eventually do. Our plan was to focus our coding on the interviewees' meanings and understandings. Conceptual approaches in the fields of communication and experimental social psychology, despite not being phenomenological or grounded in data about long-term intimate relationships, influenced our interview schedule and hence the material we gathered.

We engaged in obsessive preparation, with considerable discussion of what we were going to ask, and that preparation guided our drafting and redrafting of the interview guide (located in the book's Appendix). We planned for our interviews to go beyond the guide to capture whatever it was that interviewees had to say that might be different from, deeper than, or more nuanced than what was in the guide. The guide was also a preliminary map for thematic analysis of the data. We knew that asking the questions we were going to ask and digging into the answers to those questions with follow-up questions would be central in shaping our coding categories. We were going to ask interviewees, for example, about choices regarding what to self-disclose and not to self-disclose in their relationship, and not about what they did in their paid employment. That made sense because we expected our coding to focus a great deal on self-disclosure decisions and not at all on paid employment.

As part of coming to clarity about what we were up to and what we were going to ask, we discussed our own experiences of knowing and not knowing in close relationships (for example, in our earliest love relationships) and interviewed each other. This process established our own experiential groundings for what to ask about and code—for example, whether or not relationship history shows up in current relationships and gender issues. This process was also a step into reflexivity (e.g., Gubrium & Holstein, 1997), which we used to establish a sense of how our own selves and experiences were linked to our curiosity about the topic, our belief that the topic was important, how we framed the issues, what we thought was important to ask and code, what we thought we would hear from people, and how our being who we were might bias what we reported. It was also a way to establish what we had to bracket (Tufford & Newman, 2010), putting aside our own projections and assumptions in order to be, like any good scientist, unbiased in understanding and making sense of what our interviewees had to say. We wanted to be fully open to their lived experience and not make the mistake of coming up with coding and a research narrative that made it seem that everyone was like us. A piece of doing that well involved being aware of our own experiences in the domain of our research.

Interviewing Together

When one is both the interviewer and data analyst, considerable data analysis can occur during the interview. It is not only that one thinks about how to code something an interviewee just said, though that can be important, but also how one can press an interviewee for clarification about a topic (e.g., for illustrations or to address seeming contradictions in what she or he has said). Additionally, that might encourage an interviewee to say more about what will likely be interesting and of value in the data analysis. For example, when a man who talked in general terms about his wife hiding important things from him was asked for examples, he gave an example that made clear that what bothered him most was that she hid her intent to do things and by doing that she blocked him from offering his point of view before she acted.

We carried out every interview together, and we remained cognizant of our codes as we interviewed and listened. When either of us asked a question, summarized for the interviewee what we just heard, or pushed for additional material, that communicated to the other what might be coded and in what ways. For example, in an interview where it seemed that Paul had reached a point where he thought he understood where a woman was about self-disclosure to her partner and that she was as open as possible, Liz asked the woman a question that opened things up again, both for the interviewee and Paul. Liz asked: "Are there things that shouldn't be shared? Or is there any reason why someone in a partnership wouldn't share some things?" The woman's response made clear that things were more complicated with her than it had seemed to Paul, and she then said quite a lot that added to what we coded in her case about areas of not wanting to be known.

We took turns being the lead interviewer with the understanding that the other could interrupt at any time to follow an interview line further, to take things in a new direction, to ask for clarification, to question an answer, and so on. How each of us asked the interview guide questions and how each of us questioned in general was to some extent different, which is common with multiple interviewers (Rosenblatt, 2012). For example, Liz, who is a clinician, asked more clinical-sounding questions (e.g., about feelings and about steps an interviewee might have taken to problem solve) and was definitely better than Paul at exploring issues of sexuality. Our differences were not a problem because with both of us present and active at every interview, we had the benefit of each other's interviewing strengths.

Discussing Each Interview Immediately After Completing It

After each interview, often beginning just minutes after the interviewee left our offices or we left the interviewee's house, we discussed the interview, with discussions usually running an hour or more. We did not record these discussions but trusted our memories. The context of that trust of our memories included that we saw our research approach as postmodern and hence perspectival rather than the pursuit of precise truth. That made keeping exact records of our discussions seem unnecessary, and besides, we both had many other projects and responsibilities and were loath to add to the amount of material we would someday have to process as we moved forward with the project.

Our discussions were wide-ranging, though the core of them was always about the interviewee—the person's narratives, phenomenology, and ways of answering our questions—and what we were likely to code from the interview. Sometimes we discussed ambiguities in what an interviewee said. Additionally, after the first case we compared each case with one or more other cases. These comparisons helped identify which budding thematic categories might be more significant because of being widespread among the interviewees—for example, the value to many interviewees of knowing their partner well. These comparisons also helped us identify distinctions that might make sense to draw in coding and eventual writing—for example, withholding information from a partner that allowed the person to continue doing what the partner would not want done versus withholding information from the partner to protect them. With early cases we talked about how to add to or modify our interview guide, in the spirit of theoretical sampling (Strauss & Corbin, 1998). That meant that our ideas of what to code and what data to gather in order to code evolved, with later interviews based on a somewhat different interview guide.

There was a reflexive element to our post-interview discussions, relating what each interviewee said to our own experiences, realities, anxieties, and so on. This was a way to use self-as-researcher in making sense of what the interviewee said and deciding what was important and what we understood. These discussions were also part of ensuring that we knew where our own selves were in making sense of an interview and, by knowing that, to ensure that we were not projecting ourselves or our defensive reactions to feeling threatened by interviewee values and realities into the coding. For example, at times we both had to process our emotional reactions to interviewees who in some way reminded us of ourselves.

Some of our discussions pushed deep into analytical alternatives for working with the material. Although we were working with a general phenomenological approach and a more focused phenomenology-of-everyday-life approach (e.g., van Manen, 1990), some interviews drew us into discussions of feminist critical thought (e.g., McDowell & Fang, 2007), the anthropology of emic cultural realities (e.g., Sanday, 1979), and other analytic frameworks. These discussions did not derail our phenomenology-of-everyday-life approach, but they pushed us to think about alternative paths our analysis and writing might take and to be sensitive in our analyses and writing to other perspectives. For example, our discussions of gender (ours, the interviewees', gender in society, etc.) led us to draft personal statements about gender and to explore diverse ways in which we might write about gender.

A sticky coding issue in any qualitative study is what to do with material that for some reason one feels less confident about. In this study, one interviewee seemed to have early dementia, which raised questions for us about what to do with some of her comments. Another interviewee's self-presentation, account of himself, and realities seemed strange and implausible to us, compared to what we were hearing from other people and what we knew about our own lives and those of other people we knew. There were also several men whose narratives about their relationship life were to a large extent different from what we thought we were studying. In particular, their answers to questions about knowing and not knowing seemed to us to be mostly about sexuality, what annoyed them, and how they got their way. We then had the challenge of how much to use from their interviews and how much we had the right to exclude what they said that seemed not to be on the topic of the study. With these cases a key part of our post-interview review involved discussing how much and in what ways to use material that we thought was not about what we were studying, given that what they said to us seemed to be what they thought were appropriate answers to our questions.

In the end we decided not to discard any case. If someone gave a strange answer to a question we kept track of that answer, but unless it made sense to us as a deviant case conceptually relevant to the main line of cases, we were not going to use it. For example, a man who talked at length about being treated for alcoholism, his sexual dysfunction, and his efforts to have sex with his wife, including his assaulting her, did not seem to us to be answering the questions we were asking about knowing and not knowing. That did not mean we were prematurely locked into a coding framework. In fact, there were cases that pushed us to think about things in new ways and to expand the scope of what we thought we were dealing with. For example, some people who spoke eloquently about their own dishonesty and deception in an intimate relationship or their experience of a partner's dishonesty and deception expanded our thinking to include partner deceptions people seem to be aware of, to not confront, and to live with.

We often discussed the data (in ways that respected interviewee confidentiality) with colleagues, students, transcribers, and friends. Telling others some of what was in our data, for example, about the woman who found that her husband was secretly binge-eating food that was very dangerous to his health, was a step toward being clear with ourselves about what we had. It sometimes was also about identifying what we were having trouble being clear about—when we found ourselves not being able to describe something clearly to others. And, at times, it was about reflexivity in that the discussions pushed us to be clear about where our own personal phenomenology was in the situation. Some people we discussed cases with offered comments and questions that led us to be smarter about the material, but what was most helpful in talking with others was that it pushed us to be clear and articulate about what we were learning.

Transcribing Data and Reviewing Transcripts

For us, transcribing is a step in data analysis. Paul transcribed most of the interviews (and carefully checked the transcriptions done by volunteer transcribers). Transcribing and careful checking of transcriptions by others made it clear what riches there were to code, what the preponderance of responses to certain questions was, and what interviewee statements about various topics would make vivid quotes concerning what was likely to be central in our thematic analysis. We had 711 single-spaced pages of interview transcripts. The transcriptions were what the formal thematic analysis coding was going to involve, and with so much engagement with the audio-recorded interviews and having been present and involved throughout each interview, Paul knew each interview very well prior to the formal data analysis. Liz also had vivid recall of each interview and had the transcripts to work with, so we were both fully involved in the coding.

Preliminary Thematic Coding of the First Four Interviews

After the first four interviews were transcribed, we carried out a preliminary thematic phenomenological analysis of them. Although we had been having congenial discussions of the project and the interviews and seemed to be in agreement about everything, we felt we needed to check on (a) whether we would actually be in high agreement with regard to the data analysis and (b) whether the data we were getting could support our ambitions for what we hoped to write.

In our thematic phenomenological analysis of these four cases, we looked for dominant themes and subthemes regarding the lived experience of knowing and not knowing, being known, and now known. We were not guided by any single source on how to code, but what we did was in the spirit of van Manen's (1990) analysis of lived experience. We used all three analytic strategies proposed by van Manen—holistic, selective, and detailed. In our debriefing conversations we developed a holistic picture of each participant, and that picture was in mind as we coded. In coding, we were purposeful about focusing on particular topics (selective) and we coded and analyzed those in a way that focused on details of what people said and details of our analytic interpretation. We coded independently of each other and without a predetermined, common codebook, so we were each generating emergent codes from the interview material. Of course we were not really independent, because we had worked closely together in developing the focus of the study and the interview guide. Also, we had carried out the four interviews together and had spent considerable time processing each interview. In doing the coding we each developed a rough draft outline of our coding categories and placed interview quotes from each case in appropriate places in the outline. We saw the outlining as a big step toward the framework we would use in coding when all the data were in, what we hoped would be the outline of the book we would write.

When we completed our independent coding and sat down to review and discuss what one another had come up with we found that there was substantial overlap. For example, we both identified core themes about wanting to be known by the other and wanting to know the other. However, there were some differences in the level of abstraction that we were coding, with Liz doing more detailed coding, staying closer to words and more line by line, whereas Paul was linking data points in a more selective and holistic view. That meant that Paul was working with fewer and more inclusive coding categories and also coding a smaller percentage of each interview. We discussed our overlap and differences in detail during a long face-to-face session, which, interestingly, did not necessarily lead to eliminating any differences. In fact, keeping the differences was part of our collaboration as equals and a way to establish greater openness and flexibility in data analysis after all the interviews were transcribed. Still, the agreements between us led to our shared sense that our interview guide was working well for us, and it also led to a preliminary, shared, detailed coding outline.

Formal Thematic Analysis After All the Data Were Gathered and Transcribed

We continued gathering data after we had what seemed like a book's worth of data, something that Paul intuitively knew, given that he had previously published nine data-based books (e.g., Rosenblatt, 2006). Nevertheless, we wanted our data analysis to include more interviewees in same-sex relationships, more men, more young respondents, and more cultural diversity. We wanted a study in which a wide range of voices spoke. We were still getting lovely and moving new material with the 37th case, but by then we had met our minimum standard for diversity of material to analyze.

We had already done much informal coding through our conversations, the structure of our interviews, and the coding of the first four cases and the discussion that followed, but we needed formal holistic, selective, and detailed coding (van Manen, 1990) of all cases to clarify, affirm, challenge, and modify what we thought we had. It was also necessary to identify the interview quotes that were our evidence and that we might include in our book. Thus, when we completed and transcribed all 37 interviews, Paul conducted the formal thematic analysis, looking for relevant lived experiences that were common and important in the interviewees' lives. For example, he identified themes from the many interview transcripts that offered considerable discussion about interviewee efforts to know the other early in their relationship.

We knew that some researchers would think it necessary for the two of us (or one of us plus at least one other well-grounded coder) to do independent formal coding. That would give us a sense of something like reliability, confirmability, and dependability (Seale, 1999), help to identify conceptual ambiguities, give us more confidence in areas of agreement, and look more objective. We are, however, much too postmodern to endorse objectivity as a meaningful standard (e.g., Rosenblatt, 2012). The idea of both of us doing independent formal coding was the standard of a particular research culture and not a necessity. Besides, Paul had time to do formal coding, whereas Liz's time was stretched to the maximum with other commitments. It also did not seem appropriate to enlist someone else as a coder who had not been immersed in the study as we had been. For us it was legitimate, proper, and logical, given the time issue, for Paul to do the next step in the analysis, and we knew that Liz would closely review his results.

We agreed from the beginning that we were doing a phenomenological study, wanting to grasp the core realities, understandings, and ways of talking about things of the people we interviewed. We knew we were going to interpret what people said, but the core of what we wanted was people's realities and lived experiences as they talked about them. That meant that the outline to be used in the thematic analysis had to be shaped by everyday language terms that interviewees used, not primarily the terms of theories from social psychology, family studies, communication studies, feminist critical theory, and other academic disciplines.

We wanted from the earliest days of the project to write a book. For us, that meant that the formal thematic analysis should make use of the complexity, diversity, and depth of the interviews and yield the structure of book chapters reporting the study results. We wanted our themes and the labels for those themes to come together in a structure for the book. Then the main thematic areas would define book chapters. For example, two of our chapters are: "How couples build knowledge of one another" and "How well do you know each other? About 90%." Then the thematic material that might explain, clarify, qualify, or challenge the main thematic areas would define sections of the chapters to which they were related. The way we coded was thus not a separate process from using the results of coding to develop a book. Coding, themes, outline, and chapters were all part of a rather integrated process, which meant that when formal coding was completed we had the ingredients for the book.

The formal coding operation carried out by Paul involved marking up the printed transcript of each interview. Paul read a hard copy of each transcript page by page, marking quotes that seemed to fit the themes we had already discussed and our emergent themes. The themes would be highlighted, and in the margin would be Roman numerals, capital letters, numbers, and maybe lower case letters for where the quote might fit in the detailed but still evolving outline. This was not as daunting as it might seem. First, a number of core themes were defined by our interview guide questions, so where there was a question about, for example, not wanting to know certain things about the partner, immediately following that question in a transcript was where much of the material addressing that theme could be found. Second, because we had by this time a clear view of what we thought was the focus of the book, considerable interview material did not have to be coded. For example, one interviewee had much to say about books he had read about how to live life, but that was not coded because it did not fit our preliminary thematic framework and there were few other interviewees who talked about books. Likewise, a few people talked about abuse in the relationship they focused on, but that did not seem to us to link closely enough to the topic of the study.

Because to some extent the book outline that was the coding guide evolved as Paul's coding moved forward, at times already coded cases had to be returned to for additional coding. For example, later in the coding it became clear to Paul that it was important to code how women conceptualized men and how men conceptualized women, and that was dealt with in an additional round of coding. Doing additional coding was not time-consuming, because by then he knew the transcripts well enough to know where to look in the hard or electronic copies of the transcripts.

Paul also coded material that might be methodologically relevant. For example, if an interviewee said something about how free she or he felt to be totally honest and open with the interviewers in answering a question about lying to her partner, that material was coded, partly for us to use in deciding how much we could believe what we had and partly for possible use in a section of the book on issues of validity and data quality. Paul also kept tallies in his computer records of the number of people who said that they could be more open with us because their partner or former partner was not present and those who said they were only giving their view of the couple relationship and their partner or former partner might have a very different view. These perspectives are discussed in a section of the first chapter of our book entitled "Validity/ Data Quality." Coding that material pushed us to be as clear as possible with ourselves and our readers about what it was we had and did not have with the thematic analysis.

Before Paul started formal coding we had identified cases and areas of specific interviews that we had doubts about, which we referred to as "questionable cases." For example, there was the interviewee who seemed to have dementia (as noted earlier) and a few interviewees who seemingly did not understand key questions the way most people did (e.g., answered questions about how much a partner knows by talking about that person not having a strong sex drive). Every case is quoted in the book but, in doing thematic coding, Paul was careful not to let material from any of the few questionable cases drive a thematic code.

After Paul completed his formal coding, he organized the coding into an outline for the book along with quotes associated with the codes that would be included in each section. Paul numbered each quote with the case number (in boldface at the end of the quote) of the interviewee providing the quote. Table 4.1 shows an excerpt from the 150-page (double-spaced) document of some of the quotes in a subsection related to getting to know one's partner.

In most sections of the outline, there were more quotes than could be included in the book, but we needed to see the totality of evidence relevant to each section of the planned book to understand what was common or not in our data. That meant that the outline included a few areas of material we had little intention of using because they were supported by insufficient interview material.

Liz reviewed this document, and she used her knowledge of the cases and the fit between quotes and coding categories to check that Paul was coding appropriately. In a few instances she raised questions about how we would use specific quotes. Ordinarily, it was about quotes that not only could be framed as Paul

TABLE 4.1 Example of Book Outline Section with Interview Quotes

---

Processes for getting to know each other early in the relationship

---

Prior acquaintanceship

I saw him as a friend, and I've seen how he communicates with people, and I've heard him speak to other people. And the way he speaks to me is not the same as he speaks to other people. I know that he loves me, and I know that it's very real to him and very true to him. 01

I think we know each other really, really well. Prior to being in a personal relationship we had a very, very strong emotional connection and friendship. . . . We were best friends before we got into any kind of emotional or personal relationship. So we knew a lot about one another before we even, I mean . . . over 10 years we had gotten to know each other really well. 18

We didn't start dating for many years, like after, yeah. I think first we were just friends. 22

In the areas where I'm detail oriented, he's absent minded. And I was aware of that. We actually knew each other for like 15 years before we married. We weren't like best friends or anything, but we knew each other well enough that I had . . . noticed this about him. So I knew this would be kind of a perpetual thing in our relationship. 05

Note. The number following each quote refers to the transcript/participant number.

had but that also could be framed in other ways. She also raised a few questions about possible additions or changes to the book outline and hence the overall structure of coding. Her questions led to some changes and additions, particularly about gender (which is the focus of one of the chapters of the book), and some explorations of possible additions to the book that we eventually decided not to pursue. However, she agreed almost completely with how each quote had been classified by Paul and with the detailed outline that the 150-page document provided.

Coding continued during the drafting of the book. Paul wrote the first draft of each chapter, using the coding outline and the quotes that were included with each point in the outline. For example, each quote in Table 4.1 was used as the data core for a subsection called "Previous acquaintanceship" in Chapter 2 (titled "How couples build knowledge of one another"; Rosenblatt & Wieling, 2013, pp. 30–33). In this study, we did not do what many qualitative researchers do, which was to generate memos through the course of the study that could guide the eventual writing, but we did something else that replaced memoing. We debriefed extensively and met frequently to discuss the data. We are not opposed to memos, but in this project we felt that we could trust our conversations and memories. That does not mean that the drafting of the book was without problems. Some areas of outline and coding were found to have overlaps, ambiguities, and misclassifications, and those had to be dealt with. Also, some parts of the preliminary outline came to seem too trivial to include in the book. They seemed no longer to be about a distinction that was worth making, or were not supported by enough interview material, and all of that made the writing different from what was in the outline when the drafting of the book began.

When Paul gave the preliminary book draft to Liz, she reviewed the material from many angles, including whether (a) the assertions and data fit together, (b) there was enough data to support what was being said, and (c) the preliminary draft omitted significant issues. We did not ask anyone else to look at our drafts, though we discussed aspects of the book informally with students and colleagues. We are not opposed to sharing drafts with colleagues, but on this project we felt confident enough about what we were doing so we did not feel the need for input from others.

Reflections, Personal Insights, and New Understandings

By the time we started this collaboration we each separately had carried out a substantial number of qualitative projects. We were, of course, to some extent different interviewers, and also some of the interviewees clearly reacted to the each of us differently. That means that the interviews were richer, the discussions of what we could write were richer, and the coding was richer because we interviewed collaboratively.

Qualitative social research is, in many ways, haunted by scientific ideals of objectivity (Rosenblatt, 2012). And so, even though we felt our epistemology was sound, we were well aware that by some researchers' standards we were cutting corners. For example, using only one of us to code all the interview transcripts was an offense against the standards that some hold dear that coding is so subjective that it requires multiple coders and a quantitative evaluation of degree of agreement. However, we could not have brought this study all the way through to publication without doing things the way we did them; there were not the time resources to do all the formal things that others valued but that did not fit our postmodern thinking. By our standards, we had a very strong study scientifically. We had so many discussions of the material, there was so much cross-checking of interpretations during interviews and in the coding and writing process, and our assertions were so tied to interview quotes, that we felt what we had was rigorous, trustworthy, and would hold up if others tried to duplicate our research or were to recode our interviews.

We have both carried out qualitative studies in which coding was confined to one stage, after all the data were gathered and transcribed, but this study was different. Every stage of the project involved coding. This does not minimize the importance of the formal coding stage, because that stage challenged things conceptually, pulled together all the data and all the discussions we had had, and gave us the sense of which quotes provided the data scaffolding for what we would write. If we had been collaborating with students rather than a colleague with extensive qualitative research experience, we probably would have concentrated coding in a formal stage in order to instruct and monitor the student collaborators.

Another key to this research is that we love collaborating with each other. We enjoyed our conversations about the study, the cases, the reflexivity issues, and the different ways to conceptualize and present what we had. We were on the same page about much that had to do with qualitative research, phenomenology, postmodern thought, the complexity of close relationships, and writing. We also had differences that were engaging for us to address, some of them based in our gender, age, and ethnic differences. In fact, perhaps the key to doing this project and bringing it to completion was that we both valued and enjoyed our collaboration, and so the discussions and co-interviewing were consistently rewarding to us.

KEY WORKS INFLUENCING OUR DATA ANALYSIS

Campbell, D. T., & Stanley, J. C. (1963). Experimental and quasi-experimental designs for research on teaching. In N. L. Gage (Ed.), *Handbook of research on teaching* (pp. 171–246). Chicago, IL: Rand McNally.

> Campbell and Stanley legitimate disciplined interpretation of research findings and exquisite sensitivity to alternative interpretations. We think we followed that approach with our coding, reviewing, and interpreting throughout the study.

Strauss, A., & Corbin, J. (1998). *Basics of qualitative research: Techniques and procedures for developing grounded theory* (2nd ed.). Thousand Oaks, CA: Sage.

> Strauss and Corbin legitimate research that evolves as data are gathered, as opposed to starting out with hypotheses and then testing them, and our study certainly evolved. Also, Paul knew Strauss, and our "Knowing and not knowing" book channels what Paul thinks was Strauss's valuing of study evolution and his appreciation of studies that explore interesting, new qualitative domains.

van Manen, M. (1990). *Researching lived experience: Human science for an action sensitive pedagogy.* Albany, NY: State University of New York Press.

> We were both charmed by van Manen's articulate and accessible writing about researching the phenomenology of everyday life. His book was a touchstone in our discussions, as we aspired to be as wise and insightful as he about what people had to say about their lived experiences.

References

Campbell, D. T., & Stanley, J. C. (1963). Experimental and quasi-experimental designs for research on teaching. In N. L. Gage (Ed.), *Handbook of research on teaching* (pp. 171–246). Chicago, IL: Rand McNally.

Gubrium, J. F., & Holstein, J. A. (1997). *The new language of qualitative method.* New York, NY: Oxford University Press.

McDowell, T., & Fang, S-R. S. (2007). Feminist-informed critical multiculturalism: Considerations for family research. *Journal of Family Issues, 28,* 549–566.

Rosenblatt, P. C. (2006). *Two in a bed: The social system of couple bed sharing.* Albany, NY: State University of New York Press.

Rosenblatt, P. C. (2012). One interviewer versus several: Modernist and postmodernist perspectives in qualitative family interviewing. *Journal of Family Theory & Review, 4,* 96–104.

Rosenblatt, P. C., & Wieling, E. (2013). *Knowing and not knowing in intimate relationships.* Cambridge: Cambridge University Press.

Sanday, P. R. (1979). The ethnographic paradigm(s). *Administrative Science Quarterly, 24,* 527–538.

Seale, C. (1999). *The quality of qualitative research.* Thousand Oaks, CA: Sage.

Strauss, A. L., & Corbin, J. M. (1998). *Basics of qualitative research: Techniques and procedures for developing grounded theory* (2nd ed.). Thousand Oaks, CA: Sage.

Tufford, L., & Newman, P. (2010). Bracketing in qualitative research. *Qualitative Social Work, 11,* 80–96.

van Manen, M. (1990). *Researching lived experience: Human science for an action sensitive pedagogy.* Albany, NY: State University of New York Press.

5

SHARING EXPERTISE IN APPALACHIA

A Collaborative Feminist Content Analysis of In-Depth Interviews With Older Women Cancer Survivors

Katherine R. Allen and Karen A. Roberto

In this chapter, we address how we analyzed data from an in-depth interview study of 20 older women from central Appalachia who had experienced and were surviving gynecological cancer. We describe the process we used to analyze the data from the older women's in-depth interviews, which led to our publication in *The Gerontologist* (Allen & Roberto, 2014). Although this chapter focuses on these 20 focal women, we also used a family-level research design, which included data on an additional 33 individuals, all of whom were close family members (including biological, legal, and fictive kin). Briefly, the key findings from the study involved the women's experiences with their cancer trajectory from symptoms to diagnosis to treatment. We found four patterns of post-treatment perceptions among the 20 women: (a) 11 women had a *positive* identification of being a cancer survivor; (b) four women were *cautious* and concerned that they were at risk for reoccurrence; (c) three women *distanced* themselves from an identity of being a cancer survivor; and (d) two women were *resigned* to the belief that cancer was taking their life (Allen & Roberto, 2014). In addition to this typology, we also found that all of the women acknowledged an inner strength often bolstered by their religious faith and the ways in which they navigated their cancer experience that transcended how they viewed their prognosis.

Our methodological choices were rooted in a bigger picture of how we conceptualized the research process, of which data analysis was one core component. We did not start the analysis process with the data. As feminist family scholars, we explicitly acknowledged our commitments to the research by identifying and scrutinizing its scientific and personal components. Our practice of data analysis, which we have developed over several years working in collaboration with one another and other feminist scholars, began with the integration of (a) the context of the study; (b) our feminist theoretical perspective; (c) the sensitizing concepts derived from the empirical literature; (d) the research questions that were generated from an examination of context, theory, and literature; and (e) the data we collected directly from the participants. After having gathered together and organized all of this material, the data analysis began. Next, we describe these components and then turn to a more detailed examination of how we analyzed the data.

Context of the Study

Our investment in this project was rooted in personal and academic interests. Both of us have spent our careers studying marginalization in older families (for examples see Allen, Blieszner, Roberto, Farnsworth, & Wilcox, 1999; Roberto, Allen, & Blieszner, 2001). In addition, personal experiences have informed our work, to varying degrees. For example, the current study came about after Katherine's mother died from ovarian cancer in 2009. Karen, who directs the Institute for Society, Culture and Environment (ISCE), a research investment institute at our university, suggested Katherine put her personal knowledge into a research topic on older women's gynecological cancer, and provided an ISCE grant to pursue the study. As a principal investigator of the Appalachian Community Cancer Network, funded for more than 10 years by the National Cancer Institute and involving partners from five states in Appalachia, Karen provided resources and knowledge of the community context. Combining our respective expertise and personal investments in the study brought a more robust synergy to the project than what might have been accomplished alone.

Feminist Theoretical Perspective

Theoretically, our research is feminist, de-emphasizing hierarchal power dynamics in the research team and in the interviewer-interviewee relationship. Our commitments are to understand and ameliorate the oppressive conditions often facing marginalized populations.

We bring a heightened consciousness to data analysis, one that reflects the lived experiences of our participants as well as our own. We believe that research arises from the researcher's own experience of the everyday world (Smith, 1993). Claiming our stake in the research endeavor makes for a richer portrayal of the worlds we try to understand (Richardson, 1997). Thus, as the analysts (in terms of our own perspectives and interactions with one another), we are as much a part of the analysis as the participants. The reflexivity involved in a feminist approach is key to the conscious scrutiny we bring to data analysis and knowledge production in family science and our sister discipline of gerontology (Allen, 2000, 2016). We also often combine more mainstream theories such as a life course perspective (Elder & Giele, 2009) with critical and constructivist feminist perspectives (Sprague, 2005) to address individual, family, and social-historical time.

From the Empirical Literature to Research Questions

Our review of the literature (see Allen & Roberto, 2014) demonstrated that people in rural Appalachia suffered health disparities in under resourced communities. Older women in rural Appalachia carry a disproportionate share of the cancer burden, including greater incidence rates of primary cancers, such as cervical cancer (American Cancer Society, 2017; Wilson, Ryerson, Singh, & King, 2016). When cancer diagnosis occurs, physical and social environmental factors of this region impose major barriers to treatment and their use of supportive services. Lack of transportation, low income, low education, poor housing, lack of health insurance, few health care options, and limited access to oncology and support services (e.g., mental health) are serious risk factors for rural cancer survivors (Behringer et al., 2007; Lyttle & Stadelman, 2006).

At the same time, Appalachia is a region with a strong sense of self-reliance, traditionalism, religiosity, and family ties (Coyne, Demian-Popescu, & Friend, 2006; Schoenberg et al., 2009). Although family relationships are considered a bedrock of social support in helping individuals with cancer survive this devastating illness, assumptions about families in Appalachia are challenged by research on changing family structures and dynamics in the context of geographic isolation and economic limitations (Beesley et al., 2010; Schlegel, Talley, Molix, & Bettencourt, 2009). Shifts occur in the quantity of family members available to help women and the quality of those relationships (Allen, Blieszner, & Roberto, 2011). Older female cancer survivors are likely to be dealing with multiple illnesses and responsible for family members themselves. Their quality of life can be threatened by social and psychological stress caused by family members as well as by perceptions of how their cancer is affecting family members' lives (Bevans & Sternberg, 2012; Duggleby et al., 2011).

This combination of gender, age, geography, and family in the literature led to our research questions: (a) How do older women in rural Appalachia describe their experiences with diagnosis and treatment from gynecological cancer? (b) How do older women experience living with cancer post-treatment? These questions led to the interview questions we specifically asked of participants, which guided them through their *cancer journey*, from the onset of their cancer and how their relationships and activities had changed since diagnosis.

The Nature of the Data

The 20 older women cancer survivors were our focal research participants (Allen & Roberto, 2014). We began data collection by having each woman respond to a structured demographic questionnaire, two mental and physical health-related questionnaires, and an open-ended interview, which averaged 104 minutes. The interview questions invited the women to think and talk more deeply about their own actions, motivations, and experiences. Our use of face-to-face interviews was vital in establishing rapport and creating a climate of trust that assured the older woman that her cancer story would be treated with the respect and care it deserved. Although telephone interviews are also effective (Goldberg & Allen, 2015), we wanted to physically demonstrate our investment of time, attention, and credibility. This attention to participants at the front end of the process was essential for helping ensure that the analysis reflected the way the participants wished to present themselves.

The Data Analysis Process

Because we were guided by research questions and used sensitizing concepts (Blumer, 1969) such as cancer as a journey and the importance of family and fictive kin relationships from the outset of the study, our approach to data analysis was both deductive and inductive (Daly, 2007; Gilgun, 2016). This methodological approach fit well with critical and feminist theories that offer an emancipatory framework with the goal of challenging the status quo and empowering marginalized individuals who often live on the edges of *mainstream* society (Allen, 2016; Gilgun, 2016).

We used content analysis, a well-known qualitative methodology that undergirds grounded theory strategies. Content analysis follows the constant comparative steps of open, focused, and selective coding (Charmaz, 2006), although the labels for each of these progressively narrowing strategies of data reduction may vary depending on the *how to* text that the analyst follows (Bogdan & Biklen, 2007). Our analytic method was a process of generating and reading text over and over again. Seeing, hearing, writing about, and reconfiguring the participants' words and experiences are the skills we relied on as qualitative researchers in coming to understand what our participants were saying, feeling, and reflecting about. Our method of data collection and analysis is akin to many variations of qualitative research, and we use the standards of rigor, transparency, and full disclosure when communicating our work to others (Goldberg & Allen, 2015). In summary, our analytic approach engaged the data (i.e., the participants' perspective on their own lives), before, during, and after it was collected through the use of the scholars' tools of theory, empirical literature, reflexivity, and moments of insight forged in a collaborative process.

The Specifics of Coding and Analyzing the Data

After each interview, a professional transcribed the audio-recorded session into Microsoft Word documents for each of the 20 cases. Katherine reviewed all of the transcripts for accuracy by listening to each audiotape and comparing it to the transcribed content. In addition to correcting minor typographical errors on the transcripts, Katherine inserted pseudonyms into each transcript. The 20 older women's interview data resulted in 583 pages of mostly single-spaced transcript (on average 30 pages per person, with a range of 20 to 38 pages). This count included 443 pages of interview data and 140 pages of supplemental material (handwritten answers to interview guide questions, responses to the demographic questionnaire, responses to the depression scale, and numeric responses to the health status questionnaire). Thus, we were working with many pages of data, mostly in Word files so they could be read, marked, and analyzed either on the computer (typically used by Karen) or printed and marked on by hand (typically used by Katherine). We printed hard copies of all interview material and kept them in three-ring binders; the Word files were also stored on the computer.

In addition to the in-depth interviews, we developed a series of three family genograms (McGoldrick, Gerson, & Petry, 2008) for each woman's caregiving and health-focused relationships before, during, and after cancer treatment. Our graduate research assistant, Emma Potter, used a computer program (GenoPro; www.genopro.com) to construct the family genograms, which were stored on the computer and also printed and kept in three-ring binders. The genograms allowed us to visualize the cancer survivors' family relationships (e.g., ties to biological, adoptive, and step kin), and how they linked to their life circumstances and medical history. For the purpose of the analyses reported in our 2014 paper, we used the genograms to visually inform our understanding of the women's relationships across the cancer trajectory and remind us about the independent and interrelated roles others played in the women's cancer story as family, friends, and others entered and sometimes exited the women's daily lives. Figures 5.1, 5.2, and 5.3 show a participant's (Helen) three pathways at different points in time.

To systematically analyze the data for the 2014 publication, we used grounded theory procedures (i.e., open, focused, and selective coding), which provided flexible guidelines for developing a coding scheme that reflected the entire data set (Bogdan & Biklen, 2007; Charmaz, 2006). However, there was a lot of effort that happened behind the scenes before the actual coding and analysis process began. As we have done in previous collaborations, we decided ahead of time which one of us would take the lead on a publication (Katherine, in this case), and that person then took responsibility for directing the coding and analysis. The other person (Karen, in this case) provided the back up and served as the devil's advocate by independently reading the complete transcripts in chunks (about five at a time) and then offering insights, challenges, and new concepts/codes each step of the way. Often, we go back and forth on publications, where one of us takes the lead on the first paper, and then the other person takes the lead on the next paper. This way, we share the workload and our expertise, and both of us come to learn the

SEE FIGURE 5.1   at eResource—Helen's Pre-Cancer Relationships.

SEE FIGURE 5.2   at eResource—Helen's Cancer Treatment Relationships.

SEE FIGURE 5.3   at eResource—Helen's Post-Cancer Relationships.

data inside and out. We also tend to follow this pattern of sharing the lead when working with our graduate students and colleagues on other projects.

Thus, as first author, Katherine conducted all of the interviews and verified all of the audiotapes; this process familiarized her with the entire data set three successive times. She then read all of the transcripts again (for a fourth and fifth time) to prepare the initial drafts of the coding scheme. Karen read a random selection of five transcripts (chunks) through each iteration of the development of the coding scheme, thus providing an independent source of insight into how the scheme was developing. Ultimately, Karen also read all of the transcripts multiple times but as first author, it was Katherine's responsibility to guide the process. Because we have worked together on several research projects over many years, we have developed this system of conducting data analysis that feels second nature to us.

As we detailed in the beginning of this chapter, we brought many ideas to the corpus of data—beyond the transcripts themselves—and this initiated the open coding process. It is helpful to picture the documents before us as we sat down to conduct the initial open coding, having already read and reread the body of data multiple times. Along with the transcripts, we also had in front of us (either in paper or on the computer) the list of guiding research questions and theories, as well as the specific interview questions asked of the women (e.g., Please tell us about your cancer story. Who are the important people in your life? Who are the people that have supported you in dealing with cancer?). All of these materials helped to sensitize us to how we were interacting with the data. To do the initial open coding, Katherine wrote in pencil and colored markers on each transcript any concepts, hunches, insights, and reminders of ideas to return to (see Figure 5.4, which highlights a transcript page in which faith in God, having a positive attitude, and doubt about getting a diagnosis were noted). After she read all of the data in this unstructured way, she went through them again and generated a typed list of ideas that were common across the entire data set, as well as some ideas that were unique to each case. These ideas included a range of topics, such as (a) sources of information in learning about cancer; (b) how I now take care of myself since being treated for cancer; (c) religious beliefs and practices; (d) family crises and hardships during and after treatment; and (e) the quality and quantity of my support network.

Although at this stage we did not analyze the genograms in a formal way, they provided a valuable visual representation, of particular interest to Karen, that helped us sort out how the women viewed and talked about their relationships. For example, we saw very few major changes in the size or composition of the women's family system throughout their cancer journey. More commonly, we saw changes with the focus and intensity of the supportive roles family members played. Relationships weakened and strengthened; some changed temporarily,

SEE FIGURE 5.4 at eResource—Transcript With Katherine's Handwritten Notes.

while others were permanently altered. Women often found short-term ties (e.g., the presence of a *cancer buddy*) during the treatment and recovery process and such arrangements were more important than the help they regularly received from a spouse or adult child. Cancer often accompanied both personal and network stressors and was not experienced in a vacuum. That is, cancer was not a singular event that occurred at one point in time, but the women's diagnosis of cancer often came on top of other diseases and conditions, and into a family system with multiple problems (e.g., an adult child's incarceration) and challenges (e.g., lack of transportation; Allen & Roberto, 2014).

Another preliminary strategy we used to *learn the data* and to commit ourselves to a formal coding scheme was to write a brief case synopsis from each of the women's transcripts, and then highlight major points that we anticipated would make a difference in the next stage of coding. These case synopses were typed into a Word file containing all 20 cases (approximately one page per case). Our initial observations about the women were key in understanding how women reconstruct their kin networks and ultimately informed our preparation and understanding of the genograms we constructed. To illustrate a case synopsis, we provide an abbreviated synthesis of key points and a few observations from Grace's case, an 82 year-old woman at the time of data collection who had been diagnosed with and treated for uterine cancer.

> Grace has had a rough time. Husband is bed ridden and spent five months in a nursing home, just returning home recently. She had uterine cancer, was receiving treatment, then broke a bone, and spent five months in treatment and recovery, so couldn't care for husband—he had to go to nursing home ("a place where people go to die"). One foot was amputated, so he wasn't mobile and couldn't be left alone. Grace has no children, her brothers live out of state, her 88-year-old aunt (like a sister) is in Ohio and her aunt's husband is dying. Grace lives next door to husband's cousin, they talk on phone, but he can't do much for them. She relies on her "adopted" daughter—a woman who was interested in buying their land, but now just helps her out—buys her groceries and runs errands—her lifeline. Despite the fact that her blood family doesn't live near her and they can't visit, they are always on the phone, and that is so important to her. The woman from the cancer center who drove me out to her home (about 20 minutes away) loves Grace and said she has really been through a hard time. While I was there, an electrician was fixing her air conditioner, and she was very capably giving him instructions, and the man was very cordial and nice to her—they had a professional and caring interaction. She was wearing pajamas and a housecoat (it was 1:00 pm), and she said she never left the house. She said life was rough, but she kept going. She said she has "good genes." She also had a lot of faith. Lived in the area for 14 years; born and raised in KY.

Initial Observations From This Case Study:

1. Whatever you do, keep your loved ones out of nursing homes.
2. Kin conversion happens in most families (her aunt is just like a sister).
3. Emotional support is essential (e.g., telephone; knowing your family is out there, even if you don't physically see them).
4. Women find ways to compensate for losses—make substitutions—like with her adopted daughter. Finds emotional and instrumental support in her. Participant had a need and she worked it out by finding this support.
5. Some people have a very strong will to keep going.

As a result of these strategies, we prepared an initial coding scheme that represented the first round of data reduction (i.e., open coding). We generated a long list of about 20 codes, organized by broader categories (e.g., diagnosis, active treatment, the discourse of survivorship) that included subcodes underneath each one. This initial scheme was still very close to the data in that we mostly utilized participants' own words to indicate codes. On the coding scheme, if a code was a direct quote from a participant, we put quote marks around it. For example, if a woman had a very negative experience with her cancer treatment and had given up on receiving further treatment, we coded this type of text by using the woman's own words: "I refuse to take more treatment; it beat me." Additionally, after each coding category, we included "other" to locate topics not yet fitting into any of the previous codes. We continued to work with the data and in communication with one another to eliminate the "other" codes so that all data were accounted for. The following list is an example of how we organized codes around one main category: the diagnosis aspect of cancer:

I. Diagnosis

    A. Getting the diagnosis: Participants' reaction to cancer

        1. "Cancer is bad" (attitudes about how cancer is really bad; "life or death situation").
        2. Depends on the stage of cancer and extensiveness of recommended treatment.
        3. "I didn't let it affect me."
        4. "I knew I'd be okay."
        5. "You've just got to accept it" (being realistic; "deal with it").
        6. Other:

    B. Context of finding out I had cancer

        1. "My doctor ran some tests": Confirmed immediately.
        2. Took a while to get diagnosed: Went to more doctors; had more tests.

    3. Diagnosis is an arduous process.

    4. Other:

  C. Significance of "when I knew"

    1. "I just knew."

    2. "It took a while for me to realize it."

    3. It was a surprise.

    4. When the doctor told me.

    5. "I'd had other cancers before."

    6. I expected it ("there's a lot of cancer in my family").

    7. Other:

In the next phase of focused coding, we further reduced and synthesized our initial coding into the main topic areas of the cancer journey. To reach this point, we used the coding and analysis strategy of sorting thematic data into tables, accompanied by relevant participant demographic information. We used these data to help us organize and differentiate patterns among participant experiences. Table 5.1 illustrates this strategy. This table shows one participant per type, with her pseudonym, background information, various quotes from her transcript to support our coding decisions, and our analysis of her perceptions of post-treatment experience.

The final selective coding scheme, which consisted of two main themes, tells the story of the women's cancer experiences. We utilized this final coding scheme as the outline for writing about the findings for our publication (Allen & Roberto, 2014). The first theme was labeled "From Symptoms to Diagnosis and Active Treatment" and included the four subthemes of (a) symptoms, (b) getting a diagnosis, (c) initial reactions to the cancer diagnosis, and (d) treatment and side effects. The second main theme was "Post-Treatment: Living with and Surviving Cancer." In the final coding scheme, we also included the frequency counts (i.e., the number of cases exemplifying each type of experience) for each code. Table 5.2 shows the four types of living with and surviving cancer by frequency.

Final Reflections

As we have chronicled previously, our collaboration began over 20 years ago, and has benefitted from our willingness to share resources and learn from one another. We practice equality in our work together and take responsibility for writing our papers, not leaving one of us in the lurch or expecting the first author of a paper to do most of the work. We also share the products and accomplishments of our work together. This equality is highly feminist, and reflects our commitment to feminist theory and praxis (Allen, 2016).

TABLE 5.1 Older Women's Post-Treatment Perceptions of Being a Cancer Survivor: Examples of Four Types

Name	Age	Type of cancer	Considers herself a survivor	Words she used to describe her experience	Post-TX[a] type
Deborah	74	Ovarian	Considered herself high risk for another form of cancer because she had breast cancer	• Cancer has brought me to God. • Salvation is the perfect treatment for all diseases. • Everything in your life happens for a reason. • There are worse things than cancer (not being saved or not believing in God; no exits in hell). • I put worry in God's hands. • Thought she got ovarian cancer due to having breast cancer—that it just comes back in another form.	Cautious
Helen	68	Cervical	Doesn't say, but she's taken out her port, refusing more TX; asked doctor how long she has; cervical cancer is more aggressive than lung	• I'm just worn out, with the tests, and just not getting anywhere, and I decided, I'm just not going to do anything. • I don't trust doctors or nurses. • Things are so expensive, you can't always have the money for the food they want you to have. I go by this paper that they gave me, but it's so expensive. • Sometimes I get so tired of being poor, but there's not much you can do about it. • I worry and pray. You can't help from worrying, Take it day by day; pray a lot, seek his help, his will be done. • I'm just one of so many that's going through this horrible disease; I'm blessed to have a family that deeply care.	Resigned
Lila	64	Uterine	I am, but I don't feel like I am	• I'm very lucky; I'm very grateful and relieved. • I couldn't believe I had it. • I don't mourn the loss of my uterus. • I feel very lucky I didn't have to go through chemo.	Distanced

| Millie | 73 | Uterine | Yes, I'm a survivor; doctor tells me I'm doing good | • Will never go through chemo (breast TX) or radiation (uterine TX) again.
• Chemo much worse than radiation, ruined and aged her skin.
• Cancer is something you've got to learn to live with, and I'm living with it pretty good.
• Huge support network ("Oh Lord, write fast").
• First time I heard about my cancer, I worried about it, but it didn't scare me; you got to fight it, can't give up, but you know, everybody's got their time.
• I didn't trust woman surgeon (she quit and teaches dance).
• If you get it once, you'll get it again.
• If it's going to happen, it's going to happen.
• You've got to have faith, or you might as well forget it. | Positive |

ᵃ TX = treatment

TABLE 5.2 Typology of Post-Treatment Cancer Survivor Narratives

POSITIVE	CAUTIOUS	RESIGNED	DISTANCED
"Yes, I'm a cancer survivor"	*"Maybe, but I'm at risk for getting cancer again or I'm not cured yet"*	*"I refuse to take more treatment"*	*"I'm not a cancer victim; I do not identify with cancer at all"*
Abby	Deborah	Helen	Lila
Carla	Edie	Wilma	Nora
Fannie	Julia		Sadie
Grace	Thelma		
Iris			
Kate			
Millie			
Olivia			
Patsy			
Rita			
Violet			
n = 11	*n* = 4	*n* = 2	*n* = 3

We do not underestimate the importance of trust in one another, in our data, and in the research process. Personal and professional trust is key to having a positive, collaborative working relationship with collaborators, participants, and gatekeepers. We have been upfront with each other about what we can do and cannot do on a project, especially if life intervenes and we are dealing with a family tragedy. When we first started working together, we frequently raised our voices and jumped out of our chairs, not in anger, but in excitement of developing and crystalizing the *ah ha* moments that occurred when in the midst of data analysis. Often working in Karen's office, the graduate students next door worried and wondered why their professors were arguing. When they finally had the courage to ask us, we laughed as we explained that we indeed were yelling in disagreement but also in celebration of generating insights we were proud of!

To give an example of our differences, Katherine is much more open to using private experiences of grief and loss as a spring board to inform her research; Karen relies more on her observations of others and is much more open to using quantitative approaches in her research. As we have worked closely together over the last two decades, we have both expanded our ways of doing data analysis. Karen frequently takes the lead in qualitative analysis for some of her other research teams (e.g., Roberto, Blieszner, McCann, & McPherson, 2011), and Katherine now uses charts and tables routinely to structure and *see* patterns in her data, an approach she adopted from Karen.

We are similar in that we both are deeply committed to sharing our expertise with our students and helping them develop the methodological skills necessary to complete their graduate degrees. We share similar mentoring philosophies of high expectations of our students and intensive guidance and intellectual support as they pursue their own research. We consider the mentoring experience incomplete unless we include students on our own research and publish with them (Emma Potter in this case, who is contributing to three publications from this study), implementing the collaborative spirit with which we approach our own style with peers. That is, students publish with us (on projects we have conducted with each other, or with others), and we also give them opportunities to take the lead from our respective data sets. As feminist scholars, our goal is to coax our students toward becoming our peers by learning along with us.

Our struggles have not been in our research collaboration, but in finding the time to complete additional manuscripts and pursue external funding based on this data set. Our academic roles and responsibilities in teaching, mentoring, service, and in Karen's case, administration, often require immediate attention and like for many others, the time that takes often comes from time allocated for writing. In many ways, we have been productive with several national and international presentations, two publications from the data set (Allen & Roberto, 2014; Potter, Allen, & Roberto, 2018), and more in the works. We are still mining the women's data, and there are a host of issues to write about on the family members' perspectives as well. So, a drawback of our otherwise productive collaboration is that when another project deemed more demanding comes up, we are amenable to postponing our own work until other big projects *get off our desk*. A benefit of writing this chapter is that it has spurred renewed effort to complete our other in-progress papers.

We often find that when we go to publish our work, however, reviewers are increasingly requiring the method to be described in a way that closely follows well-regarded texts outlining the gold standard of grounded theory procedures (Charmaz, 2006; Daly, 2007; LaRossa, 2005). As qualitative research methods become more standardized, we have encountered suspicion about our description of qualitative research as *both* reflexively intuitive (inductive) and conceptually/theoretically guided (deductive), because these approaches are often viewed in opposition to one another. It seems there is little room for overtly presenting the reflexive data analysis process of filtering through private experience and the occasional clash of perspectives and egos that go hand-in-hand with collaborative data analysis. Unfortunately, we have sometimes experienced that expectation as flattening out the dynamics of our data analysis process, thus leading to somewhat sanitized versions of how we have gone *into the pit* of emotionally and intellectually disagreeing, arguing, and often sharing from personal experience (e.g., the loss or frailty of our family members) that infuse our collaborative work. Again, writing this chapter together, which provided the freedom of transparency and disclosure, was a welcome and liberating experience, rare in academic work.

Conclusion

In this chapter, we have had the opportunity to depart from the textbook approach that students are now taught, and describe some of the behind the scenes messiness and passion in conducting qualitative data analysis. At the heart of all research is the knowledge and inspiration of the researcher. Although translating the dynamic process of data coding and analysis into publication may lose some of its spark, we, as researchers, must speak the language of our discipline and translate our work into words that others will be able to understand. The attention to the importance of family support and the fact that health and illness occur in familial and community contexts provided a common language to translate multiple perspectives on women's cancer experiences into an account that is respectful of the women's reflections and true to the actual steps we took to arrive at our interpretation and conclusions.

KEY WORKS GUIDING OUR DATA ANALYSIS

Charmaz, K. (2006). *Constructing grounded theory: A practical guide through qualitative analysis.* London: Sage.

> Although we adapted grounded theory techniques to our own collaborative style, Charmaz's text is one (though not the only one) that coincides with our own. We found it particularly useful in providing a framework for conducting the phases of open and focused coding that informed the selected coding process that ultimately produced our storyline.

Schoenberg, N. E., Miller, E. A., & Pruchno, R. (2011). The qualitative portfolio at *The Gerontologist*: Strong and getting stronger. *The Gerontologist, 51*, 281–284.

> Schoenberg, our colleague from the Appalachia Community Care Network, was an associate editor for qualitative research at *The Gerontologist*, a key gerontological journal in which we publish. To facilitate the publication of qualitative research in this journal, Schoenberg and her colleagues published guidelines that are valued by the journal. These guidelines reconcile the "great divide" between qualitative and quantitative methods in publication, and identify the valuable focus on process that is contributed by in-depth textual methods.

References

Allen, K. R. (2000). A conscious and inclusive family studies. *Journal of Marriage and the Family, 62*, 4–17.

Allen, K. R. (2016). Feminist theory in family studies: History, biography, and critique. *Journal of Family Theory & Review, 8*, 207–224.

Allen, K. R., Blieszner, R., & Roberto, K. A. (2011). Perspectives on extended family and fictive kin in the later years: Strategies and meanings of kin reinterpretation. *Journal of Family Issues, 32*, 1156–1177.

Allen, K. R., Blieszner, R., Roberto, K. A., Farnsworth, E. B., & Wilcox, K. L. (1999). Older adults and their children: Family patterns of structural diversity. *Family Relations, 48*, 151–157.

Allen, K. R., & Roberto, K. A. (2014). Older women in Appalachia: Experiences with gynecological cancer. *The Gerontologist, 54*, 1024–1034.

American Cancer Society. (2017). *Cancer facts and figures 2017*. Atlanta, GA: American Cancer Society. Retrieved from www.cancer.org/content/dam/cancer-org/research/cancer-facts-and-statistics/annual-cancer-facts-and-figures/2017/cancer-facts-and-figures-2017.pdf

Beesley, V. L., Janda, M., Eakin, E. G., Auster, J. F., Chambers, S. K., Aitken, J. F., Dunn, J., & Battistutta, D. (2010). Gynecological cancer survivors and community support services: Referral, awareness, utilization and satisfaction. *Psycho-Oncology, 19*, 54–61.

Behringer, B., Friedell, G. H., Dorgan, K. A., Hutson, S. P., Naney, C., Phillips, A., Krishnan, K., & Cantrell, E. S. (2007). Understanding the challenges of reducing cancer in Appalachia: Addressing a place-based health disparity population. *California Journal of Health Promotion, 5*, 40–49.

Bevans, M. F., & Sternberg, E. M. (2012). Caregiving burden, stress, and health effects among family caregivers of adult cancer patients. *Journal of the American Medical Association, 307*, 393–403.

Blumer, H. (1969). *Symbolic interactionism: Perspective and method*. Englewood Cliffs, NJ: Prentice-Hall.

Bogdan, R. C., & Biklen, S. K. (2007). *Qualitative research for education: An introduction to theories and methods* (5th ed.). Boston, MA: Pearson.

Charmaz, K. (2006). *Constructing grounded theory: A practical guide through qualitative analysis*. London: Sage.

Coyne, C. A., Demian-Popescu, C., & Friend, D. (2006, October). Social and cultural factors influencing health in Southern West Virginia: A qualitative study. *Preventing Chronic Disease, 3*(4), 1–8. Retrieved from www.ncbi.nlm.nih.gov/pmc/articles/PMC1779288

Daly, K. J. (2007). *Qualitative methods for family studies and human development*. Thousand Oaks, CA: Sage.

Duggleby, W. D., Penz, K., Leipert, B. D., Wilson, D. M., Goodridge, D., & Williams, A. (2011). "I am part of the community but . . ." The changing context of rural living for persons with advanced cancer and their families. *Rural and Remote Health, 11*. Retrieved from www.rrh.org.au/journal/article/1733

Elder, G. H., Jr., & Giele, J. Z. (Eds.). (2009). *The craft of life course research*. New York, NY: Guilford Press.

Gilgun, J. F. (2016, November). *Deductive qualitative analysis and the search for black swans*. Paper presented at the Theory Construction and Research Methodology Workshop, National Council on Family Relations, Minneapolis, MN.

Goldberg, A. G., & Allen, K. R. (2015). Communicating qualitative research: Some practical guideposts for scholars. *Journal of Marriage and Family, 77*, 3–22.

LaRossa, R. (2005). Grounded theory methods and qualitative research. *Journal of Marriage and Family, 67*, 837–857.

Lyttle, N. L., & Stadelman, K. (2006). Assessing awareness and knowledge of breast and cervical cancer among Appalachian women. *Preventing Chronic Disease, 3*(4), 1–9. Retrieved from www.cdc.gov/pcd/issues/2006/oct/06_0031.htm

McGoldrick, M., Gerson, R., & Petry, S. (2008). *Genograms: Assessment and intervention* (3rd ed.). New York, NY: W. W. Norton.

Potter, E. C., Allen, K. R., & Roberto, K. A. (2018). Agency and fatalism in older Appalachian women's cancer-related-information seeking. *Journal of Women & Aging*. Advance online publication. doi:10.1080/08952841.2018.1434951

Richardson, L. (1997). *Fields of play: Constructing an academic life*. New Brunswick, NJ: Rutgers University Press.

Roberto, K. A., Allen, K. R., & Blieszner, R. (2001). Older adults' preferences for future care: Formal plans and family support. *Applied Developmental Sciences, 5*, 112–120.

Roberto, K. A., Blieszner, R., McCann, B. R., & McPherson, M. C. (2011). Family triad perceptions of mild cognitive impairment. *Journal of Gerontology: Social Sciences, 66B*, 756–768.

Schlegel, R. J., Talley, A. E., Molix, L. A., & Bettencourt, B. A. (2009). Rural breast cancer patients, coping and depressive symptoms: A prospective comparison study. *Psychology and Health, 24*, 933–948.

Schoenberg, N. E., Hatcher, J., Dignan, M. B., Shelton, B., Wright, S., & Dollarhide, K. F. (2009). Faith Moves Mountains: An Appalachian cervical cancer prevention program. *American Journal of Health Behavior, 33*, 627–638.

Schoenberg, N. E., Miller, E. A., & Pruchno, R. (2011). The qualitative portfolio at *The Gerontologist*: Strong and getting stronger. *The Gerontologist, 51*, 281–284.

Smith, D. E. (1993). The Standard North American Family: SNAF as an ideological code. *Journal of Family Issues, 14*, 50–65.

Sprague, J. (2005). *Feminist methodologies for critical researchers: Bridging differences*. Walnut Creek, CA: AltaMira Press.

Wilson, R. J., Ryerson, A. B., Singh, S. D., & King, J. B. (2016). Cancer incidence in Appalachia, 2004–2011. *Cancer Epidemiology and Prevention Biomarkers, 25*, 250–258.

6

REVISITING AND REMAKING THE LISTENING GUIDE

An Ecological and Ontological Narrativity Approach to Analyzing Fathering Narratives

Andrea Doucet

This chapter traces a process of revisiting a field site, a problematic of gendered work and care, and a small group of participants roughly a decade after a first phase of research in a study about primary caregiving fathers. This revisiting process led me to rethink my knowledge making practices, including the data analysis approach that I had originally used and further developed in that work: the Listening Guide. The story guiding this chapter is about how I tried to analyze the second phase of interviews (2009–2014) with the same data analysis approach (the Listening Guide) that I had used for the first phase of research (2000–2004). It was a method that I had worked with and co-developed for two decades, but was no longer working for me, mainly because my epistemological and ontological moorings had shifted. Recognizing that the Listening Guide had been developed in a particular context and was infused with specific, albeit more implicit than explicit, theoretical, epistemological, and ontological assumptions, I realized that I needed to realign this approach to the second phase of data analysis with my own evolving epistemological and ontological thinking. In fact, I had to remake the Listening Guide method, and this remaking had implications for how I conducted my data analysis processes. I address these issues in this chapter.

The case study informing this chapter is part of a 14-year-long qualitative, ethnographic, and longitudinal research program conducted mainly in Canada, but recently in the United States, on households with fathers who self-define as primary caregivers (stay-at-home fathers and single fathers) and mothers who are the main breadwinners (for details, see Doucet, 2006, 2015, 2016, 2018a). The research program included a series of interviews conducted between 2000 and 2004 with 70 stay-at-home fathers and 12 mother/father couples and follow-up interviews conducted about a decade later (2009–2014) with six of the mother/father couples (individual and couple interviews; for more details, see Doucet, 2018a). The two phases of research shared (a) a similar set of questions, (b) a visual and participatory method for collecting data on household divisions of labor (the Household Portrait; Doucet, 2006, 2016, 2018a), (c) the use of ATLAS.ti qualitative software (to read for theoretical themes across transcripts and to construct memos while analyzing and writing), and (d) attention to reflexive and relational knowing, subjectivity, and narrative, albeit in different ways between two phases of work in a longitudinal study.

In this chapter, I start by providing a brief overview of how I used the Listening Guide approach in the first phase of the project. Second, I describe my parallel project of rethinking my epistemological and ontological commitments, detailing how this affected my approach to knowledge making, narratives, concepts, and data analysis. Third, I demonstrate some of my process of remaking and using the Listening Guide data analysis approach.

Phase 1: Listening Guide and Data Analysis

In the first stage of my research (2000–2004), I was guided by one version of the Listening Guide, a data and narrative analysis approach to in-depth interviews, initially developed by Carol Gilligan, Lyn Mikel Brown, and colleagues at the Harvard University Graduate School of Education in the late 1980s and early 1990s (Brown & Gilligan, 1992). This approach has had different names (e.g., a Reader's Guide, a Listener's Guide, and a voice-centered relational method) and varied iterations across time in different projects, disciplines, and countries (for an overview and history of the Listening Guide, see Mauthner, 2017; Mauthner & Doucet, 2003). I learned the Listening Guide approach in a small data analysis group led by Carol Gilligan over a period of 17 months (1992–1993) while I was a doctoral student at the University of Cambridge.

Following that period of intensively learning and working with this approach, I continued to use and further develop the Listening Guide in collaboration with Natasha Mauthner (e.g. Doucet, 2006; Doucet & Mauthner, 2008; Mauthner & Doucet, 1998, 2003). In a nutshell, our approach to the Listening Guide utilizes four readings of the interview transcripts broadly framed as attending to (a) reflexivity, (b) narrative, (c) subjectivity, and (d) structuring contexts. The process thus calls for at least four readings of interview transcripts "each time listening in a different way" (Brown, 1998, p. 33) and also, ideally, listening to the corresponding interview tape as a way to return to the multi-sensory quality of the interview relationship. There is also a strong focus on researchers conducting their own interviews so that they develop and maintain relationships with research participants through the data collection and data analysis phases of research.

SEE FIGURE 6.1 at eResource—Listening Guide Phase 1.

Applying the Listening Guide

In my first research phase, I conducted four readings of interview transcripts using the Listening Guide. The first reading had two parts: one that focused on the central storyline or plot and a follow-up reading that added a reader-response reflexive strategy (Mauthner & Doucet, 1998, 2003). The second reading was for subjectivity, tracing the "I" (or central protagonist) in the narrative. My third and fourth readings extended the analysis from the research subjects and their narratives to their nexus of social relationships and then into wider structural relations and theoretical analyses.

As recommended in some of the early versions of the Listening Guide (Brown & Gilligan, 1992), I used a "worksheet" technique (using different colored pencils for each reading). I did all the readings separately, working on a hard copy (paper) of the transcripts with wide margins in which to make notes for each of the four readings. At the end of this process, I went through the transcripts again, reviewing my four readings, and I developed case study stories for all 12 mother/father couples and for eight fathers; for the latter, I attended to diverse characteristics (i.e., single, gay, and/or new immigrant fathers). Upon completing my four readings with the Listening Guide, I used the computer-assisted qualitative software program ATLAS.ti to code the theoretical themes developed from the final stage of my Listening Guide readings and to create research memos, which guided my writing.

Next, I briefly explore how I did these readings, using the case study of Dennis, a single, mixed race (Aboriginal/Chinese), low-income father of one daughter (aged 9 at the time of the interview) as an example (Figure 6.1).

First Reading: Reading the Story and Reading Myself in the Story

My first reading of fathers' interview transcripts began with a reading for plot or narrative. I read interview transcripts using a colored pencil to highlight recurring words, themes, events, protagonists, the central plot, subplots, and key characters. I used a different color for each reading to more easily view and compare the four different but parallel readings across the two versions of the Listening Guide. Although these colors vary each time I do the readings, in Figures 6.1 and 6.2, I used the following colors: pink and purple for the two phases of Reading 1, green for Reading 2, orange for Reading 3, and blue for Reading 4. Each of these different colors reflects the unique interpretation being carried out in each reading (discussed in this section and the next three sections).

The second dimension of this first reading was a reflexive one in that it:

> involves a 'reader-response' element in which the researcher reads for herself in the text. She places herself, her background, history and experiences in relation to the respondent. She reads the narrative on her own terms, listening for how she is responding emotionally and intellectually to this person.
>
> (Mauthner & Doucet, 1998, p. 126)

This reflexive reading attempts to maintain a continuous relationship with research participants and provides a concrete way of "doing reflexivity" (Mauthner & Doucet, 2003, p. 418). Using the worksheet technique, the respondent's words are laid out in one column and the researcher's reactions and interpretations are laid out in an adjacent column (Figure 6.1). This reading examines how the researcher's "assumptions and views might affect her interpretation of the respondent's words, or how she later writes about the person" (Mauthner & Doucet, 2003, p. 419).

Second Reading: An "I" Reading (Reading for Research Subjects)

The second reading attends specifically to the particular *person* in the interview transcripts—to the way that person speaks about her/himself and about the parameters of her/his social world—"rather than simply and quickly slotting their words into either our own ways of understanding the world or into the categories of the literature in our area" (Mauthner & Doucet, 1998, p. 132).

For this reading I again used a colored pencil to trace the instances of "I" in a hard copy of the interview transcripts. I then worked with the interview transcripts on a computer to distill these into an "I story" or an "I poem" (Gilligan, Spencer, Weinberg, & Bertsch, 2003), which is a streaming sequence of "I" and "we" statements (for an example, see Table 6.1). A key purpose of this reading was to focus on how the interviewee "speaks of herself before we speak of her" (Brown & Gilligan, 1992, pp. 27–28).

This second reading led me to highlight several important themes that guided my work over the next decade. For example, in the first research phase, I argued that this type of reading, and the related I poems, helped to illuminate how fathers spoke about themselves as men and as fathers and how they navigated the "shoulds" and "oughts" of fathering and masculinities. Their feelings of being judged as "failed males" in terms of not earning and of being under sporadic surveillance as embodied actors moving on female-dominated terrain (Doucet, 2006) were also uncovered though this reading.

TABLE 6.1 I Poem, Listening Guide Phase 1

Dennis: I poem (constructed from beginning of interview transcript)

I'm half Chinese, half Native I grew up on a reserve
I had my hair permed. . .
I was Hawaiian . . . Somalian. . .
I was passed for Greek, Italian . . . Yeah, it's gotten easier. . .
Her Mother and I didn't get along. . .
I found out that she was pregnant with her after we had broken up. . .
I just told her that I'd be there for her as a father. . .
I didn't want to separate the two kids . . . I tried to do that for awhile and then
I decided to come from Winnipeg to Toronto,
I figured there was nothing for me to do out there and I had to do something good for myself. . .
I came to Toronto. . .
I was going to school, I had a job. . .

I flew up there and picked her up, flew back, spent Christmas . . . She was six. . .
I spent most of the time bringing her up, If I was working, I was working. . .
I would be jumping back and forth from work and home So, we bonded pretty quickly.
Her Mother wasn't . . . a very nurturing person . . . I sent her back out there. . .
I had called back a couple weeks later
She was at home by herself at about eight o'clock . . . ten o'clock at night. . .
I was trying to call my father and the police and so on to get them over to the house. . .
I've heard rumors about it before. . .

I got a private investigator . . . I called social services,
I called all her old neighbours and family that knows what she's like . . . I decided okay,
I'm going to fight for custody. . .
I had decided that I wasn't telling her family . . . I figured they'd all just up and disappear,
    That's the kind of people they are.
I was doing this. . .
I went through that this summer.
So, social services got on their butt really hard. . .

She jumped up screaming . . . shouting . . . swearing to give her to her father

Cause he wants her anyway, and walked out. . .
All I had to do is get my lawyer to do up the papers, I went out there,
She signed them.
And that was that.

Source: Andrea Doucet, *Do Men Mother* (2nd ed). Appendix C, University of Toronto Press, 2018.
Reprinted with the permission of the publisher.

Third Reading: Relationships and Relational Subjectivities

The third reading of interview transcripts, which I developed with Mauthner, was informed by feminist theoretical insights on relational concepts of subjects and selves (Mauthner & Doucet, 1998, 2003). Recognizing the eminently social and relational dimensions of parental subjectivities, I traced participants' intimate relational worlds by focusing on friendships, social networks, and social support, underlining with a different colored pencil any references to these on the hard copy of the transcript (Figure 6.1). In the case of Dennis, I read for indications of his relationships with his ex-partner, his extended kin networks, other parents, the various institutional actors who were central in his children's daily lives (e.g., teachers, health care workers, other caregivers) and the social networks he created (or not) for his daughter.

Fourth Reading: Socio-Structures, Ideologies/Discourses/ Theoretical Themes

Finally, in the fourth reading, I explored intersections of class, ethnicity, sexuality, and gender while focusing on structured power relations and dominant ideologies. Broadly speaking, this reading was informed by fundamental principles gleaned from structuration theory (Bourdieu, 1977) and "relations of ruling" (Smith, 1987). This fourth reading moved away from a local, particular, micro-level, subject-centered emphasis toward a macro-level, structural, material, theoretical, and ideological/discursive focus. This process led me to make particular sociological and structural arguments about my research participants. For example, in the case of Dennis, issues of gender, ethnicity, and class mattered in his parenting; this was especially evident in his minimal access to financial resources and social capital and his circumstances of having lived on an Aboriginal reserve and then making the transition into low-income housing in the city. Ideological conceptions of fathers as breadwinners and mothers as primary caregivers also played a role in Dennis's constant search for a girlfriend to help him care for his daughter. Writing notes in the margins of the hard copy transcripts and through my ATLAS. ti coding, I read for theoretical issues of embodiment, masculinities, the relation between gender equality and gender differences. I also began to use ATLAS.ti memos to assist me in writing up several case studies that bought together my interpretations and analysis. The themes of these readings and the case studies all became central in the book (and other publications) I wrote based on this research (e.g., Doucet, 2006).

Phase 2: Shifting Ethico-Onto-Epistemological Commitments

Through the years 2009–2014, while I was conducting fieldwork for a second project on breadwinning mothers and caregiving fathers (including the case study of my revisiting fathers and mothers that informs this chapter), I also worked on a parallel project about rethinking knowledge making practices. My evolving approach to knowledge making was underpinned by a wide set of performative, ecological, non-representational, and ontologically relational resources. More specifically, I worked closely and diffractively with the writing of feminist philosopher and epistemologist Lorraine Code (2006) and with Margaret Somers' work on non-representational narratives (1992, 1994) and her genealogical approach to concepts (Somers, 1994, 2008). This led me to develop an ecological and non-representational approach to knowledge making, concepts, and narratives (for details, see Doucet, 2018a, 2018b, 2018c).

In relation to knowledge making, an ecological approach underlines how researchers are responsive to and responsible for their participation in dialogically constituted narratives and unfolding subjectivities and worlds. An ecological approach shifts our research work from gathering and *representing* data to "intervening" in (Hacking, 2002) and "intra-act[ing]" (Barad, 2007, p. 33) *with* data and with research subjects and their worlds. More broadly, this is a non-representational approach to method (Doucet, 2018c; Law, 2004; Mauthner, 2017) wherein methods, including data analysis methods, are not neutral techniques for gathering stories, narratives, or experiences, but are, rather, performative. Put differently, methods are imbued with particular ontological and epistemological assumptions about narratives, subjects, knowledges, and realities and these assumptions matter in terms of *what* narratives and knowledges are brought into being.

From this perspective, rather than study representations per se, researchers work with a "politics of possibilities" (Barad, 2007, p. 46) with the recognition that there are always many possible narratives that we can construct as scholars. This means attending to the concepts that inform our work, examining their histories, relationalities, and, where possible, their genealogies (Somers, 2008), and sometimes developing new conceptual narratives (Doucet, 2018a). There is a profound ontological shift from searching for findings to reflecting instead on how we partly *make* these findings. This shift led me to rethink how I approached narratives, the Listening Guide, and my data analysis processes.

An Ecological Approach to Narratives

My aim in this section is to highlight some key dimensions of Somers' (1992, 1994) approach to non-representational narratives and what I call, more broadly, an ecological approach to narratives (Doucet, 2018a). This approach builds partly on Code's ecological thinking and partly on Somers' (1992, 1994) work on non-representational narratives and ontological narrativity, through which she argues that most approaches to narrative analysis assume that narratives reflect, represent, or impose a narrative structure on lived experiences, life stories, or realities. In contrast to this, non-representational approaches define "narrative and narrativity as concepts of *social epistemology* and *social ontology*" (Somers, 1994, p. 606; emphasis in original).

Working broadly within an approach that entangles epistemology and ontology, Somers promotes a multi-layered approach with various dimensions and types of narratives. She argues that there are at least three kinds of nested narratives: (a) ontological narratives; (b) social, public, and cultural narratives; and (c) conceptual narratives.[1] The first type, "ontological narratives," describes "the stories that social actors use to make sense of—indeed, *to act in*—their lives" (Somers, 1994, p. 618; emphasis added). For Somers, these are not representations. Rather, they are what theorists describe as agential, performative, and generative; they are made in particular conditions of possibility and they make and remake narrative identities (see *Reading 1 [1]*). Ontological narratives are intricately tied to particular conceptions of subjects and subjectivities. Intersecting with longstanding poststructuralist concerns about how researchers aim to uncover subjectivity or experience and see subjects and subjectivities as fixed, ontological narratives focus on unfolding subjectivities and narrative identities (Ricoeur, 1985; Somers, 1992, 1994). As Somers (1994, p. 618; emphasis in original) notes: "Ontological narratives make identity and the self something that one *becomes*" (see *Reading 2*).

Social, public, and cultural narratives highlight how the stories that people tell us are constituted by and unfold within "intersubjective webs of relationality [that] sustain and transform narratives over time" (Somers, 1994, p. 618); these include how people interpret and narrate social institutions and socio-political and cultural discourses (see *Reading 3*). Finally, conceptual narratives, reflect "the concepts and explanations that we construct as social researchers" (Somers, 1994, p. 620; *see Reading 4*).

Each of these three narrative types are, in turn, structured by what Somers refers to as "four dimensions of a reframed narrativity particularly relevant for the social sciences," which are "1) relationality of parts, 2) causal emplotment, 3) selective appropriation, and 4) temporality, sequence, and place" (Somers, 1994, p. 616). Put differently, all narratives "are constellations of *relationships* (connected parts) embedded in *time and space*, constituted by. . . *causal emplotment*" (Somers, 1992, p. 601; emphasis in original). I take up these three types and four dimensions of narratives in my discussion of my remaking of the Listening Guide, briefly referring to a couple interview that I conducted with Tom (a stay-at-home dad for seven years and now a part-time health counselor) and Natasha (a pediatrician) in 2009, nine years after I first interviewed them.

Remaking the Listening Guide: From Representational Narratives to Non-Representational and Ecological Narratives

Although there are many differences between the two versions of the Listening Guide, I highlight three overarching changes. First, the concepts that underpin the version of the Listening Guide that I used (and co-developed with Mauthner) over a decade ago—narrative, reflexivity, subjectivity—were all reconfigured to embrace several new epistemological and ontological concerns that arose through my shifting from representational to non-representational ways of knowing. Second, I experienced a shift in my understanding of what concepts *are* and how they work in data analysis processes. Previously I had thought about concepts only in the theoretical formulation of my project without attending to how they were performative in data analysis processes. In my second stage, I explored the histories, relationalities, and performativity of my informing concepts and I began to revision those concepts and the effects of these revisioning processes. I rethought, for example, the concept of the stay-at-home father (Doucet, 2016), binaries of work and care, and dominant conceptions of equality, and I developed wider conceptual narratives of care and breadwinning (Doucet, 2018a).

The third change was a shift in my thinking about *what* I was doing as a researcher. My research practices, guided by the voice-centered and representationalist assumptions that were built into the Listening Guide (Mauthner, 2017), had previously led me to believe I had collected and *captured* the stories of my research participants. I realized that I had been working with narratives through a *"mode of representation"* (Somers, 1994, p. 606; emphasis in original). Like many qualitative and narrative researchers, I referred to people's stories as "their narratives," as if those narratives were "already there," removed from any intervention on my part to bring *particular* narratives into being. I came to the view that I was not collecting stories, but working with many "politics of possibilities." I was, in fact, involved in the making of various types of multi-layered narratives with different dimensions that coalesced through my data analysis processes and my knowledge making and writing practices.

Here, my four reconfigured Listening Guide readings, and how I used them, are briefly laid out. Some of my points embrace the wider research process, but I focus mainly on the concerns of this book: the analysis of interview transcripts. As in my first phase of research, with the new Listening Guide, I conducted my own interviews and worked with hard copies of transcripts (using colored pencils for different readings). I also listened to the interview tapes while I did my readings. In the latter stages of analysis, I used ATLAS.ti mainly to trace concepts and conceptual narratives across all interviews and also to envision and write about new conceptual narratives using its memo-ing capacity. Finally, I developed case studies (from a few pages to approximately 20 pages). Drawing on Abbott (1992), I worked with case studies that highlight what he calls an "instance" (p. 53), which include a "case" or a "set of social objects" (p. 53; i.e., persons) or conceptual instances (i.e., concepts and conceptual narratives). In the second stage of the research project that informs this chapter, I used both of these types of case studies, developing case studies of couples/individuals as well as of key concepts and I worked parts of these case studies into written pieces (e.g., Doucet, 2018a). I built the case studies across time, working back and forth between the Listening Guide readings, ATLAS.ti memos, my fieldnotes, and both hard copy notes (in notebooks/research journals and on hard copies of transcripts) and typed notes (in Scrivener and Ulysses writing software).

Reading 1 [1]:[2] Reading for Ontological Narratives

To focus on emplotment is not to dispense completely with thinking about elements of plot, including plot themes (Frank, 1995). A narrative can exhibit qualities of both plot *and* emplotment, thereby justifying how a narrative can be both a noun and a verb, can be approached through both *what and how* questions, and always involves processes of *"selective appropriation"* for both the teller and the listener (Somers, 1994, p. 617; emphasis in original). This view supports the idea that there is nothing inherent or representational in a narrative plot; rather, researchers take responsibility for particular readings of plot, recognizing the choices made in the telling as well as in the listening.

In the first phase of my research, my data analysis processes attended to plot and to *what* people said, not to emplotment (i.e., *how or why* people said the things they did) or what processes of selection, contexts, and conditions of possibility framed their tellings. I *did* attend to how spoken narratives were *situated* in certain ideological and structural contexts and narratives, but I did *not* recognize how narratives—approached as matters of epistemology and ontology—are *constituted by* and within "relational and cultural matrices" (Somers, 1994, p. 662) that include "*temporality, spatiality*, and *emplotment* as well as *relationality* and *historicity*" (Somers, 1994, p. 620, emphasis in original). In practical terms, this meant that the interviews transcript readings were, in my first stage of research, pulled apart so that I read for narratives, *then* for the subject within those narratives. After this, I moved toward the wider relations of the subject and, finally, I wove my theoretical concerns into the fourth reading of my Listening Guide process.

I now approach the transcript readings in a much more integrated way. In practice, this shift has meant that across my interview transcripts, I still begin by attempting to trace the readings separately (especially when I want to focus on one narrative type or when I am curious about particular issues related to my research problematic or that arise from the interview phase). However, at some point in the process—beginning, middle, or end, depending on the interview—I also do simultaneous tracings of the four readings on my hard copy versions of the interview transcripts (Figure 6.2). This work of doing transcript readings is very time consuming, iterative, intuitive, and non-linear. Moving back and forth between readings, I recognize the integral relationality of the various kinds and dimensions of non-representational narratives, my narrative analysis, and my epistemic responsibilities as a researcher and writer.

SEE FIGURE 6.2 at eResource—Listening Guide Phase 2.

Reading 1 [2]: From Reflexivity to Diffraction

Diffraction is about relationships, intervention, and "interacting within and as part of" (Barad, 2007, p. 89). As diffraction emphasizes intervening and is less about reading or listening, it is also connected to epistemic responsibility—not for what we "find," but for what we both find and make—through our "matters of concern" (Latour, 2004, p. 231), "questions about care, concern, and advocacy" (Code, 2015, p. 1), and our conceptual narratives. In short, a shift from reflexivity to diffraction strengthens the attention to our epistemic practices. This is a move from "a place from *which to know* as the language of 'perspectives' might imply, indifferently available to anyone who chooses to stand there" to a view that our situatedness "is itself *a place to know* who intricacies have to be examined for how they shape both knowing subjects and the objects of knowledge" (Code, 2006, p. 40; emphasis in original).

Diffraction can mean many things in our research practices (Mauthner, 2017; Mazzei, 2014; Taguchi, 2012). For me, building on Haraway's (1997) concept of diffraction, which is about "heterogeneous history, not about originals" (p. 273), it means recognizing ontological multiplicity in my analytic work (see Doucet, 2018c). Here, I not only attend to my reflexive responses to the interview transcripts but also consider how my concepts are performative in bringing forth particular narratives and excluding others.

Reading 2: From Subjects to Narrative Identities

Working with an ecological approach to narratives "redirects theoretical analyses toward situated knowledges, situated ethico-politics, where situation is *constitutive of*, not just the context for, the backdrop to, enactments of subjectivity. . . . This is not, then, a merely contextualized subjectivity" (Code, 2006, p. 19; emphasis in original). In my new approach, the ontological fit between narrative identities, nested narrative contexts, and conceptual narrativity is *tighter*.

What does this mean in practice? To shift from subjects to narrative identities means at least two things. First, it recognizes that identities (such as gender, class, race, sexuality, and ability) and categories (including the categories or concepts of "stay-at-home father" or "breadwinning mother") are fleshed out and remade through intersecting narrative forms and dimensions. Somers (1992, 1994, 2008) argues that we should approach all analytic categories—and what she calls narrative identities—as narrated and unfolding in specific practices and relations (rather than as assumed categories). In terms of my narrative analysis process for the project that informs this chapter, this led me to scrutinize the taken-for-grantedness of concepts such as the stay-at-home father and to argue that they must be approached as contingent, contextual, highly heterogeneous, and shaped by intersectionality (Doucet, 2016).

Another point about this second reading is that this shift from subjectivity (as something to be *found* in the interview) to narrative identities (as being *made* within multi-layered narratives) leads to a different epistemological and ontological ration-ale for the Listening Guide's "reading for the I" and writing of "I poems." I still believe that this part of the Listening Guide is a valuable heuristic device, especially when intimate or difficult topics are being covered in life history interviews and/or where there is an urgent or political need to carefully listen to and center the first person perspective. The "I" reading can provide, for example, "sensitivity to detail, to minutiae, to what precisely—however apparently small—distinguishes *this* woman" from another (Code, 2006, p. 17; emphasis added). Its purpose now, however, is different. Unlike my earlier Listening Guide approach, which leaned toward attempting to capture subjectivities through "I poems," my new approach attends to how narrative identities are *produced* in the telling of stories. This means paying attention to the dialogic quality of the interview, noting how the questions I ask and the problematics I am exploring may lead the teller to choose particular ways of speaking about themselves. I also attend more to how the teller emplots themselves, sometimes seeking to create positive enactments of their narratives and subjectivities.

My first stage of analysis, over a decade ago, identified some interview stories as "heroic narratives" (Doucet, 2006, p. 64), but neglected to deeply examine emplotment and narrative identities. My argument now addresses a broader sense of emplotment that exists in *all* interviews. Interview narratives are entanglements of plot and emplotment, constructed in particular ways for particular audiences and for particular purposes; they are entangled with the making and remaking of specific identities within particular contexts. In my second stage of research, these narrative identities related mainly to being a good/responsible mother/father and a good/responsible worker/breadwinner.

Reading 3: Social, Public, and Cultural Narratives

In this reading, I asked questions such as: What are these social, public, and cultural narratives? How did these constitute the stories people tell? As I analyzed my interview transcripts, I drew attention to how, implicitly or explicitly, specific policies (or lack thereof) affected mothering and fathering decisions, including childcare or parental leave policies. If people did not talk about these policies in their interviews, I drew attention to this gap in their parenting narratives as I recognized that connections between different narrative layers made particular stories possible. Tom and Natasha, for example, both took it for granted that their only option was for Tom to stay at home with their young children. This was because when their first child, Taylor, was born in 1993, only a short maternity leave was available for Natasha, a self-employed doctor, and daycare services were minimal. In their decision-making, Tom and Natasha thus drew on social, cultural, and public narratives about the need to have one parent at home. Taylor (16 years old at the time of their second interview) joined us for part of this second interview and, when asked about her future plans, she responded that she wanted to be a biologist and that she planned to use daycare.

She added that she would expect neither herself nor her potential partner to be a stay-at-home parent. Her ontological narrative was thus different from her parents partly because the informing social, public, and cultural narratives had changed. For example, in her home province of Quebec, publicly funded, affordable daycare and generous parental leave provisions now existed for both mothers and fathers.

Reading 4: Conceptual Narratives

This reading frames the entire process of data analysis and knowledge making. Broadly speaking, I attend to how the concepts and conceptual narratives in my informing scholarly fields play a role in how I am framing my problematic, asking questions, and analyzing my interviews. I ask: Are there new conceptual narratives that I can revision or reimagine?

How has this new approach to reading for conceptual narratives in my data analysis process shifted my thinking and my arguments about concepts and conceptual narratives? Drawing again on the case study of Tom and Natasha, I began to question concepts of gender equality (Doucet, 2015), which led me to recognize how I was overlooking the severity of job precariousness for Tom and for other stay-at-home fathers. My earlier work had been informed by a specific concept of gender equality that focused on how women's parental responsibilities impeded equality in paid work and care work. Utilizing a reconfigured concept of gender equality that attended more closely to class differences between caregiving situations and to issues of economic "vulnerability" (Fineman, 2008) for caregivers, my analysis shifted to also consider the workplace disadvantages faced by stay-at-home fathers, including Tom, who gave up paid work to be at home for several years.

With an awareness of how different conceptual narratives lead to different kinds of arguments and knowledges, in this fourth reading I also asked myself questions about my epistemic responsibilities. How and why was I emplotting the way I was? Why was I telling *this* scholarly narrative and not *that* scholarly narrative? How would I write this narrative? How and with whom would I negotiate my knowledge making? What are the possible effects of these narratives? How have my "matters of concern" (Latour, 2004, p. 231) my "questions about care, concern, and advocacy" (Code, 2015, p. 1) and my conceptual narratives played a role in bringing particular narratives into being? (Doucet, 2018a).

Conclusion

This chapter has laid out two phases of a research project on primary caregiving fathers and a reconfiguration of the Listening Guide into an ecological, ontological narrativity, and non-representational data and narrative analysis approach. A considerable difference in my reconfigured approach is that I now view my conceptual and theoretical concerns and my informing epistemological and ontological assumptions about narratives, knowledges, subjectivities, and social worlds as deeply entangled throughout the entire research process. In plain and provocative language, Arthur Frank in an interview with Eldershaw, Mayan, and Winkler (2007, p. 133; emphasis added) makes this point:

> The crucial thing is that we need to get away from this rather crude episte- mology of one person having the story inside of him- or herself and then delivering the story like the goose laying the egg in the presence of the other person, who then goes: What an egg! In fact, it's a *collaborative activity all the way through.*

My reading of this collaborative activity is wide. I now read interview transcripts as a "relationality of parts" (Somers, 1994, p. 616) where people tell and emplot stories (ontological narratives) selectively, in particular conditions of possibility, including the public, social, and cultural narratives that constitute their lives and the stories they tell. These stories are constituted, in turn, within and through the conceptual narratives of researchers, who ask particular questions from among many "mat- ters of concern" and then relay these stories as scholarly narratives within and to particular epistemic communities. I apply my new approach throughout my knowledge making process, not only in the analysis of transcripts, but in how I read authors (Doucet, 2018a), work with concepts, and understand my epistemic responsibilities. My interview transcript work is also guided by a few simple yet powerful questions: What makes *that* story possible?[3] What narratives will I assem- ble? What scholarly narrative will I tell? Why am I telling *that* narrative?

KEY WORKS GUIDING MY DATA ANALYSIS

Code, L. (2006). *Ecological thinking: The politics of epistemic location.* New York, NY: Oxford University Press.

I drew on this book as well as Code's four decades of writing on the political, ethical, epistemological, and ontological dimensions of knowledge mak- ing and the development of her ecological thinking approach. Her work is rooted in several epistemological strands (e.g., naturalized, social, virtue, feminist, and epistemologies of ignorance) and, among others, the work of Deleuze and Guattari, Latour, Bourdieu, Foucault, Castoriadis, Ricoeur, and Haraway. Ecological thinking has been my guiding framework for the devel- opment of a relational, non-representational, and politico-ethico-onto- epistemological approach to narratives, subjects, social objects, social relations, and to knowledge making and its multiple effects.

Somers, M. R. (1994). The narrative constitution of identity: A relational and network approach. *Theory and Society, 23,* 605–649.

> This is a highly challenging, rich, and foundational piece for working with a non-representational and epistemological-ontological approach to narratives. It lays out several interlocking narrative types and dimensions of narratives. It is also rooted in Somers' larger 30-year program of work on relational sociology, narrative theory in the social sciences and humanities, and her work on the "historical sociology of concept formation" (Somers, 2008, p. 172), which is a genealogical approach to concepts and conceptual narratives. I began to draw on Somers to remake the Listening Guide in my co-authored earlier work, but it took many years for me to figure out how to work in a way that would be underpinned by her larger research program.

Frank, A. W. (2010). *Letting stories breathe: A socio-narratology.* Chicago, IL: University of Chicago Press.

> This is an excellent overview of dialogic narrative analysis in practice. Although it has synergies with the work of Somers, it engages less with larger debates on epistemologies and ontologies, and, rather, is rooted in some of the key qualitative research and narrative debates. On my reading, it also provides a very good overview of how to work with narratives in ways that balance non-representational theory and representational concerns, especially when studying cases of human suffering or disadvantage.

Notes

1. Somers also has a fourth category of narrative, metanarratives that I did not apply in this research project (Somers, 1994, 2008; see Doucet, 2018c).
2. As with the earlier version of the Listening Guide, I still work with a two-part approach to the first reading, attending to plot/emplotment and diffraction/epistemic reflexivity.
3. I am grateful to Natasha Mauthner for sharing this question with me.

References

Abbott, A. (1992). What do cases do? Some notes on activity in sociological analysis. In C. C. Ragin & H. S. Becker (Eds.), *What is a case? Exploring the foundations of social inquiry* (pp. 53–82). Cambridge: Cambridge University Press.

Barad, K. (2007). *Meeting the universe halfway: Quantam physics and the entanglement of matter and meaning.* Durham, NC: Duke University Press.

Bourdieu, P. (1977). *Outline of a theory of practice.* Cambridge: Cambridge University Press.

Brown, L. M. (1998). *Raising their voices: The politics of girls' anger.* Cambridge, MA: Harvard University Press.

Brown, L. M., & Gilligan, C. (1992). *Meeting at the crossroads: Women's psychology and girls' development.* Cambridge, MA: Harvard University Press.

Code, L. (2006). *Ecological thinking: The politics of epistemic location.* New York, NY: Oxford University Press.

Code, L. (2015). Care, concern, and advocacy: Is there a place for epistemic responsibility? *Feminist Philosophy Quarterly, 1*(1), 1–20.

Doucet, A. (2006). *Do men mother?* (1st ed.). Toronto, ON: University of Toronto Press.

Doucet, A. (2015). Parental responsibilities: Dilemmas of measurement and gender equality. *Journal of Marriage and Family, 77,* 224–242.

Doucet, A. (2016). Is the stay-at-home dad (SAHD) a feminist concept? A genealogical, relational, and feminist critique. *Sex Roles, 75,* 4–14.

Doucet, A. (2018a). *Do men mother?* (2nd ed.). Toronto, ON: University of Toronto Press.

Doucet, A. (2018b). Feminist epistemologies and ethics: Ecological thinking, situated knowledges, epistemic responsibilities. In R. Iphofen & M. Tolich (Eds.), *The Sage handbook of qualitative research ethics* (pp. 73–88). London: Sage.

Doucet, A. (2018c). Decolonizing family photographs: Ecological imaginaries and non-representational ethnographies. *Journal of Contemporary Ethnography.* Advance online publication. doi:10.1177/0891241617744859

Doucet, A., & Mauthner, N. S. (2008). What can be known and how? Narrated subjects and the Listening Guide. *Qualitative Research, 8,* 399–409.

Eldershaw, L. P., Mayan, M., & Winkler, A. (2007). Through a painted window: On narrative, medicine, and method. Interview with Arthur W. Frank conducted by the International Institute for Qualitative Methodology EQUIPP Students. *International Journal of Qualitative Methods, 6*(3), 121–139.

Fineman, M. A. (2008). The vulnerable subject: Anchoring equality in the human condition. *Yale Journal of Law and Feminism, 20*(1), 1–23.

Frank, A. W. (1995). *The wounded storyteller: Body, illness, and ethics.* Chicago, IL: University of Chicago Press.

Gilligan, C., Spencer, R., Weinberg, M. K., & Bertsch, T. (2003). On the listening guide: A voice-centered relational model. In P. M. Camic, J. E. Rhodes, & L. Yardley (Eds.), *Qualitative research in psychology: Expanding perspectives in methodology and design* (pp. 157–172). Washington, DC: American Psychological Association.

Hacking, I. (2002). *Historical ontology.* Boston, MA: Harvard University Press.

Haraway, D. J. (1997). Modest_Witness@Second_Millennium.FemaleMan©_Meets_Onco Mouse™*: Feminism and Technoscience.* New York, NY: Routledge.

Latour, B. (2004). Why has critique run out of steam? From matters of fact to matters of concern. *Critical Inquiry, 30,* 225–248.

Law, J. (2004). *After method: Mess in social science research.* London: Routledge.

Mauthner, N. S. (2017). The listening guide feminist method of narrative analysis: Towards a posthumanist performative (re)configuration. In J. Woodiwiss, K. Smith, & K. Lockwood (Eds.), *Feminist narrative research: Opportunities and challenges* (pp. 65–91). London: Palgrave Macmillan.

Mauthner, N. S., & Doucet, A. (1998). Reflections on a voice-centred relational method of data analysis: Analysing maternal and domestic voices. In J. Ribbens & R. Edwards (Eds.), *Feminist dilemmas in qualitative research: Private lives and public texts* (pp. 119–144). London: Sage.

Mauthner, N. S., & Doucet, A. (2003). Reflexive accounts and accounts of reflexivity in qualitative data analysis. *Sociology, 37,* 413–431.

Mazzei, L. A. (2014). Beyond an easy sense: A diffractive analysis. *Qualitative Inquiry, 20,* 742–746.

Ricoeur, P. (1985). *Time and narrative. Volume 1* (K. Mclaughlin & D. Pellauer, Trans.). Chicago, IL: University of Chicago Press.

Smith, D. E. (1987). *The everyday world as problematic: A feminist sociology*. Milton Keynes, England: Open University Press.

Somers, M. R. (1992). Narrativity, narrative identity, and social action: Rethinking English working-class formation. *Social Science History*, *16*, 591–630.

Somers, M. R. (1994). The narrative constitution of identity: A relational and network approach. *Theory and Society*, *23*, 605–649.

Somers, M. R. (2008). *Genealogies of citizenship: Markets, statelessness, and the right to have rights*. New York, NY: Cambridge University Press.

Taguchi, H. L. (2012). A diffractive and Deleuzian approach to analysing interview data. *Feminist Theory*, *13*, 265–281.

7

AUTHENTICITY IN QUALITATIVE DATA ANALYSES

Notes on Racial and Gender Diversity in Team Ethnography of Young Men of Color

Kevin Roy, John R. Hart, and Laura Golojuch

Questions of social justice and scientific rigor shape how we conduct "good" qualitative research—in particular, how the gender and racial composition of research teams is related to social inequality and lived experiences of men of color (Twine, 2000). Researchers must grapple not only with their own constellation of "stances" and social locations through critical, reflexive discourse (Best, 2003; McCall, 2005), but also with how this critique informs relationships between researchers and community members in the real world and methodological techniques for data collection and analyses. Some advocate for matching researchers with participants based on race and gender characteristics (Rhodes, 1994). However, a research team with a diversity of lived experiences (as simultaneous "insiders" and "outsiders" to the experiences of community members; Merton, 1972) can provide a strengths-based approach. Such a team can also reflect an ethical obligation to counter concerns over misrepresentation in fieldwork and interpretation (Stanley & Slattery, 2003).

In the fall of 1997, Kevin Roy (first author) was a 30-year-old single, White male doctoral student who had worked for two years in a community-based fatherhood program on the South Side of Chicago with young, low-income, nonresident Black fathers. These men had persevered in their pursuit of "being there" for their children in spite of job loss, relationship conflict, police sweeps for gang activity, and court appearances for child support. These fathers opened up to Roy in interviews to discuss intimate relationships such as their relationships with their own fathers.

Dr. Phil Bowman was a senior scholar of African American families and one of Roy's doctoral committee members. He listened to how Roy struggled to respect these fathers' experiences given that he was not yet a father himself. Bowman asserted that these young men would disclose things that they seldom told anyone, even if Roy did not share many lived experiences with them. In some ways, he argued, that was exactly why they could share: "you have to respect the sacred ground that you're walking on . . . they are trusting you to present their stories with honesty and integrity" (Bowman, personal communication, 1997).

Insights about sacred ground continue to shape Roy's research, including the collaborative team ethnography that he developed more than a decade after his doctoral project. In this chapter, we explore methodological decisions about balancing the perspectives and expertise of a diverse research team during data analyses. We present a framework of *authenticity* that is critical to effective analyses. This approach began with prolonged time and interaction in communities, as well as the emergence of trust, reciprocity, and rapport with team members and family members. As we developed an appreciation of inequality rooted in relationships, our analyses were deeper and more insightful.

Our team's experience provides evidence of how data analyses seep into the earliest moments of data collection (Daly, 2007). In this chapter, we briefly discuss data collection processes, including explicitly paired team facilitation of program sessions, tailored individual relationships to develop rapport with participants, and weekly team meetings to work through complicated and, at times, contradictory understandings of young men's experiences. Next, we describe in detail our team's decision making with regard to data analysis processes that were based in grounded theory methodology. As a group, we open coded the data, and then created carefully selected small clusters of codes for axial coding related to specific research questions. As we moved forward to craft dimensions of a specific concept, we relied on a process of selective coding.

Ethnography of Young Men of Color in the Transition to Adulthood

Our commitment to respecting sacred ground necessitates prolonged engagement in local communities, which promotes credibility in data quality (Krefting, 1999) and is commonly encouraged by prominent family ethnographers (see Lareau, 2011). This approach contrasts with "drive-by" research, which is common in our field and characterized by few hours spent in community contexts, avoidance of interaction with local gatekeepers often based on fear and anxiety, and limited contact with participants. We believe that a one-time interview or focus group strains trusting relationships with families and communities. Without immersion in the physical and social spaces that shape the lives of research participants over an extended period of time, researchers may proceed with inaccurate data analyses that lack contextual understanding of critical phenomena.

The focus of our ethnographic study was the transition to adulthood for young men of color (Roy, Messina, Smith, & Waters, 2014)—the methodological details of which we discuss here. Our research team conducted data collection for 24 months in two youth development programs, as well as pilot research in a correctional facility, in the Baltimore/Washington DC metropolitan area. The first program, Urban Progress (UP), helped out-of-school youth and young adults to "turn their lives around." This sprawling one-story brick facility sat underneath an expressway overpass alongside strings of row houses that were home to generations of African American families. Our research team facilitated two weekly life skills sessions in conflict management, coping with exposure to violence, and stress and depression. Twenty-one African American men between the ages of 17 and 24 agreed to participate in the study. The second program, Diversity Matters (DM), was also a youth development project, located in a former high school and tucked into the back streets of a community of single-family homes. We offered similar life skills sessions in the DM facility, from which we recruited another 20 men (five African American, two West African, and 13 Salvadoran, which reflected the racial and ethnic variation in the program). Although young men of color are often characterized as "hard-to-reach populations" by social scientists, we spent time with them in settings of their choosing, where they were comfortable and ready to engage with staff.

Configuring a team of ethnographic researchers took careful consideration. Nineteen students (doctoral, masters, and undergraduate) voluntarily approached Roy to serve as interviewers or coders over the seven years of the project. As principal investigator, Roy considered each team member as a unique colleague, adding to a complex set of insights that the full team could offer. The composition of the team was not preplanned based on knowledge of urban Baltimore; growing up in a White, Black, or Latino family; or life experiences based on being a man or woman. Thirty-two percent of team members ($n = 6$) were students of color, and another 37% were White women. Initially, nine students collected data during fieldwork and interviews, and another 10 joined the team during coding (and as original team members transitioned off the project). Further, half of the team members were licensed couple and family therapists, with months of training in listening skills with hundreds of client families.

Roy asked each team member to start with a simple commitment to respect the "sacred ground" of participants. At any moment, any of us could be confused, inexperienced, or unaware of the nature of the young men's lived experiences in our ethnography, and we had to rely on others to provide insight through team discussion. We had to ask each other, "Do we know what's going on with these young men? Does our story feel right? Who can help us understand?"

Data Collection and Early Stages of "Field-Based" Analyses

We used two primary methods of data collection: participant observation and individual life history interviews. For many weeks, the research team took extensive fieldnotes after sessions and interactions with staff and participants in each site. This method provided information on ecological processes (such as negotiation of peer networks, exposure to violence, limited job and educational opportunities, and physical mobility), community barriers and supports for youth development, mental health considerations, and close relationships with friends and family members. After we developed a consistent and trusting relationship with most participants, we mentioned to each of the young men in the life skills sessions that we would like to interview them.

Each team member met a young man one-on-one in a private classroom in each site to conduct a one- to two-hour interview. These life history interviews examined how parents and close kin supported sons in the transition to adulthood. A semi-structured format provided a general guide to discuss their daily routines, next steps for work and education, support networks, and what it meant to be an adult. In many interviews, we also discussed family conflict (such as divorce or domestic violence), immigration and fluid residential change, masculinity, intimate relationships, incarceration and gang activity, and depression or related trauma.

We were explicit in choosing methods of data collection that would enhance trustworthiness and provide rigorous analyses (Krefting, 1999; Lincoln & Guba, 1985; Maxwell, 2002). Credibility and dependability of the data were enhanced by use of multiple sources of data and multiple methods of data collection, as well as prolonged engagement in the field. During later stages of data analyses, in-person discussions with young men (i.e., member checks) were used to check our understanding of how their experiences as adolescents shaped their own expectations of being adults.

These considerations reflect common ethnographic techniques that researchers use in a social service setting. But it proved hard, if not impossible, to represent adequately the challenges that these young men confronted in their communities using the jargon of methodology. These men spoke emotionally about their frustrations, only to then disengage and disconnect emotionally. They constructed complex narratives of their experiences, shifting across time and place easily, borrowing familiar words from hip hop lyrics and images from movies. For example, a young man acknowledged the difficulty of avoiding friends who continued to deal drugs, even as he tried to move on, with a reference to the film *The Godfather*: "Every time I try to get out of the game, it pulls me back in." Another echoed the words of an infamous character, Omar, in the Baltimore-based television show, *The Wire*, as he thought about how he remained vigilant to anyone who might seek to hurt him: "When you come at the King, you best not miss." Yet, they repeatedly insisted that, "I've never told this to anyone before." We struggled with what was overlooked in our fieldnotes, and we noticed contradictions and gaps of silence in interviews. These early data analyses made us second-guess our data and push ourselves to represent experiences with subsequent participants with even more detail.

Likewise, our team encountered real challenges in returning to these communities each week, expecting to focus on conducting a study with little preparation for what we might encounter. The team developed abilities to persevere over many months. Roy and Hart spent months in the field to collect data, bringing it back to a larger team for analysis, only to return to the field for more data. As fieldwork continued, Golojuch moved from data analyses back into the field to collect new data with Roy and Hart. We would travel for an hour to the programs to find that sessions had been canceled with little explanation, no one showed up for a class, or young men had been placed in lockdown in sessions offered in correctional facilities (Hart, 2017). We developed a sense of humor to get through tough days. Our team felt a real sense of accomplishment when we connected with men through empathy, even if it did not lead to a recorded data session. However, it was also common that we all felt degrees of vulnerability to being traumatized by constant returns to talk with young men living in toxic circumstances. This anxiety or stress varied by who we were: some days, Hart, as a young Black man, was more susceptible to feeling down about men's shared stories, and on other days, it was Golojuch or Roy who felt disconnected due to White privilege and the sheer number of men and extent of discrimination or oppression that we had never experienced ourselves.

Conversations in the car were the earliest stage of analyzing data, as well as a vital mechanism for us to communicate and learn from each other. After leaving some of our first field sessions, we would drive back to campus and debrief about the fieldwork. At times, we vented frustration or excitement, and we asked each other for help in translating "what just happened in that classroom?" In these car conversations, our team developed a shared analytical language and more nuanced ways to ask questions of data. We audio recorded a few of these conversations, but more often took copious jottings of insights and confusion while we drove in the car. For example, we were shocked that young men's parents had cut them loose from support years earlier, when they were 13 or 14 years old. We debated how the parents of these young men "loved their sons but raised their daughters" (Mandara, Varner, & Richman, 2010, p. 48). Our understanding of independence during emerging adulthood shifted dramatically when we compared notes to find that many men had lived on their own for six or seven years already.

It became clear that each team member's "fit" with an ethnography of young men of color went far beyond consideration of gender and racial characteristics. The most integral and successful team members (a young Black man, a middle aged White man, and a young White woman) could understand their own experiences through a critical lens. Roy was attuned to the mix of insider and outsider statuses that each of us carried into the team. For example, when we worked with young fathers, Roy brought many years of lived experience as a father of his own children. As a White middle aged man, however, he was also unlike the young Black men who were team researchers and may have grown up in the same communities as our participants. In turn, clinical training benefited Hart and Golojuch, who were more attuned to addressing mental health challenges and group dynamics. We found how we could complement each other.

Authenticity and Data Analyses

A frame for this complex sense of individual identities and resources that make up a team project must go beyond a flattened consideration of race and gender as binaries. We propose that *authenticity* should pervade the team as a whole. For example, clear comfort with our own complicated identities allowed us to be confident but open to critique our own assumptions as we moved into the phase of conducting interviews (and continuing data analyses). Being authentic with young men in the study, and with each other, meant that we did not pretend to understand how it felt to watch a friend get shot, or to be picked up by police in front of one's home, and participants in the study did not expect that of the team. Knowing the limits of our own understanding opened up moments of trust and rapport, as well as opportunities for reciprocity when our team could contribute from training as therapists or teachers with knowledge about mental health, parenting practices, or human development.

For example, interviews often touched on how men found ways to protect themselves in dangerous neighborhoods where policy or gang members pursued them. Roy did not understand how critical this pursuit was to daily life in their communities, when young Black men would look at him and honestly ask, "You have no idea what I'm talking about, do you?" If he was to be authentic with them, he had to admit that he did not, and simply ask them if they would explain to help him better understand. During the many months that Roy conducted interviews, Hart—as a young Black man, even one who was a doctoral student—"schooled" him on what it meant for young Black men to be "on point" and vigilant of who was in the proximity and what kind of threat they might bring. In order to be "true to the data" and sacred ground, authenticity was a critical tool in collection and analyses. We struggled with our own limited perceptions, which could obscure the real experiences of young men as they conveyed them in interviews. In other words, authentically informed analyses were not grounded in our ability to parrot current headlines from the *New York Times* or findings from academic articles on the Baltimore uprising, but in the months of interaction that each of us had with each young man in the study, in program sessions, in the hallways of the youth development program, or in one-on-one discussions in closed-door classrooms.

This level of authenticity had many challenges. Although participants knew the team collectively though life skills sessions, interviews were conducted by a single team member. One team member, a young Black woman with extensive expertise in trauma and homicide survivorship, grew to expect flirtation that was present in each interview session. Relatedly, when she began fieldwork, Golojuch, a white female, had discussions with Roy and Hart about how we would dress or present ourselves as a team, to downplay gendered interactions that might even threaten to take over interview sessions. That dynamic could obscure a true engagement in an interview, or it could present a real chance for meaningful exchange. As a team, we protected each other in these situations, but we realized that we were being honest in who we were and that we did not want to meet these young men as generic researchers trying to hide our own unique identities. Reflecting back, we believe that the interaction that the three of us modeled— a respectful and vulnerable give and take, playing to each of our strengths as therapists, teachers, or researchers—allowed young men to trust us and to disclose deeply personal stories.

For faculty facilitators of such projects, is there a threshold for authenticity in recruiting students on the team? In other words, how do we know if a team researcher is comfortable in their own identity enough to be challenged, be confused, or admit to not being an expert? Moreover, is there a threshold for a faculty researcher to be comfortable in their own identities? We can say that the relentless challenging of one's assumptions—even for the young men of color on the team—requires a commitment to constant education. We were careful not to bring anyone into fieldwork without consensus from the team that the new researcher appeared confident in who they were and ready to cope with the difficult experiences at hand. Moreover, there were always roles that interested students could play that did not involve fieldwork and interviewing.

The daily experiences of young men were unexpected, terrifying, exhilarating, even marked with boredom and depression. Researchers engaged in data collection, for example, must be ready to unlearn and relearn, to accept that many months of prior research may not prepare them for the demands of relating to young men exposed to toxic urban environments of police, gang, and family violence. In effect, a team project is, at its most basic, a call to grow and develop together, an emergent process of surprise discovery and hard work.

Retaining Authenticity During Coding and "Out-of-the-Field" Analyses

For the study, all 41 interviews were digitally recorded on audiotapes and then transcribed by either the original interviewer or another team member who worked in tandem to clarify sections of the interview that were unclear or confusing. Team members also transcribed their own jottings and fieldwork notes. Transcriptions in Microsoft Word documents were then imported into Dedoose software. Dedoose is qualitative analysis software program that uses an online platform for storing data in a secure virtual cloud and which also allows for simultaneous coding by multiple coders. Coding began after all interviews were conducted, but while transcription was still underway.

Following a modified grounded theory framework (LaRossa, 2005), data analysis consisted of three phases of coding: open, axial, and selective. Prior to examining transcribed data to open code, our team held three meetings over the course of two months specifically to brainstorm a working set of sensitizing concepts (van den Hoonaard, 1997) as the basis for a codebook. Each of us drew eclectically from existing studies of disadvantaged young men and emerging adulthood, including adultification (Burton, 2007), generativity, knifing off (Laub & Sampson, 2006), survival strategies (Rich, 2011), cultural scripts (Harding, 2010), masculinity (Way, 2013), soft skills, the youth control complex (Rios, 2011), and aspirations/expectations (Fader, 2013). As we then began to open code data, we also discovered codes that were unexpected and which were usually described by the young men themselves. These included the process of "ghosting," or disappearing from school, work, family, and friends for set periods of time (Richardson & St. Vil, 2016); and being "man of the house," which had specific meaning for young men raised by single mothers and who had important caregiving responsibilities for their siblings (Roy et al., 2014).

Each text segment was coded by at least two team members. Roy assigned researchers who served as initial interviewers to take the lead on coding, but we also involved researchers who had not conducted interviews as secondary analysts. At times similar codes showed overlap and agreement; often, however, a second coder introduced a new set of codes that expanded the interpretation of an event or phrase. This approach was not meant to result in a numeric agreement value (coder reliability), but to provide checks and balances for analysis and interpretation.

In a collaborative ethnography, it was important to distinguish analysis from interpretation, in that we needed multiple voices to agree to "what is going on" in each text unit, but to agree and disagree about "what it means" as well (Wolcott, 1994). For a primary coder, a first check on an appropriate code was their coding partner; a second check was Roy, as principal investigator; and a final check was the group as a whole. Similar to tag team data collection, we strived to take advantage of the diversity of perspectives on our team (May & Pattillo-McCoy, 2000; Stanley & Slattery, 2003).

For the team as a whole, we developed two basic processes to deliberate coding decisions. First, coding pairs communicated with each other through the memoing function in Dedoose software. They raised questions with each other ("Don't you see his decision to leave home related to his conflict with his mother, not just a need for independence?"), which led either to agreement on a single code or on a set of linked but different codes. Dedoose memos resembled post-it notes on the transcription text (see Figure 7.1 for an example), and memos could also be marked with the same codes, to allow for quick retrieval and comparison. In effect, memos became another set of data for analysis. Second, we came together in weekly team meetings to discuss coding decisions. We selected key interactions to untangle and deliberate face-to-face. The goal here was to agree as a group about how to best code a section of text.

SEE FIGURE 7.1   at eResource—Use of Memos in Dedoose Software Program.

Coding partners challenged each other on a regular basis. For example, De'Onte, a young man in Baltimore had been "flat" in one interview, in that he repeatedly asserted, "I don't want to talk about" relationships with his peers, his childhood relationship with his mother, or his gang involvement. A team member, a young Black man who grew up in similar community settings to those partici-pants from Baltimore, stressed that a "cool pose" was a protection strategy with cultural roots. His coding partner, an older White woman with very divergent lived experiences, had more training in mental health and trauma. She suggested that these responses might also reflect depression, disengagement, and emotional disconnection. As a result, this text was marked with a complex mix of codes for mental health, cultural scripts, traumatic response, and masculinity. We realized that we could not dismiss "I don't want to talk about it" as a lack of information, but as a window into a single complicated expression that borrowed from both of their insights. We would only have appreciated this expression by not privileging one insight over the other, rigorous conceptualization over depth of lived experi-ence, or visa versa. This iterative process of reviewing and revising codes played to the strengths of students trained as therapists, who integrated additional skills and ways of processing data.

Given these experiences of the young men we interviewed, coding partners needed to support each other as well. We carried the imprint of many days in impoverished communities, or for some of us, in correctional facilities work-ing with young men, and it was imperative that we processed our experiences while coding. Team members felt vulnerable to being traumatized by field-work to talk with another young man living in toxic circumstances, including gunshots, depression, boredom, getting high, or highs and lows of romantic relationships. Returning to these difficult conversations when we shifted to transcribing and then coding text, we felt at risk for a degree of vicarious trauma. Hart, as a young Black man, felt as if he was just a breath away from the same experiences, wondering what made him different than these men, who could have grown up next door to him. He turned to other team members, often those of us who were not men or not Black, to gain perspective, to pull him out of the depths of coding where he saw only the dark sides of each man's interview responses.

The media portrayal of police involvement in the murders of Black youth throughout the country, in Ferguson, Cleveland, and of course Baltimore, only heightened the impact of the simple act of reading and then coding. The fact that young men of color were being killed played on our minds and hearts as we coded; as a group, we prioritized the need to "check yourself" and examine if we were entering the data with a healthy mind frame, not allowing our personal relations to cloud our interpretations of text. Emotional check-ins were common, especially for student-clinicians who valued and understood self care. This required time and space that was distinct (but related) to coding deliberation, to process emotions.

Axial coding involved identifying conceptually similar categories while noting the overlapping and distinguishing characteristics of the codes (Daly, 2007; LaRossa, 2005). Working across 41 cases, we explored variation in specific codes. We used two primary tools to examine differences across each site, and by cultural context. First, Dedoose offers a "descriptors" function to tag an entire case interview with demographic information. The software program also creates ways to explore data by this information; we could choose cross-tabs, bar graphs, even word clouds to examine how a code varied by specific axes, such as participants' age or race/ethnicity. Second, we stepped outside Dedoose to create spreadsheets in Microsoft Excel. Each case was a line, and each descriptive code was a column, and we explored the data to look for patterns along specific axes. Figure 7.2 shows an example of one of these Excel spreadsheets about how five young men's residential histories (by row) were coded with five distinct but related codes (by columns) to compare and contrast complex narratives of where they lived and how their residences changed over time.

For example, participants were initially given the title "man of the house" after a range of specific events, such as departure of their fathers, their mothers' loss of a job, or bringing home money for the first time. We found that some parents stepped back to let their sons perform adult duties; others carefully extended these duties step by step; and a few never asked their sons to take on accelerated responsibilities in care or provision. The concept of man of the house, in all of its forms and nuances, was common across the majority of cases, and we realized that we had nearly saturated this theme when it described most—but not all—of the cases in the analysis.

This second wave of coding was often implemented outside of the Dedoose online environment, in real-time discussions in team meetings. We printed up decontextualized paragraph-sized texts on a specific code, asked a cluster of five team members to sift through the different pieces with a pen or pencil in hand and to take notes, add insights, and compare and contrast across cases. The paragraphs that appear in Table 7.1 are verbatim coding reports produced by Dedoose, as examples of text units coded as "ghosting."

Coming back together as a group, team members identified patterns or illustrated shifts in meaning. For these two paragraphs, we compared how young men used the metaphors of "being dead" or "falling off" to describe the process of disappearing from interaction with their friends and families. Coders scribbled notes by hand, swapped pages, and drew arrows to link text units that complimented or contrasted with each other. In this case, we created multiple dimensions for "ghosting," which included disappearance, social isolation, and safety.

Again, the diversity of the team became a strength and not a signal of disagreement. Even if one of us conducted the interview itself, or if we "matched" the

SEE FIGURE 7.2   at eResource—Use of Spread Sheet to Search for Data Patterns.

TABLE 7.1 Text Units Coded as "Ghosting"

Title: FASIT 003.doc
Codes Applied: Transitions   Staying   Precocious Knowledge   Ghosting   Mother
Partner

(So how long you been dead?) I mean two years now. (Wow, and you're able to lay
low). I don't go through the neighborhood or nothing no more. And if I go through
the neighborhood, I'm shaking everybody hands and they're like, "Yeah, Mike,
I thought you was gone . . ." And a lot of people bust out crying or fall out crying and
everything, like "daaang, Mike Mike." (Is that what they call you on the block, Mike?)
Lil Mike, Puerto Rican, Mike.

Title: FASIT 017.docx
Codes Applied: Fears   Ghosting   Social Support/Social Capital   Self

(so what's your greatest fear?) My greatest fear is falling. (What do you mean, falling?)
Falling. Falling off . . . you don't get it? Off of life, falling off. (so how could you fall
off?) I mean, basically, just fall off for real. Like you know how the junkies and the little
homeless people just be—that's falling off of life and that's where I get falling from, just
falling. (I'm glad I asked cause I thought you were just talking about disappearing but
you were talking about a whole different kind of thing) and you like the term I came
up with so that's basically seeing me falling off and I ain't trying to fall like that and
that's falling off hard, for real, no home, no house nothing you feel me. A bum, I'm not
tryin to be a bum. So that's a good term that I came up with right now, so that's falling,
for real.

SEE FIGURE 7.3   at eResource—Ambiguous Loss and Mid-Range Theories.

participant's race or gender, it was always better to get feedback on coding from
another team member. We might collectively agree on a process, or use a term
from the literature. Clinically trained coders have been drawn to the familiar
concept of ambiguous loss (Boss, 2004), for example, to describe family members'
experiences of young men's physical disappearance from daily interaction while
they also maintained an emotional presence in family relationships. In Figure 7.3,
we show some of the whiteboard brainstorming sessions when the team explored
how axial coding—by virtue of comparison and contrast—gave us insight into
variation in our interview text, which then led to ideas for mid-range theorizing
of ambiguous loss. This concept was not familiar to other coders on the team,
however, and we found that applying ambiguous loss allowed some team members to better grasp the ambivalent presence of young men, as well as the emotional toll it took on their families. We regularly used whiteboards to illustrate our
deliberation process, and we captured these discussions by snapping photos on our
cell phones, as they reflected an emergent set of theoretical notes for the project.

We also pushed each other at times: *why* do you find that this young man was justified in his lack of trust in family members who did not see the depth of his change, staying clean of drugs and avoiding prison? Maybe he was just telling a good story and making excuses. Another threshold is evident here as well. What threshold does the group hold for a "secondary" team member who did not collect the interview or who might not share the lived experiences of young men whom we interviewed? In other words, how did we know that Golojuch was not "tripping" (overreacting or getting upset over small details) on Hart's interview? Her ability to offer useful insight into interpretations was linked to her own authenticity. To the extent that a coder understood her own insider and outsider statuses from a critical perspective (Merton, 1972) and brought a long-nurtured appreciation of difference, her insights were important contributions. Perhaps more importantly for rigorous methodology, these deliberations about interpreting axial codes enhanced credibility of our data analysis. Use of multiple coders who challenged each other's interpretations minimized distortion from a single biased coder. More importantly, the give and take captured multiple realities, and it allowed us to get closer to an interpretation of experiences that would be recognized by the young men themselves.

Finally, during the last stage of selective coding, we identified a centrally relevant major code that was linked to multiple minor codes. LaRossa (2005) identified this kind of code as a "core variable" that is theoretically saturated, which allowed us to describe a theoretical story line. Figure 7.4 illustrates whiteboard notes from a discussion in which our team selected "transformation" as a core code. Prior to this stage, we had open coded 40 cases and carefully examined individual codes during an axial coding stage. We began to discuss broad relationships between these codes, careful to capture individual differences in men's experiences as well as common pathways. We built a story line that described how young men in our study experienced a developmental transformation when they become fathers (or father figures, even at a young age as "man of the house"). Related to this overarching theme were four related processes: (a) establishing connection to a child, (b) navigating relationships with mothers of the children, (c) moving beyond a preoccupation with fate ("things happen"), and (d) moving toward a focus on agency.

This final wave of coding is always the most difficult dimension of grounded theory data analysis to describe. In journal articles, this is the point at which most authors exclaim, "and then it all came together, magically." We offer the concept of "qualitative integrity" to urge researchers to tie together all the various aspects of their study, from epistemological stance to sample decisions, to discussion of theoretical and data saturation (Roy, Zvonkovic, Sharp, Goldberg, & LaRossa, 2015). In this chapter, we are challenged to spell out how we reached a "saturated" story, a full understanding and account of the experiences of young men in the

SEE FIGURE 7.4   at eResource—Transformation as Core Category.

ethnography. Authenticity in data analyses (and data collection, as the early stages of analyses) fortifies rigorous research by drawing on the strengths of divergent and complementary experiences, across race and gender. Our interpretation of data became more credible when team members earned their voices and their authority through spending time in the field with programs, through trusting relationships with young men and staff, and through an authenticity acknowledged by their co-researchers as well as participants in the study.

Final Reflections

The true test of authenticity in team ethnography, particularly in a project that tries to offer insight into family survival in toxic environments, is providing a common-sense daily logic of the lives of young men of color. If an analysis can offer this logic, it is based in a language that begins deep with men's own words and perspectives, through shared team understanding, and through moving toward other researchers, policymakers, and an engaged public. As a team, we explained young men's decisions to go straight, walk away from the streets, or step up as fathers by referring to their own words, supported by our understanding and situating them in everyday contexts of how inequality reaches into households and neighborhoods. We knew that we had viable insights when we recounted these narrative patterns, and we saw each of the participants in the study nod their heads in affirmation. This was, for us, the real member check. Through some form of collective authenticity, we could present an honest and enriched account of their lives.

KEY WORKS GUIDING OUR DATA ANALYSIS

Daly, K. (2007). *Qualitative methods for family studies and human development*. Thousand Oaks, CA: Sage.

> This is an excellent primary textbook for qualitative methods in family research. Daly not only describes basic "nuts and bolts" decisions for data analysis and data collection, but also shows how to integrate epistemological and ontological assumptions into a rich understanding of the strengths of a qualitative approach.

LaRossa, R. (2005). Grounded theory methods and qualitative family research. *Journal of Marriage and Family, 67*, 837–857.

> LaRossa's article is a deep application of this approach to data analysis and theory development. He translates primary sources on grounded theory for use in family science and offers a variable-centered language that can bridge mixed methods research.

Merton, R. (1972). Insiders and outsiders: A chapter in the sociology of knowledge. *American Journal of Sociology, 78,* 9–47.

Merton discusses how one moves from being an outsider to being an insider by translating a different worldview into one's own language. Ultimately, the researcher is then able to think and act according to that worldview. These insights are valuable for qualitative researchers as they recognize their own complicated life experiences—as simultaneous insiders and outsiders—to contexts of race, ethnicity, gender, and class in particular.

References

Best, A. L. (2003). Doing race in the context of feminist interviewing: Constructing whiteness through talk. *Qualitative Inquiry, 9,* 895–914.

Boss, P. (2004). Ambiguous loss research, theory, and practice: Reflections after 9/11. *Journal of Marriage and Family, 66,* 551–566.

Burton, L. (2007). Childhood adultification in economically disadvantaged families: A conceptual model. *Family Relations, 56,* 329–345.

Daly, K. J. (2007). *Qualitative methods for family studies and human development.* Thousand Oaks, CA: Sage.

Fader, J. J. (2013). *Falling back: Incarceration and transitions to adulthood among urban youth.* New Brunswick, NJ: Rutgers University Press.

Harding, D. J. (2010). *Living the drama: Community, conflict, and culture among inner-city boys.* Chicago, IL: University of Chicago Press.

Hart, J. R. (2017). *Fathering after incarceration: Navigating the return of young Black men to families, jobs and communities.* (Doctoral dissertation). Retrieved from ProQuest Dissertation and Theses (umd17946).

Krefting, L. (1999). Rigor in qualitative research: The assessment of trustworthiness. In A. Miliniki (Ed.), *Cases in qualitative research: Research reports for discussion and evaluation* (pp. 173–181). Los Angeles, CA: Puscale.

Lareau, A. (2011). *Unequal childhoods: Class, race, and family life* (2nd ed.). Berkeley, CA: University of California Press.

LaRossa, R. (2005). Grounded theory methods and qualitative family research. *Journal of Marriage and Family, 67,* 837–857.

Laub, J. H., & Sampson, R. J. (2006). *Shared beginnings, divergent lives: Delinquent boys to age 70.* Boston, MA: Harvard University Press.

Lincoln, Y. S., & Guba, E. G. (1985). *Naturalistic inquiry.* Beverly Hills, CA: Sage.

Mandara, J., Varner, F., & Richman, S. (2010). Do African American mothers really "love" their sons and "raise" their daughters? *Journal of Family Psychology, 24,* 41–50.

Maxwell, J. (2002). Understanding and validity in qualitative research. In A. M. Huberman & M. B. Miles (Eds.), *The qualitative researcher's companion* (pp. 37–64). Thousand Oaks, CA: Sage.

May, R., & Pattillo-McCoy, M. (2000). Do you see what I see? Examining a collaborative ethnography. *Qualitative Inquiry, 6,* 65–87.

McCall, L. (2005). The complexity of intersectionality. *Signs: Journal of Women in Culture and Society, 30,* 1771–1800.

Merton, R. K. (1972). Insiders and outsiders: A chapter in the sociology of knowledge. *American Journal of Sociology, 78,* 9–47.

Rhodes, P. J. (1994). Race of interviewer effects: A brief comment. *Sociology, 28,* 547–558.

Rich, J. A. (2011). *Wrong place, wrong time: Trauma and violence in the lives of young Black men.* Baltimore, MD: Johns Hopkins University Press.

Richardson, J. B., Jr., & St. Vil, C. (2016). 'Rolling dolo': Desistance from delinquency and negative peer relationships over the early adolescent life-course. *Ethnography, 17,* 47–71.

Rios, V. M. (2011). *Punished: Policing the lives of Black and Latino boys.* New York, NY: New York University Press.

Roy, K., Messina, L., Smith, J., & Waters, D. (2014). Growing up as "man of the house": Adultification and transition into adulthood for young men in economically disadvantaged families. *New Directions in Child and Adolescent Development, 143,* 55–72.

Roy, K., Zvonkovic, A., Sharp, E., Goldberg, A., & LaRossa, R. (2015). Sampling richness and qualitative integrity: Challenges for research with families. *Journal of Marriage and Family, 77,* 244–261.

Stanley, C. A., & Slattery, P. (2003). Who reveals what to whom? Critical reflections on conducting qualitative inquiry as an interdisciplinary, biracial, male/female research team. *Qualitative Inquiry, 9,* 705–728.

Twine, F. W. (2000). Racial ideologies and racial methodologies. In F. W. Twine & J. W. Warren (Eds.), *Racing research, researching race: Methodological dilemmas in critical race studies* (pp. 1–34). New York, NY: New York University Press.

van den Hoonaard, W. C. (1997). *Working with sensitizing concepts: Analytical field research.* Qualitative Research Methods Series 41. Thousand Oaks, CA: Sage.

Way, N. (2013). *Deep secrets: Boys' friendships and the crisis of connection.* Cambridge, MA: Harvard University Press.

Wolcott, H. F. (1994). *Transforming qualitative data: Description, analysis, and interpretation.* Thousand Oaks, CA: Sage.

8

WHAT DOES THIS MEAN TO YOU? PARTNERING WITH *AMIGAS DE LA COMUNIDAD* TO ANALYZE THE HOUSING CONDITIONS OF UNDOCUMENTED LATINA IMMIGRANTS

Colleen K. Vesely, Bethany L. Letiecq, Rachael D. Goodman, Marlene Marquez, Liciane Alves, Wendy E. Lazo, and Roberto C. Martinez

In this chapter, we detail how we worked in partnership with Latina immigrant community members who are a part of our community-based participatory research (CBPR) project to analyze data exploring overcrowded housing conditions experienced by undocumented Latino immigrant families (Letiecq et al., 2017). All phases of our research process, including the analysis of data, were guided by our Community Advisory Board (CAB), which is comprised of Latina immigrants and community agency partners. This chapter illustrates our process and our reflections about the benefits gained and struggles faced as we worked with CAB members to analyze data as a collective.

At the outset, we (Vesely, Letiecq, & Goodman, 2017) acknowledge our "outsider" (White, non-Latina, academic) positionality (Minkler, 2004) when analyzing qualitative data collected from research participants whose countries and cultures of origin and languages are different from our own. As we discuss, we use rigorous methods to ensure trustworthiness of the data and analyses (e.g., prolonged engagement with participants, member checking, bracketing, reflexivity, thick and rich descriptions of context; Morrow, 2005). Yet, questions linger about what might be lost in translation or misunderstood because our lens or judgment is colored by our standpoint epistemology. We also question how our work is impacted by implicit bias—or the subtle cognitive processes operating at an unconscious level that affect our understanding, actions, and decisions—particularly when working across cultures and contexts (Staats, Capatosto, Wright, & Jackson, 2016). We are committed to processes that ensure our analyses of participants' stories reflect their truth, and not merely our interpretations of their truth.

To this end, we practice "cultural humility," which requires those from majority cultures (and those who occupy seats of power in relationship to others) to humble themselves to other ways of knowing (Tervalon & Murray-Garcia, 1998). This differs from "cultural competency," which focuses on achieving full understanding of someone who is culturally different (DeAngelis, 2015). As Trevalon and Murray-Garcia (1998) note, cultural humility incorporates a commitment to self-evaluation, redressing the power imbalances in relationships, and developing mutually beneficial and non-paternalistic relationships. To systematically integrate cultural humility along with reflexivity and critical consciousness in our approach to research, we turn to CBPR.

Community-Based Participatory Research (CBPR)

Using a CBPR approach demands that researchers work to shift the balance of power from the researchers to the participants in research, creating a partnership that is dialogical, egalitarian, and often centered on social justice ends (Hallett et al., 2017; Israel, Eng, Schulz, & Parker, 2012; Minkler & Wallerstein, 2008). A CBPR approach engenders a reflexive, collaborative, and iterative process that is community-driven (Israel et al., 2012). This approach builds on community strengths, ensures benefits to the community, and promotes co-learning between community and academic partners (LaVeaux & Christopher, 2009).

In principle, CBPR should foster mutual ownership of research processes, data, decisions about the data and findings, and how budgets are allocated (Minkler & Wallerstein, 2008; Stoecker, 2009). Ideally in CBPR, community partners engage in all phases of research and co-author publications (Ospina et al., 2004). Of no surprise, as Hallett et al. (2017) note, there are few examples in the literature where researchers have fully actualized all CBPR principles. Especially lacking are examples of partnering during data analyses. In this chapter, we share our processes of collaborative qualitative data analysis.

Background and Context of the Project

Beginning in 2014, Goodman, Letiecq, and Vesely met with two community-based service providers and a group of Latina immigrant mothers who were concerned about the well-being of their children, the safety of their community, and threats of deportation and family separation. As a collective, we committed to a CBPR project (*Amigas de la Comunidad* or *Friends of the Community*; hearafter *Amigas*) and began implementing a five-step process to build our research and action program (Faridi, Grunbaum, Gray, Franks, & Simoes, 2007; Israel et al., 2012; Letiecq & Schmalzbauer, 2012; Minkler & Wallerstein, 2008). These steps included: (a) establishing a research team (to include faculty and students) and a CAB (to include Latina community members, service providers, and bilingual community organizers); (b) establishing partnerships with NGOs and governmental agencies; (c) garnering funding for our project; (d) collaborating with the CAB on all phases of research; and (e) implementing community-driven and research-informed action steps.

As we engaged in on-going research activities in 2016, we frequently heard community members express concerns and fears about deportation and family separation. These concerns, which were present under the Obama Administration, grew while Donald Trump was ascending to the Republican Party nomination for president (Law, 2017). To address community fears and build trust, we began offering a series of "Know Your Rights" (KYR) immigration clinics, offered in partnership with immigration advocacy organizations.

Following the election of Trump in November 2016, community members grew more uncertain about the immigration policy landscape, if Deferred Action for Childhood Arrivals (DACA) would be rescinded, and who would be targeted for deportations. Simultaneously there was also an increase in Immigration and Customs Enforcement (ICE) raids both nationally and locally. Those targeted by the Trump Administration included a much broader group of immigrants than those targeted under the Obama Administration (Law, 2017). Responding to CAB members' concerns about their community and child well-being following nearby ICE raids, we pivoted from our formal data collection processes to conduct additional KYR clinics where we practiced responding to ICE agents. We also offered legal clinics, staffed by volunteer lawyers, translators, and notaries, to assist families in completing legal paperwork, such as Power of Attorney forms, to protect their children should they be detained or deported. The sociopolitical context of our CBPR work challenged our ability to conduct interviews and stalled data analysis efforts. Community members rightly assessed their safety and capacity to engage, while we (university partners) moved cautiously as to do no harm to our community partners and research participants. Although these KYR and legal clinics were time consuming and shifted us away from our planned research, we felt it a necessary and important use of our time and resources. In addition, these efforts contributed to building and maintaining trust and rapport with the community.

The Current Study—Living With Strangers in Overcrowded Housing

Using an iterative CBPR approach in partnership with a Latino immigrant community has yielded many threads of research and action steps, which we detail elsewhere (Goodman, Letiecq, & Vesely, 2016; Goodman, Letiecq, Vesely, Marquez, & Leyva, 2017; Vesely et al., 2017; Vesely, Letiecq, Goodman, Marquez, & Leyva, 2016). The context of Latino immigrant families engaged in our on-going CBPR project also drove our research questions. In this chapter, we focus on our most recent CAB-directed study (Letiecq et al., 2017) to qualitatively interrogate the overcrowded housing conditions experienced by undocumented immigrant families from Central America who are "living with strangers." Our entire CAB assisted with study design and participant recruitment. Moreover, given the importance of involving the community in all aspects of the research, based on the principals of CBPR, a subcommittee of the CAB, which consisted of four undocumented Latinas from Central America (three) and Mexico (one), volunteered to engage in our collaborative data analysis process. These four women expressed a particular interest in housing issues and could devote the time necessary to data analysis. Our *Amigas* university team was three faculty, three graduate students, and three undergraduate students. Students on the project (including co-authors Alves, Lazo, and Martinez) represented a variety of racial, ethnic, and linguistic backgrounds and perspectives that were especially important to our reflexive and analytical processes. Marquez, our Salvadorian-American bilingual community organizer, was part of the CAB and university team. She lived in the community where our project is located, and was a student in social work at George Mason University while serving on this project.

From September 2016 to May 2017, after developing an interview protocol with the CAB and receiving Institutional Review Board approval, *Amigas* faculty and Marquez conducted 16 in-depth interviews with undocumented immigrant Central American mothers living with their families in apartments shared with strangers. All participants completed audio-recorded interviews conducted in Spanish with consecutive English interpretation. Specifically, Marquez helped interpret, both linguistically and culturally, during each interview. Audio files were transcribed in Spanish and English, and the Spanish components were fully translated into English by a trained member of the research team.

We identified three themes in the data that illustrate the contexts of families' lives as they resided in overcrowded housing with strangers. First, *organization of space and housing situation* detailed the arrangement of space in terms of sleeping, eating, and raising children, and how families creatively put together their living spaces depending upon who was in the housing unit. The second theme titled *living with strangers: relationship processes and power dynamics* illustrated the relationships among everyone in the household, as well as how activities of daily living were accomplished through schedules and negotiation across lessees (those who informally rented from leaseholders) and leaseholders (those whose names were on the formal lease). We explored how these rules and routines were established amidst the hierarchy resulting in the leaseholder having more power than the lessee, and the lessee being vulnerable and sometimes fearful. Finally, the third theme, *"doing family" while living with strangers,* illustrated how participants raised their children in these environments and how they negotiated their couple relationship in these spaces.

Our Analytical Process

In accordance with CBPR tenets, we analyzed data in consultation with CAB members. Because studies of overcrowding among undocumented immigrants living with strangers are nascent, we used an exploratory, constructivist grounded theory approach (see Charmaz, 2005). Like most qualitative work, our initial analyses began in the field while conducting interviews and observations (Maxwell, 2012). Marquez and a faculty member (Letiecq) conducted each interview, dialogued with each other, and recorded their fieldnotes following each interview.

Fieldnotes (see Table 8.1 for an example) included physical descriptions of participants, their homes, and overall tone of the interview. These notes included details such as whether or not the participant made conflicting statements, any background information garnered outside of the recording, or if there were any methodological issues (e.g., recorder stopped working). These fieldnotes were added to the interview transcriptions and coded during the analysis phase to more fully understand the participants and their homes. Throughout the data collection process, we (the university team) held face-to-face meetings with the CAB to ensure we were continuing to ask the right questions and focus on the most meaningful topics related to housing. For example, as a research team, we wondered about couple intimacy so we checked with CAB members to find out if such inquiries were appropriate and then proceeded to add this line of inquiry to our interviews.

Community Coding Strategies

The second phase of our analyses included three waves of formal coding including open, axial, and selective coding (LaRossa, 2005). We integrated this approach with Flicker and Nixon's (2015) DEPICT model (pp. 618–621), which consists of "dynamic reading" (open coding); "engaged codebook development" (open coding); "participatory coding" (open, axial, and selective coding); "inclusive reviewing

TABLE 8.1 Fieldnote Excerpts

Excerpt 1	We met Luciana back in 2015 when the incident with her son had just happened. She came to one of our meetings to sell tamales. She was trying to raise money to send the body of her son back to Guatemala.... We have visited Luciana on different occasions to see how she is doing. We did not have contact with her for about a year ... we reached out to her and she agreed to do a housing interview.
Excerpt 2	Lola was welcoming and talkative. We observed the apartment to be clean and the kitchen to be organized. She said that she is the only one that uses the kitchen. There was a lot of space in the living room where Lola's son played during the interview.
Excerpt 3	Both the survey and the housing interview took place at a local McDonald's.... At times it seemed like she was making things up. For example she said that she was single but when talking to her she kind of mentioned the father of her younger son and it seemed like they still had a romantic relationship. She had somewhat of an issue with us recording the interview.

and summarizing of categories" (axial and selective coding); "collaborative analyzing" (open, axial, and selective coding); and "translating" (open, axial, and selective
coding)—such that each part of the DEPICT model was represented within at
least one wave of coding. Our community coding meetings ranged in length from
approximately 1½ to 2½ hours. Prior to beginning formal community coding,
we conducted coding training with the university team to help ensure a uniform
approach to and understanding of the formal coding process.

Community Open Coding

During open coding, the university team met with our four CAB member subcommittee. In alignment with CBPR principles, CAB members were paid for
their time. We met at a CAB member's home (an apartment not unlike those
of our study participants) because the community space in which we typically
met for CAB business was being renovated. Although unplanned, meeting in the
apartment allowed for a deepening of our relationships. We began by discussing
the coding process with the CAB member subcommittee, detailing reasons for
coding the data as part of the analysis, and discussing the specifics of how to code
data using examples of labeling text. We were sensitized by recent work of Hallett
and colleagues (2017) with the Apsaalooke Nation in Montana, which depicted
how the community opposed some of the traditional academic ways of coding
data, especially the breaking apart of individuals' stories. Thus, we openly discussed
the coding process with the CAB to learn if they anticipated aspects of this process being objectionable. The CAB supported the three waves of coding that we
outlined. Taking guidance from aspects of Hallett et al.'s (2017) methods for analyzing data, and the "dynamic reading" aspect of the DEPICT model (Flicker &
Nixon, 2015, p. 617), we began by first reading through excerpts from a single
transcript out loud to the CAB members. Then, we began the process of "engaged
codebook development" (Flicker & Nixon, 2015, p. 617) by discussing as a large
group overall impressions of what was heard (Hallett et al., 2017) and how we
might label or code different aspects of the passage. For example, as the CAB read
the following excerpt, they discussed a few different codes, including "comunica-
cion" (communication), "prioritad" (prioritize), and "compartir" (sharing):

INTERVIEWER: So there is some sharing of space. If you are cooking, she waits
for you and vice versa?

TRANSCRIPT 31–32: No. Yo si a ella le pregunto a ella a veces si le precisa mucho.
Yo lo que hago es que dejo lo que estoy haciendo y ya dejo que ella cocine
porque no. Yo así hago porque cuando vienen los niños de la escuela todos
vienen con hambre y al mismo tiempo. Sí, casi al mismo tiempo vienen.
Entonces yo como no trabajo a veces preparo algo pero no mas, a veces de
calendar nomas. [Translation: No. I ask her sometimes if she really needs to
use it. What I do is stop what I am doing and let her cook because no. That

is what I do because once the children arrive from school they are hungry and at the same time. Yes, they come around the same time. So since I do not work I sometimes prepare something but only, sometimes just for reheating.]

As we discussed this passage further, the CAB focused even more on "prioridad" or the prioritizing of who was able to use the kitchen or other shared spaces, and noted that there seemed to be an underlying and somewhat forced respect among lessees for the leaseholder—due to power dynamics—as well as prioritizing based on work schedules and the needs of children in the household. Following this discussion we read a few more passages out loud and the CAB members discussed possible codes. After three passages from a single interview were read and coded as a large group, reflecting aspects of "participatory coding" as outlined in DEPICT (Flicker & Nixon, 2015), we read a fourth passage (the final part of the interview) and had the CAB members individually assign codes by hand on hard copies of Spanish transcripts that included English translations, and then discussed as a large group. During this discussion, codes were recorded on a whiteboard in Spanish and English, and we began linking codes that were similar in meaning (Figures 8.1 and 8.2). We continued through the first transcript examining excerpts focused on different components of the interview. This took place over the course of two 2-hour long meetings scheduled one week apart.

During this process, the CAB corrected any misinterpretations of the data. For instance, the university team misunderstood the passage: "Entonces les dice a las niñas cuando yo voy saliendo, 'ah no hijas, aprovechen.'" ["So she tells the girls when I am leaving, 'Oh daughters, make the best of it.'"] The university team assumed a neutral or positive tone in which the leaseholder was encouraging her children to enjoy a bit more space while the interviewee/lessee and her children were out of the apartment. The CAB, however, noted the hostile meaning of the word *aprovechen*, revealing that this exchange was indicative of the leaseholder's disdain for the interviewee/lessee. This also prompted us to add codes for "hierarchy and power" and "lessee/leaseholder relationship quality." Additionally, the CAB helped clarify this same participant's guarded comments regarding intimacy. In particular, as the participant discussed her sexual relationship with her partner, she did not specifically use the words "intimacy" or "sex," but the CAB noted that when the participant stated, "No hay espacio por eso." ["There is no space for this."], she was referring to why they did not have sexual intercourse. By the time initial coding of this interview was completed, 31 original codes were identified.

SEE FIGURES 8.1 AND 8.2   at eResource—Whiteboard Images Reflecting Collaborative Open Coding Conducted With the George Mason Team and the CAB.

Next, for the sake of time and with the CAB's approval, the university team used these codes to code a second interview. This coding was done in Microsoft Word using the comment tool. This coding on hard copies was printed out, reviewed by the CAB to ensure that the initial codes were used correctly, and to have them review and discuss new codes. This interview described 13 people living in a two-bedroom apartment; lessees paid relatively high rents to the leaseholder, which covered the leaseholder's total rental payment entirely. During coding, the CAB noted what they considered exploitation of lessees and a need for "roommates to have rights." As a research team and community outsiders, we sought to determine whether this was exploitation or outside of the norm from the perspective of the community members, instead of making our own assumptions about what was appropriate. The CAB clarified that they saw this leaseholder (and others) as taking advantage of the lessees' desperation for housing and work due to lack of legal status.

As we continued through the interview with the CAB, we noted the "typicality" of cohabiters having to "wait in line" for showers in the morning, as well as the "atypicality" of the situation given the high degree of stress due to overcrowding (e.g., worrying about a newborn baby's cries at night waking others in the household). We discussed the normative and non-normative experiences being uncovered during the interview process and vulnerabilities (e.g., being evicted from one's housing because of overcrowding and unauthorized status). The CAB also pointed out the gendered aspects of certain spaces in the apartment, reflective of their own experiences. Specifically, they shared that men did not use the kitchen and tended to eat outside the home, whereas women in the household coordinated the kitchen schedule with each other. Consequently, in households in which there were single men, the negotiation of kitchen space occurred among the women in the apartment. At another point in the interview, the participant (a lessee) described how the leaseholder regularly talked to her about some of the men in the apartment who were not paying their rent on time. The participant did not understand why the leaseholder discussed this with her as she did not previously know these men. The CAB noted that the leaseholder may have been using his power over the participant to bring about peer pressure and shaming of the men who were not paying their rent on time.

A section of the interview focused on the bathroom and the participant discussing toilet training of her toddler-aged son and using a small potty or *banito* in her bedroom. The participant noted that her older children sometimes used this *banito* if the bathroom was occupied by other tenants. When the CAB members read this, they expanded the previous code focused on "health concerns" ("problemas de salud") to include "unsanitary conditions" ["condiciones no sanitarías"]. These examples illustrate the insight that the CAB provided via rich reflections and discussions of the interviews. The research team surely would have missed or misinterpreted many nuances emergent from these discussions.

TABLE 8.2 Excerpt From Final List of Codes

CODIGO (Spanish)	CODE (English)
1. organización	1. organization
1a. planeamiento	1a. planning ahead
1b. orden de quién cocina/usa el baño primero	1b. order of who cooks/uses the bathroom first
1c. sin otra opción excepto planear	1c. no other option but to plan
2. prioridad	2. prioritizing based on. . .
2a. respeto	2a. respect
2b. persona sin trabajo	2b. person (not) working
2c. necesidades de los niños	2c. children's needs
2d. quien tiene la mayor necesidad	2d. who has the greatest need
3. (ausencia de) espacio/tiempo	3. (lack of) space/time
3a. áreas separadas para dormir	3a. separate areas for sleeping
3b. áreas separadas para guardar comida	3b. separate areas for storing food
3c. útiles separados para el baño	3c. separate bathroom supplies
3d. falta de espacio para crecer los niños (comparado con país de origen)	3d. lack of space for raising children (compared to back home)
3e. configuraciones para dormir	3e. sleep configurations
3f. falta de espacio para intimidad	3f. lack of space for intimacy
3g. falta de espacio para comer	3g. lack of space for eating

Following the coding of this second interview, we updated our working version of the codebook in Word to a more finalized version that reflected the new codes that were developed with the CAB (see Table 8.2 for an excerpt from the list of codes). Working in pairs, the university team (Vesely, Goodman, Marquez, and Alves) continued to open code the interviews. Each member of the coding pairs was familiar with the codebook as they contributed to the development of the codes by both coding the initial interviews and being present during CAB meetings in which the codes were developed.

All interviews were double coded, with a lead and secondary coder assigned to each interview (Table 8.3). The lead coder conducted the initial coding of the interview, and the secondary coder reviewed the codes and noted any discrepancies. These discrepancies usually resulted from the lead coder missing a code, rather than disagreement on an assigned code. If discrepancies occurred, the two researchers discussed them until consensus was reached. Sometimes this resulted in adding a new subcode or consolidating or reorganizing already existing subcodes. For example, as Vesely and Marquez began coding interviews of leaseholders, the relationship with the apartment building management and processes for collecting and paying rent were identified as important. They discussed how to best capture these phenomena in the code list, and decided to add two subcodes to a larger existing code to capture this relationship. Shortly thereafter, the university

TABLE 8.3 Sample Open Coding Assignments

Interview ID	Lead coder[a]	Secondary coder	Final reviewer	Status	Entered into ATLAS.ti
001	ALL[b]	ALL	ALL	DONE	Yes
002	ALL	ALL	ALL	DONE	Yes
003	LA- done	CV- done		DONE	Yes
004	MM- done	CV- done		DONE	Yes
005	CV- done	MM- done	MT[c]	DONE	
006	MM- done	CV- done		DONE	
007	CV- done	RG- in progress			
008	CV	MM			
009	MM	BL			
010	CV	MM- done	MT	DONE	

[a] LA, CV, MM, BL, RG represent the initials of coders (i.e. CV = Colleen Vesely).
[b] ALL: Mason team and CAB.
[c] MT: Member of Mason team.

team met with the CAB to discuss these changes in the code list. Additionally, every fifth interview was checked by a third coder. The bulk of open coding was conducted by Vesely and Marquez, with Goodman and Letiecq as university team members who were final reviewers of these coded documents.

Community Axial and Selective Coding

In preparation for axial coding, we transferred the open coding completed with the comment tool in Word documents into ATLAS.ti, a qualitative data management software tool. During axial coding, we worked with the CAB to determine how some codes might be combined (e.g., organization and communication/schedule of who cleans/cooks). We discussed each code by examining what was coded under each individual code across all participants or by looking across the participants' data. For example, using ATLAS.ti we pulled all excerpts of participants' interviews that were coded as "lack of space/time," and began reading this text to understand the varied dynamics within this code based on all participants' experiences. The university team met to discuss the codes identified as most salient (e.g., lack of space/time; lack of equality/hierarchy) based on the volume of data coded under each code. This was easily garnered examining ATLAS.ti's "grounded" column in the "codes" tool, as well as how much the CAB discussed its importance. We used this level of salience to inform how we ordered our discussion of codes/groups of codes with the CAB. For example, the CAB consistently remarked on the hierarchy and lack of equality among lessees and leaseholders. Coupled with a high volume of data being coded as such, this indicated to us the salience of this particular code for understanding these families' experiences, and where to commence our axial coding. During this phase of coding we first met with the CAB to further understand hierarchy, as well as how this related to other codes. Building on this discussion, we continued to move through the major groups of codes to understand the dynamics.

During these discussions we moved into the third wave of coding—selective coding—during which we started to make sense of how individual codes went together and coalesced into three themes to help tell the story of these immigrant mothers' experiences living with strangers in overcrowded housing. In particular, we began to understand how the power and hierarchy among the leaseholder and lessee shaped the physical organization of the space, all the leaseholder-lessee relationships, and the family (i.e., parent-child and couple) relationship dynamics.

We met with the CAB for two hours to discuss these three themes and how the codes parsed into each theme. The purpose of this meeting, and our overall work, was to ensure that the information we would share about families' experiences of living with strangers would be accurate and would help individuals and organizations better understand and meet the needs of community members. The CAB described how important it would be, especially for teachers, principals, and service providers to gain a better sense of the complexity of families' lives such that they could more sensitively, compassionately, and effectively work with immigrant families. We then described each theme and discussed the codes that we thought aligned with each theme. Due to time constraints, we created an initial list of codes that we suggested aligned with each theme (see Table 8.4). CAB members were quick to note if they disagreed with our organization of the codes and themes. For example, as we reviewed the code "limited options/forced choices," a CAB member shared how she thought this code could be a part of two different themes. During this conversation, the university team gained even more understanding of the codes as the CAB shared more examples from their lives. Specifically, we learned the breadth

TABLE 8.4 Example of Organization of Theme and Associated Codes Developed Collaboratively with University Team and *Amigas*

Theme 2: Negotiation of processes and power dynamics across people in the housing space (i.e., living with strangers)

• organization	• rights for roommates
• prioritizing	• lack of equality/hierarchy
• house rules	• stress/worry/fear
• schedules for kitchen and bathroom cleaning	• get in line
• cleaning rules	• gender
• children's schedules vs. adult work schedules	• relationship with roommate and leaseholder
	• getting out or closing in
	• (not) sharing of resources

of "house rules" and "hierarchy" when one of the CAB members shared that a friend's leaseholder told her that after certain hours in the evening she could not pass through the living room (where another lessee was sleeping) to leave the apartment. Consequently, the CAB member's friend sometimes used her window on the second story to exit and enter the apartment after hours to not break the rules and, in turn, lose her housing. Throughout axial and selective coding, we employed aspects of the DEPICT model (inclusive reviewing and summarizing of categories and collaborative analyzing) to ensure that we were discussing all perspectives as the data were interpreted, and not solely relying on the university team's interpretations (Flicker & Nixon, 2015). Specifically, as we began to summarize the themes we brought them back to the CAB for review. As the CAB reviewed the themes and subthemes, and provided feedback we adjusted our written findings.

Reflections on Our Process

Analyzing data with the CAB ensured greater understanding of participants' stories and accuracy in interpreting their experiences. It provided opportunities to further develop trusting relationships with and among CAB members, and to understand more about each CAB member's individual story. We noted on a number of occasions following coding meetings with the CAB that this analytical process seemed to strengthen the university team and CAB relationship. Additionally, the CAB shared how much they enjoyed working with the data and described how hearing others' experiences helped ease their burdens, and helped them to know they were not alone in their struggles to navigate life in the U.S. Moreover, as we worked through the various stages of coding with the CAB, it also helped us to thoughtfully consider our own standpoint epistemology, and critically reflect on our positionality.

Despite the strengths of analyzing the data with the CAB, there were a number of challenges including language and translation, meeting time and space, and competing demands of the larger CBPR project. Analyses were conducted in both English and Spanish with the CAB members working in Spanish and the university team primarily working with the English version of the transcripts. Thus, in coding with the CAB, we relied on student research assistants as translators, spent time discussing points of confusion, and held multiple meetings with the CAB. As others have noted, analyses with community members can be time consuming (Cashman et al., 2008), and researchers should identify components of the analysis process that best capture the community's strengths (Cashman et al., 2008; Flicker, 2008; Hallett et al., 2017). In this case, our CAB members were very interested in examining data and in assisting with the analysis, as well as continuing with on-going action steps underway in the community.

We also experienced some particular challenges related to scheduling, often tied to aspects of the larger project and our community advocacy work. Coordinating CAB members' and the university team's schedules, coupled with meeting space options, sometimes presented logistical challenges that delayed the process. Certainly, our data analysis process was slower than it might have been had the community not been involved. However, it was clear during each community meeting how important their inputs were to accurate interpretation of the data.

Conclusion

Participating in a CBPR project in partnership with Latina immigrant community members—and engaging in a collaborative data analytic strategy in particular—was transformative for us. This process confirmed what we once opined as limitations in our prior, academics-only qualitative analyses: our "outsider" positionality rendered us vulnerable to misinterpretations of the lived experiences of participants from cultural and contextual spaces different from our own. Engaging in this shared analytical process has given us greater confidence that the stories we are sharing are more accurate depictions of undocumented immigrant women's experiences living with strangers in overcrowded housing. We began this chapter thinking about our practice in terms of cultural humility. We end this chapter with a deep sense of personal humility and gratitude for the commitment that our friends, *Amigas,* have made to us and to making their community a better place to live and raise their children, particularly at a time socio-politically when this work poses such risk to their safety and to their families.

Acknowledgment

The activities of the project described in this chapter were conducted with generous support from the Bruhn Morris Family Foundation, George Mason University Faculty Research Awards, and George Mason University Office of Student Scholarship, Creative Activities, and Research (OSCAR) Program.

KEY WORKS GUIDING OUR DATA ANALYSIS

Flicker, S., & Nixon, S. A. (2015). The DEPICT model for participatory qualitative health promotion research analysis piloted in Canada, Zambia and South Africa. *Health Promotion International, 30,* 616–624.

Researchers have noted that involving the community, especially those with limited research experience in data analysis, is time consuming and potentially not the best use of community members' time on CBPR projects. The authors push back against this rhetoric, and describe the DEPICT model, which is a collaborative approach to qualitative data analysis used in CBPR as researchers work to analyze data with communities. They note for each step of this process—"dynamic reading," "engaged codebook development," "participatory coding," "inclusive reviewing and summarizing of categories," "collaborative analyzing," "translating"—team members' roles, questions to ask during each phase, and the logistics and preparations for each phase. The authors review the use of the DEPICT model in six studies, as well as the benefits and challenges of using this model.

Hallett, J., Held, S., McCormick, A., Simonds, V., Real Bird, S., Martin, C., . . . Trottier, C. (2017). What touched your heart? Collaborative story analysis emerging from an Apsáalooke cultural context. *Qualitative Health Research, 27*, 1267–1277.

The authors of this study detail the development of a collaborative process for analyzing qualitative interview data with the Apsaalooke nation. This method emerged in reaction to the multiple incompatibilities of traditional academic data analysis processes with Indigenous story data, and the lack of existing alternatives for approaching these data. The authors, who were from Montana State University as well as Crow Agency and Bighorn Valley Health Center, specifically noted that the breaking apart of data—that is, participants' stories, and the loss of participants' voices, as well as the interpretation of participants' stories for others' use rather than using traditional methods of story interpretation, were especially incompatible with Indigenous communities' traditions. They describe how analyses were conducted while keeping participants' stories intact, and through discussion developed a conceptual framework for intervention development.

References

Cashman, S. B., Adeky, S., Allen, A. J., Corburn, J., Israel, B. A., Montaño, J., . . . Eng, E. (2008). The power and the promise: Working with communities to analyze data, interpret findings, and get to outcomes. *American Journal of Public Health, 98*, 1407–1417.

Charmaz, K. (2005). Grounded theory in the 21st Century: Applications for advancing social justice studies. In N. K. Denzin & Y. S. Lincoln (Eds.), *The Sage handbook of qualitative research* (3rd ed., pp. 507–535). Thousand Oaks, CA: Sage.

DeAngelis, T. (2015, March). In search of cultural competence. *American Psychological Association's Monitor on Psychology, 46*(3), 64. Retrieved from www.apa.org/monitor/2015/03/cultural-competence.aspx

Faridi, Z., Grunbaum, J. A., Gray, B. S., Franks, A., & Simoes, E. (2007). Community-based participatory research: Necessary next steps. *Preventing Chronic Disease: Public Health Research, Practice, and Policy, 4*(3), 1–5 [series online]. Retrieved from www.ncbi.nlm. nih.gov/pmc/articles/PMC1955426/

Flicker, S. (2008). Who benefits from community-based participatory research? A case study of the Positive Youth Project. *Health Education & Behavior, 35,* 70–86.

Flicker, S., & Nixon, S. A. (2015). The DEPICT model for participatory qualitative health promotion research analysis piloted in Canada, Zambia and South Africa. *Health Promotion International, 30,* 616–624.

Goodman, R. D., Letiecq, B. L., & Vesely, C. K. (2016, March). *Using CBPR with refugee and immigrant women: Trauma, stress and resilience.* Paper presented at the American Counseling Association Annual Meeting, Montréal, Canada.

Goodman, R. D., Letiecq, B. L., Vesely, C. K., Marquez, M., & Leyva, K. (2017). Community practice with immigrants and refugees. In A. Hilado & M. Lundy (Eds.), *Models for practice with immigrants and refugees: Collaboration, cultural awareness, and integrative theory* (pp. 204–225). New York, NY: Sage.

Hallett, J., Held, S., McCormick, A. K. N. G., Simonds, V., Real Bird, S., Martin, C., . . . Trottier, C. (2017). What touched your heart? Collaborative story analysis emerging from an Apsáalooke cultural context. *Qualitative Health Research, 27,* 1267–1277.

Israel, B. A., Eng, E., Schulz, A. J., & Parker, E. A. (2012). *Methods for community-based participatory research for health* (2nd ed.). San Francisco, CA: Jossey-Bass.

LaRossa, R. (2005). Grounded theory methods and qualitative family research. *Journal of Marriage and Family, 67,* 837–857.

LaVeaux, D., & Christopher, S. (2009). Contextualizing CBPR: Key principles of CBPR meet the Indigenous research context. *Pimatisiwin: A Journal of Aboriginal and Indigenous Community Health, 7,* 1–16.

Law, A. O. (2017, May 3). This is how Trump's deportations differ from Obama's. *The Washington Post,* Monkey Cage Analysis. Retrieved from www.washingtonpost.com/ news/monkey-cage/wp/2017/05/03/this-is-how-trumps-deportations-differ-from-obamas/?utm_term=.de11725e3e32

Letiecq, B. L., & Schmalzbauer, L. (2012). Community-based participatory research with Mexican migrants in a new rural destination: A good fit? *Action Research, 10,* 244–259.

Letiecq, B. L., Vesely, C. K., Moron, L., Goodman, R. D., Marquez, M., Shah, P., & Alves, L. (2017, November). *Living with strangers: Overcrowded housing among immigrant families.* Paper presented at the Annual Meeting of the National Council on Family Relations, Orlando, FL.

Maxwell, J. A. (2012). *Qualitative research design* (3rd ed.). Washington, DC: Sage.

Minkler, M. (2004). Ethical challenges for the "outside" researcher in community-based participatory research. *Health Education and Behavior, 31,* 684–697.

Minkler, M., & Wallerstein, N. (2008). *Community-based participatory research for health: From process to outcome* (2nd ed.). San Francisco, CA: Jossey-Bass.

Morrow, S. L. (2005). Quality and trustworthiness in qualitative research in counseling psychology. *Journal of Counseling Psychology, 52,* 250–260.

Ospina, S., Dodge, J., Godsoe, B., Minieri, J., Reza, S., & Schall, E. (2004). From consent to mutual inquiry: Balancing democracy and authority in action research. *Action Research, 2,* 47–69.

Staats, C., Capatosto, K., Wright, R. A., & Jackson, V. W. (2016). *State of the science: Implicit bias review, 2016 edition.* Retrieved from the Kirwan Institute http://kirwaninstitute. osu.edu/wp-content/uploads/2016/07/implicit-bias-2016.pdf

Stoecker, R. (2009). Are we talking the walk of community-based research? *Action Research,* 7, 385–404.

Tervalon, M., & Murray-García, J. (1998). Cultural humility versus cultural competence: A critical distinction in defining physician training outcomes in multicultural education. *Journal of Healthcare for the Poor and Underserved, 9,* 117–125.

Vesely, C. K., Letiecq, B. L., & Goodman, R. D. (2017). Immigrant family resilience in context: Using a community-based approach to build a new conceptual model. *Journal of Family Theory & Review, 9,* 93–110.

Vesely, C. K., Letiecq, B. L., Goodman, R. D., Marquez, M., & Leyva, K. (2016, November). *Partnering with undocumented immigrant families for health and justice.* Paper presented at the Annual Meeting of the National Council on Family Relations, Minneapolis, MN.

9

LOST IN THE DATA

Strategies Used to Analyze a Large-Scale Collaboratively Collected Qualitative Dataset of Low-Income Families

Katherine E. Speirs, Colleen K. Vesely, and Kevin Roy

The *Welfare, Children, and Families: A Three-City Study* (hereafter, the Three-City Study) is a longitudinal examination of low-income families from Chicago, Boston, and San Antonio. With its large sample (*n* = 256) and two years of ethnographic data collection for each family, the study promised to provide the first two authors (Speirs and Vesely; hereafter referred to as we) a unique opportunity to understand childcare instability within the context of families' lives and larger policy structures. Our excitement about using this dataset was tempered, however, when we were confronted with thousands of pages of interview and fieldnote data, summary documents, and confusing participant identification numbers and file names. We very quickly found ourselves *lost in the data*. Here we tell the story of how we found our way out.

This chapter begins with a brief description of the Three-City Study dataset and our findings concerning childcare instability and transitions. We then detail the strategies that we used to become familiar with a large-scale qualitative dataset, select an analytic sample, and code the data. We end the chapter with reflections on analyzing a large-scale qualitative dataset.

The Ethnographic Component of the Three-City Study

The Three-City Study was designed to explore the impact of welfare reform on children and families; a detailed description can be found at http://web.jhu.edu/threecitystudy. For the project described in this chapter (Speirs, Vesely, & Roy, 2015), we used the study's ethnographic component, which involved 256 families. For 12 to 18 months ethnographers visited each family at least once a month to conduct semi-structured interviews and participant observations during everyday events at the family's home, doctor visits, and appointments with social workers. Semi-structured interviews were conducted using 10 required topical interview guides (e.g., daily routine, welfare and employment experiences) and 10 optional protocols (e.g., childcare and father involvement). Interviews were transcribed verbatim. Observations were recorded as detailed fieldnotes that also included the ethnographer's insights. Data collection is described in detail in our original report (Speirs et al., 2015). Given the prolonged engagement and frequent contact, many families had at least 20 data collection points and hundreds of pages of data. When first opening these files we were overwhelmed by the amount of data for each family and the prospect of attempting to read through them multiple times, but also excited about the level of detail this much data could provide.

Speirs and Vesely, who led the secondary data analysis described in this chapter, were not involved in data collection and had not used the dataset before this project. The third author, Roy, was a lead ethnographer for the Three-City Study, coordinated data collection for the Chicago site, and had published from the dataset (e.g., Roy & Burton, 2007; Roy, Tubbs, & Burton, 2004). Roy worked with Speirs and Vesely (as doctoral students) to navigate the complicated set of study documents and brainstorm preliminary analyses, and then handed over primary data analysis to them so that they could carve out a topic of shared interest.

Overview of Study Findings

We identified four types of stability and instability (Speirs et al., 2015). Mothers who organized *planned transitions* made changes to their care arrangements that were planned in advance and supportive of their families' well-being. *Averted transitions* were the work mothers did to maintain functional care arrangements that were supportive of their child's healthy development and/or their own ability to maintain employment. Mothers who experienced *forced transitions* had to leave a preferred care arrangement. *Failed transitions* occurred when mothers were not satisfied with their care arrangement but were unable to secure a new one. We also detailed the factors that led to each of these types of transitions. For example, we found that mothers were able to make planned transitions when they had time (either by being able to anticipate transitions or having reliable and flexible secondary care arrangements); organizational and planning skills; and support from family, friends, and caseworkers.

Becoming Familiar With the Dataset

Most qualitative researchers become familiar with their dataset and begin analysis by writing memos during data collection. This was not possible for our project as we did not collect the data. Instead, we reviewed summary documents created by the original study team to familiarize ourselves with the dataset and begin analysis.

Timelines

Timelines for each family that graphically illustrated changes in several areas (e.g., employment, income, childcare arrangements, health conditions, and housing) were the first summary documents that we used (see Figure 9.1). We received the timelines as hard copies printed in color on legal-sized paper and as electronic files (one per family) in Microsoft Excel. The timelines allowed us to quickly orient ourselves to each family by providing an overview of every time a family transitioned from one care arrangement to another as well as how changes in one life domain (e.g., employment, childcare, housing) preceded or followed changes in another. We could immediately appreciate the complexity of families' lives with this concise visual tool.

SEE FIGURE 9.1   at eResource—Timeline Excerpt for a Family From Chicago

Family Profiles

The second summary documents, multi-page (range: 20–80 pages) family profiles, were developed by ethnographers at the main Penn State office during data collection to organize chunks of relevant text from fieldnotes and interview transcripts into one Microsoft Word document. These family profiles were a critical "way-in" to the data and served as first-pass summaries of the entire set of data for each family.

Family profiles included four sections: (a) enrollment and study information (e.g., participant ID and study entry date); (b) participant background information (e.g., names and descriptions of family members); (c) data collection details (e.g., date data were collected, file names, and interview or fieldnote content); and (d) detailed notes from each data collection time point. The fourth section was the essence of the profile. It began with a description of how the family was recruited to the study, their home, neighborhood, and their social network. Most importantly, there were summaries of the relevant information from each interview or fieldnote organized by topic. See Table 9.1 for an excerpt from the childcare section of a profile.

The length and complexity of the family profiles varied depending on how long the family was enrolled in the study and how many interviews and observations they had completed. For the full sample we had thousands of pages of family profiles.

We began familiarizing ourselves with the dataset by noting major events on each family's timeline, and then reading their family profile to flesh out the details. We started with the childcare section of the timelines and family profiles and then read other related sections (e.g., employment, daily routines). We had anticipated strong links between employment and childcare, but were also able to see how

TABLE 9.1 Excerpt From Childcare Section of a San Antonio Family's Profile

---

[Fieldnote Date and File Name] When Lorene was working at McDonald's, Jordan's
  father (Adam) watched Jordan. He also had a job and scheduling was difficult.
  Sometimes Jordan was watched by his grandmother but it did not work well. Lorene
  could not find childcare and had to quit her job.

[Interview Date and File Name] Lorene is upset with her daycare center. It is
  inadequately staffed. Jordan developed a rash because the staff did not change his
  diapers. Lorene did not say anything. Recently, it looked like Jordan was bitten and
  the staff tried to hide it. Lorene is going to take Jordan to the doctor and if it is a bite,
  she is going to say something to the daycare. Lorene says, "They can sanction me, take
  what they want, but they have to give me a chance to get another daycare and do an
  investigation."

[Fieldnote Date and File Name] Adam and Lorene broke up and Lorene was left without
  his help which impacted her childcare situation. She had to miss work.

[Fieldnote Date and File Name] Lorene had her children in a state-sponsored daycare,
  but was not able to meet the participation requirements of the Texas Workforce
  Commission and lost this daycare.

Note. All names are pseudonyms.

health issues and housing instability related to care arrangements. While reviewing the summary documents, we each took individual notes concerning potential study aims and how different aspects of families' lives were associated with
childcare. We made these notes in Word documents that we each kept to record
questions, ideas, and memos. At this point our notes included what was not available in the timelines and family profiles (e.g., detailed information about mothers'
motivations for childcare transitions) and that data were uneven across families
(e.g., some families did not complete a childcare interview).

Formulating Study Aims and Early Analyses

After each reading 10 families' timelines and profiles, we began meeting with
Roy two to four times a month to discuss our notes, overall impressions of the
data, and potential study aims. One note that Speirs wrote early on in this process
concerned differences across types of care: "Should we look at the kind of care
(center, kin care, home-based) mothers switch to and from? Is it easier to switch
to or from one kind? What are the complications with switching to and from different kinds of care?" (Speirs, memo, 2014). The three of us discussed these kinds
of questions at our meetings, came to consensus (or agreed to put off making a
decision), and used that decision to guide our subsequent reading of the data. We
continued to move through the dataset in this manner: reading timelines and family profiles for a few families, then meeting to discuss our initial ideas about the
data. We also began to review the literature on childcare stability (e.g., Adams &
Rohacek, 2010; Chaudry, 2004) and decision making (e.g., Van Horn, Ramey,

Mulvihill, & Newell, 2001) to have a sense of the questions other researchers were addressing and how our data could add to this conversation.

We decided to focus on mothers' transitions between care arrangements and how and why they made these transitions. Our literature review had suggested that there was limited research on childcare transitions and instability and the extant research was largely quantitative. We thought we could use the Three-City Study ethnographic data to bring to light mothers' perspectives and lived experiences as well as generate findings that might inform efforts to develop policies and programs to help mothers find supportive childcare.

Creating Our Own Summary Document

We decided an important first step would be to count the number of childcare transitions for each family and document the reasons for them. We wanted to be sure we were capturing all of the childcare transitions that we had data for, not just those that were the most interesting or frequently discussed. We also attempted to document the number of school and work transitions in order to explore relationships between childcare, work, and school. We created a spreadsheet to organize this work (see Figure 9.2) and stored it in a Dropbox folder so that all three of us could view and edit the same spreadsheet.

Although some of this information was already summarized on the timelines and in the family profiles, creating our own summary spreadsheet proved a critical step in developing our familiarity with the dataset and "owning" the analyses. In putting together the summary spreadsheet we were forced to identify which aspects of the family's lives were important to our analyses (childcare, school, and work) and dig through the available documents to find as much information about these transitions as we could or acknowledge where data were missing. This process helped us move from reading through the original study team's summaries and ideas about the data, which were often included in the family profiles and interview transcripts, to developing our own insights into families' childcare stories and drawing conclusions about childcare stability. Engaging with the dataset in this way helped us begin to take ownership of the data and our analyses.

As we put together this spreadsheet, we started to define different kinds of transitions. In looking at the motivation for each care transition, we realized that some were out of the mothers' control (e.g., a center unexpectedly closing). We recorded our ideas about the different kinds of transitions as notes and memos in Word documents that we kept separately on our own computers. Speirs, Vesely, and Roy also discussed the different transition types during hour-long meetings, held once or twice a month. At least one of us would take

SEE FIGURE 9.2   at eResource—Excerpt From Our Summary Spreadsheet.

notes by hand. After the meeting one or both of us would update our electronic notes to reflect any new ideas generated at the meeting. We were probably not as systematic in this note keeping as we should have been. There were times we forgot to update our electronic notes and instead relied on our memories and handwritten notes. We likely lost details from some of our discussions. When we did write notes, they included a description of the transition (e.g., some mothers make plans to move their child from home-based care to a preschool to prepare them for school) and examples from the interviews or family profiles illustrating the transition.

Engaging With the Literature

While we were creating our summary spreadsheet, we continued to read the literature to be able to situate our analyses within what was already known about childcare transitions and instability. As we read the literature, we deposited relevant articles as pdf files into our Dropbox folder. We compiled article summaries in a shared spreadsheet that included one row for each article and columns for the research question and hypotheses, dataset or sample, definitions of stability or transitions, type of analysis, results, and notes about (among other things) how the article was relevant to our study. If we found something particularly interesting, we shared it over email or at our meetings.

In reading the literature we were influenced by two discoveries: (a) the distinction between *changes* (predictable planned childcare transitions) and (b) *instability* (unanticipated changes; Lowe, Weisner, & Geis, 2003). We had seen this distinction in our data and noted that although some mothers were able to plan transitions, others (or sometimes the same mothers) were left to respond to unanticipated or unwelcomed changes. We came to think of this second transition type as being forced on the mothers.

Our second discovery was that many quantitative studies (e.g., Pilarz & Hill, 2014; Tran & Winsler, 2011) assumed that childcare stability would be associated with positive child outcomes and instability with negative outcomes. However, we noted that there were several mothers in our sample who desperately wanted to change their childcare arrangement but could not find a suitable alternative. These "failed transitions" were impossible to ignore because of the psychological toll that some mothers described. These cases seemed to challenge the assumption in the quantitative literature that childcare stability should be associated with positive outcomes.

Having identified three kinds of transitions (planned, forced, and failed), we explored how they were related. We realized that they could be defined by two dimensions, whether they represented stability (failed transitions) or instability (planned and forced transitions) and whether they should be supportive of child and parent well-being (planned transitions) or not (forced and failed transitions).

TABLE 9.2 Two-by-Two Matrix of Childcare Transitions

	Childcare instability	*Childcare stability*
Supportive of general well-being	Planned transition	Averted transition
Unsupportive of general well-being	Forced transition	Failed transition

Note. From Speirs et al. (2015). Reprinted with permission of Elsevier.

Having defined three cells in a two-by-two matrix (Table 9.2), we turned our attention to the fourth cell—stability that was supportive of well-being. We began looking for examples and realized that many of the mothers in our sample worked hard to maintain childcare arrangements that provided safe and enriching environments for their children and allowed the mothers to work or attend school.

Selecting an Analytic Sample

Having defined four types of transitions using the timelines and family profiles, we wanted to use the full interview transcripts and fieldnotes to confirm that we had an exhaustive list of transition types and that they were relevant for large proportions of the sample. However, we were overwhelmed by the thought of coding multiple transcripts and fieldnotes for 256 families. Luckily, around this time we traveled from Maryland to North Carolina to meet in person with Linda Burton, the principal investigator of the Three-City Study ethnography, and she suggested selecting a smaller analytic sample so as not to lose depth and detail by attempting to analyze the full sample (L. Burton, personal communication, June 26, 2012).

Guided by our research question, we drew an analytic sample of 36 families. In order to preserve the purposive sampling built into the original dataset, we selected 12 families from each of the three cities and race/ethnic groups (African American, Latino, and non-Latino White) sampled from for the original study. Our original report includes a detailed description of sample selection (Speirs et al., 2015).

We also limited the number of interviews that we coded. For the families in our analytic sample we had access to 10–20 interviews conducted by Three-City Study ethnographers, as described in the second section of this chapter. Transcripts for each interview ranged from five to 35 single-spaced pages. We quickly realized that not all of these interviews would be useful as not all of them addressed childcare. We found it most useful to focus on the childcare, employment, and family routines interviews. Skimming by hand and text searching (using the find function in Microsoft Word) for keywords such as "childcare" or "work" in the remaining interviews indicated that we should also read the support network interviews as they often included details about kin care and secondary care arrangements. We also continued to use the family profiles to gain an overall portrait of participants' lives. The contextual details found in the family profiles (e.g., who was in the household and how money was allocated at different points in the month) helped us to interpret how each transition unfolded.

Coding and Finalizing Our Analysis

After determining that we would focus on the childcare, employment, family routines, and support network interviews, we divided the 36 families in our sub-sample between the two of us. Speirs took the Chicago families, Vesely the Boston families, and the families from San Antonio were divided between us. We each uploaded the interview transcripts, fieldnotes, and family profiles (all of which were Word documents) for 18 families into ATLAS.ti software. We had one file per interview, fieldnote, or profile. We then began coding in order to confirm the four transition types we had identified. As we coded, we moved between summary documents and full interview transcripts. Before coding an interview, we reviewed the timeline and family profile to orient ourselves to each mother's major childcare and employment transitions. We would then code the transcripts and once again consult the summary documents to ensure we had not missed any important transitions. We used ATLAS.ti to code any section of interview text that described a childcare transition as a "planned," "forced," "failed," or "averted" transition, or as "unsure how to code" (see Figure 9.3).

We worked through the sections of text coded "unsure how to code" one at a time. Some were easily resolved after reviewing the text a second time with fresh eyes. Others required discussions at our in-person meetings. For example, we were initially unsure if the following text described a planned or forced transition.

> When I moved down here with (my husband), I supported him. [laughs] While I was working, he was with (target child). I didn't have no problems with it. But then, I got kind of pissed off about it, cause I got kind of tired of going to school and working at the same time while he was sitting at home, watching (target child). I didn't consider that 50/50. Until after, I kind of thought about it and was like, well, wait a minute. I do need a sitter. Who's going to watch the child for free, besides his own daddy? But then, at that point, he was sick and in the hospital and I kind of regretted that. Getting into that little argument with him about that. But—I let him know I loved him, and after he got well then he could come back.

We debated if this was (a) a planned transition because this mother wanted her husband to work rather than care for their child and seemed to take action to make this happen, or (b) a forced transition because she eventually saw having her husband care for her child as a beneficial arrangement, but was forced to find another

SEE FIGURE 9.3   at eResource—Screenshot From ATLAS.ti.

caregiver after her husband became sick. After searching the rest of the interview transcripts and the family profile, we found no evidence that the father had actually stopped caring for the child after the mother mentioned that she was not happy with this arrangement but before he became ill. We therefore decided that this was a forced transition. Additionally, the mother's statement that "after he got well then he could come back" suggested that she was ultimately happy with the father caring for their child and was forced to find another caregiver after he was hospitalized.

After coding all transitions as planned, failed, forced, or averted, we used ATLAS. ti to produce four reports. Each report listed all of the quotes associated with one transition type (i.e., all sections of interview or fieldnote text that had been coded as a planned transition). We each took responsibility for two transition types: Speirs coded failed and forced transitions and Vesely planned and averted. We shared the reports so that we each had all of the quotes associated with our two transition types. We independently uploaded these reports into ATLAS.ti and began reading through them to understand how and why each transition happened. We focused on factors that promoted transitions because one of our goals with this paper was to provide information that could inform policy and program development.

We moved through three stages of coding: open, axial, and selective (LaRossa, 2005) as described in our original report (Speirs et al., 2015 and Figure 9.4). We began by identifying questions that would shed light on how and why transitions happened, then created open codes that answered these questions. For example, for the code "failed transitions," one question we were interested in was why mothers wanted to transition. We applied open codes that described their motivations for attempting to change care providers and then grouped these codes into three categories (or axial codes). "Concern about quality or safety of care arrangement" was for codes related to mothers' concerns about health and safety or the caregiver's ability to provide appropriate care. "Logistics" included codes for inconvenient operating hours for centers, provider not available at agreed on times or dates for kin care; and inconvenient location. "Child missing an important experience" was for mothers' concern about their child missing opportunities to promote social-emotional or cognitive development.

In reading through the quotes associated with the "Child missing an important experience" code, Speirs noted that one mother responded to not being able to enroll her daughter in a preschool program by teaching her some of the skills (e.g., writing her name, counting) that she would have learned in preschool. She wrote the following memo: "This mother has found another way to provide these experiences for her child. Suggests resilience and planfulness even in the context of a failed transition. Are other mothers doing this?" (Speirs, memo, 2014).

SEE FIGURE 9.4   at eResource—Open and Axial Coding for Why Mothers Who Experienced Failed Transitions Wanted to Move to a New Care Arrangement.

During the next meeting, Vesely confirmed that she had also seen examples of this. After the meeting, Speirs went back to the data and coded additional examples. Looking for these examples and thinking more about how mothers responded to failed transitions lead to the realization that an important dimension of failed transitions was that some seemed to have a greater impact than others (e.g., using an unsafe care arrangement was more distressful than using an inconveniently located one).

We coded independently and then met to talk through our findings. At this point in the project, we were living in different parts of the country so we held these meetings over the phone. One person would present her conclusions and the other would support or challenge them. At one point, Vesely suggested that having at least one secondary care provider could allow mothers to make planned transitions by providing emergency care and time to carefully search for a new provider when a primary provider was suddenly and permanently unavailable. Speirs expanded on this idea by offering examples where short-term emergency care from a secondary care provider meant a mother did not have to find a new primary care provider if her current one was unavailable for a short period of time (e.g., during a vacation). We fed off each other's excitement. If one person suggested a theory or conclusion about the data, the other would often jump in with examples supporting it. However, we were not shy about challenging each other's conclusions. At this point, we had worked together for several years and had a great deal of mutual respect. We were quick to introduce examples that contradicted each other's conclusions and speak up when we thought the other person was incorrectly interpreting the data. At this point in the coding process, Roy was not joining our phone calls, but was available when we needed to run something by him or for general guidance.

We took different approaches to organizing and recording our open and axial coding. Vesely loaded the interview transcripts into ATLAS.ti and applied an initial set of open codes. She then switched to a Word document for axial coding by creating documents that listed all of the quotes associated with each code. As her standard analysis process, Vesely stores data and conducts initial analyses in ATLAS.ti so that she has an electronic record that includes all of the codes and their definitions. This can be easily updated and used to aggregate data by code. Vesely has gotten into the habit of using Word documents during axial coding, as she typically works on large research teams that include community members who may not have access to ATLAS.ti, and she has experienced difficulty sharing ATLAS.ti projects with other researchers especially across PC and Mac operating systems.

In contrast, Speirs prefers coding entirely in ATLAS.ti because it offers two features that she has come to rely on. First, ATLAS.ti provides a window where code memos can be written and easily edited (see Figure 9.3). She uses this window to write definitions for each code and then refers back to that definition to ensure that her understanding of the code has not changed. If it has changed, she either widens the definition or creates new codes. Second, she likes the ability to quickly see all of the quotes associated with a code. During and after an initial coding pass she will look at all of a quote's associated codes to ensure that all quotes describe the same phenomenon and that additional codes do not need to be added.

Selective coding came after we had completed open and axial coding and had begun writing the findings section of our manuscript. We decided that the central theme organizing our findings was the idea that both stability and instability could be positive or negative. This was the central theme that all of our open and axial codes spoke to and the largest take-away message from the paper.

Reflections

When we began a secondary data analysis of the Three-City Study ethnography, we did not realize how different it would be to work with a dataset of this size than it had been to work with smaller datasets. We quickly realized that this project would require creative analytic strategies. In the following, we reflect on lessons learned and effective approaches, and provide cautions for researchers embarking on similar analyses.

Throughout this project we navigated a tension between using the full potential of the dataset and being realistic about the amount of data we could analyze. At two points we made decisions to limit the data that we would use: we selected an analytic sample of 36 families from the full sample of 256 and focused on four of the 10 to 20 interviews available for each family. It would not have been realistic for two people to read thousands of pages of interview transcripts and fieldnotes multiple times to analyze the full dataset. Using the full dataset would have meant relying more heavily on summary documents, skimming interview transcripts, and using text searches to find relevant passages, ultimately losing the depth of detail that two years of data collection allowed. In limiting the dataset to 36 families we were able to follow a childcare transition across multiple interviews and observe how it started as an idea or a mother's desire to make a change, became a plan, met roadblocks, and either resulted in a transition or the mother starting over. We were able to track down passing references to conflicts with childcare providers or trace out how a family feud meant a mother lost her most reliable source of childcare when her mother stopped talking to her.

These decisions to limit the sample size and number of interviews were made with careful consideration. We fought the idea that we could not use the full sample for some time and were only convinced to do so because Linda Burton (a researcher we greatly respected) suggested it. We had internalized the idea that a larger sample size is always better. What this line of thinking led us to ignore was that in using the full sample, we would have lost some of the depth of detail that this longitudinal dataset offers and which qualitative coding is uniquely suited for exploiting.

We encourage other researchers working with large-scale qualitative datasets to consider limiting their sample size or the amount of data they use for their analyses. These decisions should be made strategically and with the study aims in mind (Roy, Zvonkovic, Goldberg, Sharp, & LaRossa, 2015). It may be possible to use the full dataset for some parts of the analysis and an analytic sample for others. We were able to use the full sample in our initial analysis that identified four transition types largely because of how the summary documents were structured. The timelines allowed us to easily catalogue all of the major childcare (and employment and housing) transitions for one family and the family profiles allowed us to quickly understand the most important details for these transitions and other attempted transitions.

The summary documents allowed us to quickly orient ourselves to the dataset and begin analysis. We were fortunate to not have to create these ourselves, but would encourage anyone working with a large dataset to expend the resources and time to create similar materials. There are many strategies for doing this and the exact format will be dictated by the study structure and aims, but the goal should be to produce short documents that provide an overall picture of the data available for each unit of analysis. It was also important that we were able to link the information in the timelines and family profiles back to the interviews and fieldnotes (through file names embedded in the summary documents).

Although summary documents are valuable resources, it is important to consider how their content and structure may affect analytic strategies and conclusions. Our decision to focus on childcare transitions may have been influenced by using the timelines—which inherently highlight transitions—to orient ourselves to the dataset. It is also likely that the information emphasized in the timelines (and to a lesser extent the more comprehensive family profiles) influenced our thinking about the areas of the families' lives to consider. For example, because housing and health were included on the timelines it is likely that we gave them more attention (at least initially) than other aspects of the families' lives not captured on the timelines (e.g., intimate relationships).

Finally, it is important to note that these analyses took place over several years. They reflect a "generative" scenario in which a young scholar shared a rich and promising dataset with two doctoral students, who then took the lead in conducting the analyses as they left graduate school and emerged as independent scholars. The depth of detail and volume of data found in large-scale qualitative datasets allows for multiple generations of family scholars to develop a long line of supported inquiry.

Conclusion

Using a large-scale qualitative dataset to explore an interesting research question offers unique challenges and rewards. The amount of data available can be daunting and may require producing short summary documents and selecting a smaller analytic sample. However, the depth of detail that this kind of dataset offers can be unparalleled. We found it particularly rewarding to be able to explore child-care transitions in a longitudinal dataset that allowed us to observe the transitions before, during, and after they happened. It is our hope that this chapter inspires and prepares qualitative researchers to conduct their own analysis of a large-scale dataset.

KEY WORKS GUIDING OUR DATA ANALYSIS

Chaudry, A. (2004). *Putting children first: How low-wage working mothers manage child care.* New York, NY: Russell Sage Foundation.

> Chaudry's book gave us direction in our early conceptualization of child-care transitions and helped us think through how to integrate multiple data sources (e.g., timelines and interviews).

Hunt, G., Moloney, M., & Fazio, A. (2011). Embarking on large-scale qualitative research: Reaping the benefits of mixed methods in studying youth, clubs and drugs. *Nordic Studies on Alcohol and Drugs, 28,* 433–452.

> This article provides a practical guide for all aspects of working with a large-scale qualitative dataset. It is useful to read before embarking on this kind of project for help anticipating and planning for common challenges.

LaRossa, R. (2005). Grounded theory methods and qualitative family research. *Journal of Marriage and Family, 67,* 837–857.

> LaRossa summarizes and synthesizes classic texts concerning grounded theory methodology and provides an honest portrait of areas of confusion and disagreement. His description of and suggestions for carrying out open, axial, and selective coding, which includes examples, was particularly helpful.

Maxwell, J. A., & Miller, B. A. (2008). Categorizing and connecting as components of qualitative data analysis. In S. Hesse-Biber & P. Leavy (Eds.), *Handbook of emergent methods* (pp. 461–477). New York, NY: Guilford Press.

> This article presents two approaches to analyzing qualitative data: categorizing and connecting. The description of connecting strategies was particularly useful as it is not often discussed in qualitative methods texts and provided a new way for us to approach the dataset.

References

Adams, G., & Rohacek, M. H. (2010). *Child care instability: Definitions, context, and policy implications.* Washington, DC: The Urban Institute.

Chaudry, A. (2004). *Putting children first: How low-wage working mothers manage child care.* New York, NY: Russell Sage Foundation.

Hunt, G., Moloney, M., & Fazio, A. (2011). Embarking on large-scale qualitative research: Reaping the benefits of mixed methods in studying youth, clubs and drugs. *Nordic Studies on Alcohol and Drugs, 28,* 433–452.

LaRossa, R. (2005). Grounded theory methods and qualitative family research. *Journal of Marriage and Family, 67,* 837–857.

Lowe, E. D., Weisner, T. S., & Geis, S. (2003). *Instability in child care: Ethnographic evidence from working poor families in the New Hope intervention.* New York, NY: MDRC. Retrieved from www.mdrc.org/publication/instability-child-care

Maxwell, J. A., & Miller, B. A. (2008). Categorizing and connecting strategies in qualitative data analysis. In S. N. Hesse-Biber & P. Leavy (Eds.), *Handbook of emergent methods* (pp. 461–477). New York, NY: Guilford Press.

Pilarz, A. R., & Hill, H. D. (2014). Unstable and multiple child care arrangements and young children's behavior. *Early Childhood Research Quarterly, 29,* 471–483.

Roy, K. M., & Burton, L. (2007). Mothering through recruitment: Kinscription of nonresidential fathers and father figures in low-income families. *Family Relations, 56,* 24–39.

Roy, K. M., Tubbs, C. Y., & Burton, L. M. (2004). Don't have no time: Daily rhythms and the organization of time for low-income families. *Family Relations, 53,* 168–178.

Roy, K. M., Zvonkovic, A., Goldberg, A., Sharp, E., & LaRossa, R. (2015). Sampling richness and qualitative integrity: Challenges for research with families. *Journal of Marriage and Family, 77,* 243–260.

Speirs, K. E., Vesely, C. K., & Roy, K. (2015). Is stability always a good thing? Low-income mothers' experiences with child care transitions. *Children and Youth Services Review, 53,* 147–156.

Tran, H., & Winsler, A. (2011). Teacher and center stability and school readiness among low-income, ethnically diverse children in subsidized, center-based child care. *Children and Youth Services Review, 33,* 2241–2252.

Van Horn, M. L., Ramey, S. L., Mulvihill, B. A., & Newell, W. Y. (2001). Reasons for child care choice and appraisal among low-income mothers. *Child and Youth Care Forum, 30,* 231–249.

10

UPROOTING GROUNDED THEORY

The Messy Reality of Understanding Low-income Couples' Cohabitation Transitions

Tyler Jamison

Grounded theory (GT) methods were developed by Barney Glaser and Anselm Strauss in the 1960s as a response to the problematic gap they perceived between theory and empirical research in sociology. They argued that their field had come to rely too heavily on testing a few grand theories (Glaser & Strauss, 1967). In their 1967 book, *Discovery of Grounded Theory: Strategies for Qualitative Research*, they articulated a set of techniques for building conceptual models from the "ground up" so that more researchers would be empowered to engage in the work of theory building. Glaser and Strauss, however, later disagreed about the correct approach to data collection and analysis in GT and subsequently published separate manuals on GT methods (see Glaser, 1992; Strauss & Corbin, 1990, 1998). Glaser is credited with adhering more closely to the original formulation of GT in which the researcher approaches the data without preconceptions and engages in data analysis for the purpose of creating an organized, theoretically meaningful set of concepts (Glaser, 2004). In his view, GT methods are purely inductive and purposefully flexible to allow researchers freedom to follow emerging theoretical insights without the need for "worrisome accuracy" (Glaser, 2004; "Introduction," para. 2). In contrast, Strauss and Corbin argued that GT was designed to facilitate induction as well as deduction and verification. Consequently, they were more specific about data analysis techniques (Corbin & Strauss, 2008, 2015; Strauss & Corbin, 1990, 1998).

In this chapter, I explain how I used GT analysis in a study about cohabitation transitions among low-income couples (Jamison, 2017). I have used GT in most of my work either because the topic of inquiry was largely unexplored (e.g., stayover relationships; Jamison & Ganong, 2011) or because I was interested in understanding family processes (e.g., post-divorce coparenting resilience; Jamison, Coleman, Ganong, & Feistman, 2014). My GT approach is more consistent with the method described in Corbin and Strauss's 2008 and 2015 publications. Like many qualitative studies, this data analysis was messy and took unexpected turns from its inception through writing the results. I used several techniques for analyzing the data, including open coding, writing theoretical memos, making tables, organizing lists, and asking questions of the data. The detailed retelling of this process highlights the complexity of generating a cogent narrative from raw data, the benefits of flexibility in GT, and the challenges of striking a balance between rigorous data analysis and the improvisation that makes qualitative research interesting and exciting.

Background: One Study Becomes Two

Originally, the data for this investigation were collected to explore the coparenting experiences of unmarried couples based on their cohabitation status. However, during data collection and analysis for the study, I reworked the research question to remove the cohabitation piece and simply focus on coparenting in unmarried families. Although it could not be used in the first study, the data about cohabitation experiences was substantive enough to become a second study. For the sake of clarity, I will refer to the study about unmarried coparenting as Study 1 and the study about cohabitation transitions discussed in this chapter as Study 2.

My original research question for Study 1 was: *How does cohabitation status (i.e., living together full-time, staying over, living apart) impact the coparenting experiences of unmarried couples?* The interview protocol contained questions about cohabitation throughout the couples' relationships and questions about their experiences coordinating efforts to parent with their partners. Consistent with GT, the interviews were semi-structured, leaving room to ask questions in the protocol and probe and follow participants' leads. I started each interview with a genogram and a timeline of the relationship. In the timeline, I documented all changes in residence and any breakups and reunions that occurred over time. Interviews were conducted individually, so the perspectives of each member of the couple were reflected in separate timelines and transcripts. For more detailed discussions of this process see Jamison, Ganong, and Proulx (2017).

As data analysis for Study 1 progressed, it became clear that comparing couples based on cohabitation status as I had originally planned would be challenging. It was difficult to categorize couples because they often reported transitioning back and forth between living together full-time, part-time, and living apart throughout their relationships. Given this problem, one option was to categorize couples based on their cohabitation status at the time of the interview. However, this seemed to artificially create categories where they did not clearly exist. I ultimately dropped consideration of cohabitation status in Study 1 and reframed the research question to: *How do unmarried couples coparent?* Charmaz (2014) asserted that the flexibility of GT extends to the reworking of a research question in response to insights about the data. Because I was analyzing the data concurrently with data collection, it did not take long to realize the issue and change course.

Because Study 1 unfolded this way, I had some interesting data about cohabitation patterns and transitions that were not used in the first study publication (Jamison et al., 2017). By subsequently exploring the published research on residential mobility and cohabitation among low-income, unmarried families, I discovered that these data had the potential to fill a significant gap in the literature. Specifically, studies about housing instability and residential mobility (e.g., Clark, 2010; Phinney, 2013) tend to focus on external influences such as neighborhood quality and employment opportunities rather than the interpersonal factors that might motivate changes in residence. Conversely, research about low-income couples emphasizes the frequent disruption in relationships and cohabitations, but generally fails to account for the external forces that may be influencing housing arrangements. To address this gap, Study 2 answered the question, *How do interpersonal relationships and socioeconomic conditions intersect to shape cohabitation transitions for low-income couples?* I found that coresidential transitions were motivated by both interpersonal issues (e.g., pregnancy, breakup, conflict with co-resident family) and external forces (e.g., eviction, poor housing quality). Within each of these categories couples experienced push factors that led them out of their current living arrangements and pull factors that drew them into new ones (for complete findings, see Jamison, 2017).

Sensitizing Concepts

Sensitizing concepts are prior knowledge or experience that guide how the researcher thinks about and organizes the data. Corbin and Strauss (2015) note that previous experience in the area of research is not a detriment to the coding process as long as the researcher keeps the data central to the analysis and remains open to the emergence of ideas challenging their assumptions. Because I had previously worked with these data, I was already aware of some themes related to cohabitation within the transcripts. I also worked with most of the participants in a relationship education and enhancement program for unmarried, low-income new parents. Acting as a program facilitator made me interested in the ways in which low-income families negotiated their relationships within the constraints imposed by poverty. As I prepared to analyze the data again, I explored the research on housing instability (i.e., a circumstance in which difficulty paying for housing, overcrowding, or low housing quality threatens to compromise a family's living arrangements; Clark, 2010) and residential mobility (e.g., Phinney, 2013). These sensitizing concepts shaped open coding and became particularly important as I moved through the later stages of analysis.

Open Coding

Open coding involves systematically working through the data to identify concepts that "represent [the] analysts' interpretation of the meaning expressed in the words or actions of participants" (Corbin & Strauss, 2015, p. 76). NVivo 11 qualitative data analysis software was used for open coding, primarily with pulling out relevant data about cohabitation from the larger dataset and providing some initial organization by themes. This program was a useful starting point, but I discontinued its use after open coding because I found it easier to step away from software for higher order thinking about the data. Also, having dyads and multiple data sources (i.e., timelines, genograms, and interviews) would have required using aspects of NVivo that I had not used in the past. I tend to use NVivo for open coding and organizing participant quotes because I prefer writing memos and making diagrams on paper or in Microsoft Word. Humble (2012) argued that using only the basic features of a software package is common, and there are areas of concern and discussion about the theory-building tools available in these programs.

Because I had a sense of the study's direction, open coding was admittedly the most straightforward part of the analysis. During open coding, I worked through each transcript and assigned selections of data to new or existing concepts. Although Glaser (2004) articulated the need for "line-by-line" coding, I have found that investigating complex processes often requires a broader approach. It may be necessary to consider a sentence or two or a whole paragraph to identify a meaningful concept. To do this without losing the multiple meanings within a passage, I often assigned more than one code to a section of text. At the end of open coding I had identified 10 concepts: (a) beliefs about cohabitation, (b) breaking up and moving out, (c) cohabitation as a testing ground, (d) doubled up, (e) housing instability, (f) how they came to live together, (g) circumstances that led to cohabitation, (h) other ideas about housing, (i) residential transitions, and (j) staying over.

Because concepts are identified throughout the open coding process, there is often a need to "clean up" redundancies before progressing to higher order analysis. Ideas that may have initially seemed distinct, and were therefore coded into separately created concepts, often seem too closely related in the end to stand on their own. For example, in this study, two concepts eventually blended together: "circumstances that led to cohabitation" and "how they came to live together." During coding, I assigned many passages to both of these concepts without being able to really distinguish their differences. Looking back, I believe I created "circumstances that led to cohabitation" to describe things that were external to the couple (e.g., having a fight with a roommate), whereas "how they came to live together" referred to the couple's decision-making process around moving in together (e.g., desiring to spend more time together). As data analysis progressed, I realized that the lack of clarity about these two categories was the first inkling of a central finding in the study. External forces and interpersonal motivations *were* intricately linked to produce residential transitions. It took teasing apart the reasons for each individual move (see Making Tables section) and organizing them into themes (see Making Lists section) to really understand how and why these concepts were connected. I kept coding to both codes and thought of any quote coming from either code as belonging under the same general theme (NVivo has a "merge" function for combining codes, but I was not aware of this function at the time).

Axial coding, or reorganizing finely differentiated concepts into broader, inter-connected themes, has long been considered the next step in data analysis. In 2008, Corbin and Strauss discontinued use of the term "axial coding" in favor of a more general process called "elaborating the analysis." The authors do not provide a rationale for removing axial coding, but I saw this as an attempt to move away from rigid "steps" in the coding process. Because GT data analysis is inherently nonlinear, it makes sense to discuss coding as a set of interrelated strategies for gleaning well-supported conclusions from the data. Although axial coding may be one part of that process, it should not be viewed as the only logical step after open coding. Because I already had a strong sense of the data and themes related to cohabitation transitions, the most logical step after open coding was writing theoretical memos and building a strategy for further analysis using those early written insights.

Theoretical Memos and Other Writing

Open coding immerses the researcher in her data and, therefore, lends itself to exploring the phenomenon of interest in writing. Paired with a researcher's experience with the topic and knowledge of the literature, initial impressions are an important jumping off point for the rest of the analysis. By recording some of my initial impressions in a theoretical memo in Word, I was able to demonstrate that the data on cohabitation were substantial enough to support a new publica-tion. In the memo, I articulated three themes I saw in the data (a) Cohabiting with a new partner is sometimes a response to housing instability rather than an indication of relational commitment, (b) Partnering expands an individual's potential housing resources, and (c) Moving out may not mean breaking up. Note that these themes all begin with a verb; this strategy helped me to think about my participants as actively engaging in the process I was studying and to focus on what people were *doing*. For each assertion, I gave a brief explanation of the idea and then wrote out an example or two from the data (see Table 10.1 for an excerpt). Each theme could have been its own theoretical memo, but I combined them to see how the ideas fit together. Additionally, I began consult-ing with a senior colleague and experienced qualitative scholar on the project. Writing this memo gave me something to share with her that would explain what I thought the study was going to be about. Although she was not directly involved with the study, she became an invaluable resource during data analysis and writing. She is mentioned several times throughout the description of the research process.

At this point, I needed to explore whether the ideas in the memo applied across the sample or whether they were individual stories that stood out to me

TABLE 10.1 Excerpt From Theoretical Memo

Theme	Explanation/example
Cohabiting with a new partner is sometimes a response to housing instability rather than an indication of relational commitment.	Across socioeconomic groups, couples report that their motivations for moving in together are both practical (sharing expenses) and interpersonal (taking the relationship to the next level). Among low-income couples, practicality may be particularly salient because moving in together can also solve housing problems. Unlike more financially stable couples that do not want to pay two rents, individuals dealing with housing instability may move in with a new partner to avoid homelessness or to escape poor living conditions. Beth and Allen moved in together before becoming romantically involved. Beth lived with her sister whom she felt was controlling and unreasonable; their conflicts were becoming increasingly heated when she met Allen at a party. The next day, Allen offered Beth a place to stay in the trailer he owned in exchange for light housekeeping. She moved in within days and shortly thereafter they began a romantic relationship and became pregnant with their daughter. In this case, the romantic relationship turned what would have been a temporary housing solution for Beth into a more permanent one. She transitioned from being an acquaintance in need of help to a partner and de-facto home-owner. At the time of their interviews, their daughter was 14 months old and they continued to live together in the trailer. Theirs was the most stable living situation of any couple I talked to, yet it started with a response to housing instability.

as particularly interesting. To address this issue, I wrote brief memos about how each couple came to live together initially (they all did at some point) and their journey into and out of cohabitation over time. Memos were written in a Word document, with a new page for each couple to allow for easy reference later in the process. Writing memos allowed me to combine the stories of both members of the couple into one narrative. Partners nearly always agreed about the reasons for living together (or apart), but they filled in gaps that the other person did not to elaborate on. Here is an example of a memo:

> Josie and Lamont moved in together about six weeks after they met using an online dating website. Josie was living a couple of hours away in her

aunt's house—she was there to cover her aunt's job and rent while her aunt cared for another family member. However, when she met Lamont he offered for her to move in with him to get them closer and have her help with his son. She admitted that she was having trouble making her aunt's rent, so she moved in with Lamont and his father (who had popped back into the picture after a long absence and said he had nowhere to go). I think Josie wasn't experiencing housing instability yet, but her situation didn't seem sustainable from the way she described it. Lamont's father got himself put on the lease and got Josie and Lamont evicted, so they moved to another city and into Lamont's mother's house. They lived with her and several roommates for about four months rent-free while they got on their feet and found jobs. This sounds like it was a good experience for everyone—they were grateful for her help and seemed to get along well with everyone in the house. Then they moved into their own home.

Push and Pull

Prior to beginning data analysis, I read a report by Clark (2010) in which she drew upon Ravenstein's (1976) push-pull theory of migration to explain the reasons why low-income families are particularly mobile. Having completed open coding and written a set of theoretical memos, I began to see connections between Clark's version of push-pull theory and the data I was analyzing, and so I decided to use push and pull as an organizing tool in the next stage of analysis. To do this, I needed a set of working definitions for what "push" and "pull" meant in the context of residential transitions for couples. In its original form, the push-pull theory of migration referred to the movement of large groups of people from one geographic region to another, typically due to war or famine (both push) or new opportunities (pull). Clark (2010) adjusted these definitions to consider what motivated families to move from one neighborhood to another (e.g., employment opportunities, securing a housing voucher). I had to redefine push and pull yet again for my study. I conceptualized push factors as anything that drove an individual or couple out of their current living situation (e.g., conflict with roommates or co-resident family members). Pull factors were anything that attracted the individual or couple to a new living arrangement (e.g., moving in together to share expenses). I originally recorded these definitions in a draft of my literature review because at the time I was playing with whether I *could* derive a meaningful conceptualization of push and pull for my own purposes. Ultimately, I put the definitions to work as a new approach to analyzing the data.

Making Tables

To understand "push" and "pull" as central concepts in the study (i.e., how I could characterize or define push and pull in the context of cohabitation transitions),

SEE FIGURE 10.1   at eResource—Example of Table Markup.

I needed to explore their properties (Corbin & Strauss, 2015). To achieve this, I organized the data about each residential transition by creating a table for each couple (see Figure 10.1 for an example). Although Corbin and Strauss do not specifically mention tables as a way to explore properties, Miles, Huberman, and Saldaña (2014) suggest that tables may be a useful tool for exploring the "variability or range" of a concept (p. 170).

Using the information from the timelines and transcripts, I documented all residential transitions for each couple in the left-hand column. I then searched the transcripts for the reasons couples moved and categorized them as push or pull. During this part of the process I solicited a second coder to corroborate or challenge the categorizations I was making. I had so much experience with the data that I was concerned my conclusions would be biased toward the emerging themes I was writing about in theoretical memos. Because she had no prior experience with the study, I briefed my research assistant on the data (similar to the background provided earlier in this chapter) and made sure she understood the working definitions of push and pull factors. Then we used the original transcripts (I shared electronic copies with her) to separately, but concurrently, fill in the tables about the reasons for each residential transition. After we completed our tables, we met to compare our work and make final decisions about why couples moved and whether their reasons were best classified as push or pull (see Figure 10.1 for an example of the markup I made during our meeting).

Working through the tables together, we identified three types of discrepancies in our work. First, there were times when one of us omitted a relevant push or pull factor. Because I was more familiar with the data, I often listed reasons that my research assistant overlooked. The second type of disagreement involved inferring the reason for a move based on context, without evidence that the participant actually said anything about it. For example, Krystal and Mike moved to another city together about a year into their relationship. I listed that Krystal's parents lived in the new city as a pull factor. Although it was true that her parents lived in the new city, once we went back to the data it was clear that neither member of the couple mentioned that as a *reason* why they moved. In this case, my familiarity with the data led *me* to make more errors. For each of these issues we returned to the transcripts and identified the specific passage where something was mentioned. When we could not do that, we did not include the reason in the final table. Finally, we sometimes mis-categorized a push or pull factor. This issue required us to discuss our understanding of what was motivating the couple to move and make a judgment together about whether the primary force was away from their current living situation or toward a new one. This proved challenging in some cases because each reason for moving inherently had complementary push and pull factors. For example, moving away from a place the couple could

TABLE 10.2 Final Table for Sarah and Carlton

Transition	Push factors	Pull factors
Sarah moves in with Carlton and his mother	Sarah's conflict with her mother whom she lives with	New relationship
Sarah moves back in with her parents	Carlton's mom is a drug addict and her home is not safe/clean for a baby (bugs)	
They move in together into a house of their own	Family conflict Difficulty coparenting while living apart	Can make safety improvements to home (e.g., baby-proofing) Smarter financial investment to own a home

not afford meant they were also moving toward a home that was more afford-able. We relied on participants' accounts of their residential transitions to decide whether they were primarily motivated by a push away from the old arrangement or a pull toward the new one. After the meeting, I compiled our decisions into a set of final tables (see Table 10.2 for an example).

Making the tables yielded two important insights about the data. First, despite the challenges we faced in categorizing the reasons for a move, the concepts of "push" and "pull" were an excellent tool for organizing the data. Second, one of the unique features of the study was that I had data from both members of the couples. Pulling out the reasons for each residential transition from the perspec-tive of each partner would have highlighted areas of dispute within the couples. However, there was only one instance in which the members of the couple iden-tified conflicting accounts for why they moved. Because couples' accounts were so consistent, I did not pursue further analysis of agreement or disagreement within them. In qualitative research, there is almost always more information than the scholar can realistically analyze, so making informed decisions about what lines of inquiry *not* to pursue is an important part of data analysis.

Writing as Analysis

Once I finished open coding, writing memos, and making tables, I began writ-ing a draft of the results. I decided on a general outline for the findings (i.e., describing push and pull factors) and began searching for examples for the com-mon reasons participants cited for their moves. Writing the results was part of the data analysis process because it highlighted gaps in logic and areas where my impressions were not adequately supported by the data. Writing also helped me perceive broader, more complex processes after having broken the data down in great detail. Consistent with where I was in the analysis, the results started strong, but the organization was weaker with each new section. For example, I had a clear sense of how interpersonal relationships (both the couples' relationships and those with co-resident family) shaped residential transitions, and I was able to easily identify examples of the push and pull factors that emerged out of interpersonal interactions. However, after I wrote all of the reasons that seemed most salient to me, and for which I had clear examples, I still had not discussed many of the issues participants mentioned during their interviews (e.g., housing quality). What I had written was an accurate reflection of the data, but the narrative was incomplete and largely descriptive. I shared this early draft with my colleague, who gave me feedback about my organization and suggested I make a list of all reasons for residential moves and how many times they were mentioned. This drove me back to the data and allowed it to guide the next steps for organizing the results.

Making Lists

I created two lists of all reasons why participants moved—one for push and one for pull (see Figure 10.2). When I encountered the same reason for more than one move within or across couples, I noted the duplication. This provided me with two lists including every reason for moving that participants reported and the total number of times each was mentioned in the dataset (e.g., pregnancy- 3). The lists included 17 push factors and 18 pull factors. Next, I used different color highlighters to identify clusters of similar reasons for moving within each list. I needed broader themes to organize the reasons for moving for presentation in the results. Some themes came together quickly from reading through the lists (e.g., conflict with resident family, conflict within the couple, and breakup = interpersonal conflict). After coding the push list, I had identified five different themes: (a) interpersonal conflict (e.g., breakup); (b) financial constraint (e.g., could not afford current living situation); (c) condition of home (e.g., no running water); (d) social relationships (e.g., lack of privacy); and (e) normative push (e.g., lease was up). I then coded the pull list and found complementary themes to those derived from the push factors, using the same highlighter color for similar themes so that I could make an easier comparison between lists. I identified five themes from the pull list: (a) interpersonal benefits (e.g., coparenting support); (b) finances (e.g., freedom to pay no rent or less rent); (c) benefits of a new home (e.g., can make safety improvements); (d) social benefits of new home (e.g., help with childcare); and (e) convenience (e.g., moving toward more permanent arrangement).

SEE FIGURE 10.2 at eResource—Lists of Reasons for Moving.

At this point I had another meeting with my colleague and we discussed how I should interpret and present the complementary nature of the themes I generated from the lists. As we talked about them, she challenged what constituted a unique reason for moving. For example, one reason in the push list was "did not want to burden roommates with a new baby." She asked me, "Isn't this just another way of saying the pregnancy pulled them into living together?" There was a sliver of nuance there about social connections and being courteous to others, but she was correct. At its core, the move was precipitated by the pregnancy. Our conversation led to some reorganization of the highlighted lists (e.g., pregnancy/coparenting support was combined with pregnancy/live as a family) and a decision to focus only on the moves that involved a couple entering into cohabitation or exiting from it. I decided not to include residential transitions that made no change to the cohabitation status of the couple because they made the narrative of the results less clear and added little to the study results.

At the end of this process, 11 push factors and 12 pull factors remained. Most of the eliminated factors referred to residential transitions that did not change whether the couple lived together or apart. Moreover, after scaling down, some of the original themes (five for each list) only had one or two reasons for moving left within them. I decided that only three themes were truly robust in terms of clear definition and examples from multiple couples across multiple moves: (a) interpersonal negotiations (this included both conflict and benefits), (b) finances, and (c) housing quality. These themes were present in both the push and pull lists, which made the direction for organizing the findings much clearer. I provided examples of how each theme included both push and pull motivations for moving and articulated the differences using examples from the data. Acknowledging that push and pull factors were not always completely separate was another step in understanding the complexity of the phenomenon I was studying. I returned to the writing process to organize the findings accordingly and found that they came together more easily and major assertions were easier to support.

Broader Conclusions

After composing a set of findings about why couples moved, there was still a need to explore the influence of contextual factors such as poverty and other mechanisms that might be at work in cohabitation transitions. The final part of the analysis focused on "asking questions." This is a GT technique that helps researchers explore the meanings in the data (Corbin & Strauss, 2015). In this case, the answers to my questions gave rise to some theoretical conclusions that elevated the findings beyond description and enriched the contribution of the study to the cohabitation and housing instability literatures.

Sensitizing concepts played an important role in shaping the questions I asked during this stage of the analysis. Having worked with low-income couples in an intervention, I was aware that their lives were sometimes shaped by a lack of resources rather than their desires for their families. This prompted me to ask the question, *Is moving in together (or out) always a choice?* Returning to the raw data as well as the early memos and tables provided evidence that moving was not always a choice, but rather involved a combination of choice and necessity. By seeking examples within the data I was able to flesh this out conceptually and it became the first theoretical conclusion of the study.

I am also a relationship researcher, and I have conducted several studies about cohabitation (Jamison & Ganong, 2011; Jamison & Proulx, 2013). Within the cohabitation literature it is common to assume that couples who live together must be romantically involved and couples who end a cohabitation must have broken up. This observation paired with my knowledge of the data prompted me to ask, *Do couples move in and out in response to changes in their romantic relationships?* Again, the answer was "no." Exploring the circumstances under which couples moved in or out without a relevant change in their romantic relationships provided evidence for a second theoretical conclusion.

Finally, despite the lack of compelling findings about the dyads, participants' stories were repeatedly intertwined even when their residential transitions did not directly involve the relationship. I asked, *How are couples' stories of residential transitions related to one another?* The answer had actually occurred to me in the first long memo I wrote after open coding. What was interesting about the dyads was not whether they agreed or disagreed about whether they moved. Rather, it was that being together opened up new housing opportunities by expanding their social network. Taken in the context of poverty, this provided some interesting insight about how people with relatively few resources expand their options for housing (and other resources) through their partnerships.

Reflection

Despite their heated disputes about the application of GT methods, both Glaser (1992) and Strauss and Corbin (1990) suggested that data analysis should provide enough flexibility for the researcher to follow the data to its natural conclusions. Although GT is characterized by its flexibility, scholars tend to stick with a few core techniques and terms in their descriptions of GT analysis (e.g., open and axial coding, constant comparative technique, saturation). These are valid (and some would argue necessary) techniques for conducting GT, but they are far from the only ways to make meaning from GT data. The consequence is that many GT articles contain generic descriptions of data analysis that include familiar terms but lack specificity about the process.

This problem emerges, in part, from the tension between reporting what researchers actually did and using the language reviewers and readers will be looking for to ensure that GT was applied with fidelity. Corbin and Strauss (2015) emphasize that data analysis can be tailored to the researcher. They offer a list of possible ways to engage the data for the purpose of analysis; many of which are rarely mentioned in GT publications (e.g., using the flip flop technique, making use of life experience, looking for words that indicate time, thinking in terms of metaphors or similes). Researchers rarely report the idiosyncratic aspects of these data analysis processes. A need to use GT language and core techniques remains, but expanding the scope of acceptable data analysis techniques allows for richer descriptions of the research process. Readers can contextualize and understand qualitative findings more fully when they know how researchers arrived at their conclusions.

In qualitative data analysis, the researcher is the analytical tool, which has notable advantages in terms of untangling the complexity of lived experience, but it also has drawbacks because we bring imperfections into the data analysis process. Defining acceptable data analysis methods too narrowly creates a tendency to hide mistakes and mis-steps because they appear to undermine the rigor of the study. For example, during open coding I created two codes that were nearly identical ("circumstances that led to cohabitation" and "how they came to live together"). In hindsight, I should have stopped the coding process midstream and considered more carefully the similarities and differences between the concepts so that I could use them more purposefully. Grounded theorists describe this process as exploring the *properties* of an idea (Corbin & Strauss, 2015). I did not do this and instead continued coding using both categories as a catch-all for ideas around why the couple moved in or out. I realized later that I had not adequately defined them and had to grapple with how to proceed. Although I did not adhere perfectly to GT in this instance, I was able to gain significant insight about my data by working through the mistake. I ultimately had to distinguish between these closely related concepts, and doing so led to some of the most interesting findings in the study.

Conclusion

Qualitative data analysis is full of decisions about how to process, organize, and present the narrative of the findings. Fully articulating each step of that process for this study revealed how much I tend to leave out of my descriptions of data analysis in journal publications. It also highlights the powerful implications of providing more transparency about the way qualitative scholars arrive at the study findings. Uprooting GT means embracing more improvisation in the data analysis process, and viewing creativity as a strength rather than something that undermines rigor. The key is to explain what we have done with enough detail that readers can adequately vet and interpret the process, whatever that may be.

KEY WORKS GUIDING MY DATA ANALYSIS

Corbin, J., & Strauss, A. (2015). *Basics of qualitative research: Techniques and procedures for developing grounded theory.* Thousand Oaks, CA: Sage.

This is one of the most commonly cited works for grounded theory researchers, and for good reason. It lays out the logic of grounded theory and provides specific examples of how real data can be analyzed using grounded theory techniques. The explanation of theoretical memos as a way to facilitate understanding during coding is particularly useful. The authors illustrate how to engage in analysis through writing, a skill that can easily be lost if researchers are too focused on breaking the data down into themes.

LaRossa, R. (2005). Grounded theory methods and qualitative family research. *Journal of Marriage and Family, 67,* 837–857.

This article is an accessible and succinct description of the core tenets of grounded theory. LaRossa provides context by briefly reviewing the debates within grounded theory, but the majority of the piece is dedicated to carefully defining and explaining the language of grounded theory. Although it is not a substitute for one of the more substantial grounded theory manuals, LaRossa offers a practical and articulate guide for understanding or conducting grounded theory.

References

Charmaz, K. (2014). *Constructing grounded theory* (2nd ed.). Thousand Oaks, CA: Sage.

Clark, S. L. (2010). *Housing instability: Toward a better understanding of frequent residential mobility among America's urban poor* (Report #001–009). Retrieved from www.partnering-for-change.org/wp-content/uploads/2014/11/Hoursing-Instability-Toward-a-Better-Understanding-of-Frequent-Residential-Mobility-Among-America%E2%80%99s-Urban.pdf

Corbin, J., & Strauss, A. (2008). *Basics of qualitative research: Techniques and procedures for developing grounded theory* (3rd ed.). Thousand Oaks, CA: Sage.

Corbin, J., & Strauss, A. (2015). *Basics of qualitative research: Techniques and procedures for developing grounded theory* (4th ed.). Thousand Oaks, CA: Sage.

Glaser, B. G. (1992). *Basics of grounded theory analysis.* Mill Valley, CA: Sage.

Glaser, B. G. (2004). Remodeling grounded theory. *Forum Qualitative Sozialforschung/ Forum: Qualitative Social Research, 5*(2), Art. 4. Retrieved from http://nbn-resolving.de/urn:nbn:de:0114-fqs040245

Glaser, B. G., & Strauss, A. L. (1967). *The discovery of grounded theory: Strategies for qualitative research.* Chicago, IL: Aldine.

Humble, A. M. (2012). Qualitative data analysis software: A call for understanding, detail, intentionality, and thoughtfulness. *Journal of Family Theory & Review, 4*, 122–137.

Jamison, T. B. (2017). Cohabitation transitions among low-income parents: A qualitative investigation of economic and relational motivations. *Journal of Family and Economic Issues, 39*, 73–87.

Jamison, T. B., Coleman, M., Ganong, L. H., & Feistman, R. E. (2014). Transitioning to post-divorce family life: A grounded theory investigation of resilience in coparenting. *Family Relations, 63*, 411–423.

Jamison, T. B., & Ganong, L. (2011). "We're not living together:" Stayover relationships among college-educated emerging adults. *Journal of Social and Personal Relationships, 28*, 536–557.

Jamison, T. B., Ganong, L., & Proulx, C. M. (2017). Unmarried coparenting in the context of poverty: Understanding the relationship between stress, family resource management, and resilience. *Journal of Family and Economic Issues, 38*, 439–452.

Jamison, T. B., & Proulx, C. M. (2013). Stayovers in emerging adulthood: Who stays over and why? *Personal Relationships, 20*, 155–169.

Miles, M. B., Huberman, A. M., & Saldaña, J. (2014). *Qualitative data analysis: A methods sourcebook* (3rd ed.). Thousand Oaks, CA: Sage.

Phinney, R. (2013). Exploring residential mobility among low-income families. *Social Service Review, 87*, 780–815.

Ravenstein, E. G. (1976). *The laws of migration.* New York, NY: Arno Press.

Strauss, A., & Corbin, J. (1990). *Basics of qualitative research: Techniques and procedures for developing grounded theory.* Newbury Park, CA: Sage.

Strauss, A., & Corbin, J. (1998). *Basics of qualitative research: Techniques and procedures for developing grounded theory* (2nd ed.). Newbury Park, CA: Sage.

11

CHARTING THE COURSE

Analytic Processes Used in a Study of Residents' Care Networks in Assisted Living

Candace L. Kemp, Mary M. Ball, and
Molly M. Perkins

With an emphasis on meaning, experience, as well as contradictions and tensions in everyday life, qualitative research has much to contribute to the understanding of relationships, including complex and dynamic social processes such as those found in social, family, and care networks. Research that captures and reflects the nuances of family life demands approaches to data collection and analysis that are as complex, fluid, and dynamic as the experiences and relationships they purport to understand. Such approaches are time-consuming, costly, logistically challenging, and rare (Kemp et al., 2017). Moreover, when they are used, it is not common for researchers to share detailed insight into their analytic procedures. Our goal in this chapter is to do just that, providing an in-depth account of the methods used to analyze data from the longitudinal qualitative study, "Convoys of Care: Developing Collaborative Care Partnerships in Assisted Living" (hereafter the Convoy Study).

The Convoy Study

This study was guided by our Convoys of Care model (Kemp, Ball, & Perkins, 2013), which was developed based on a synthesis of theoretical and empirical data, including our own grounded theory research set in assisted living and involving older adults, their family members and friends, and care workers. Care convoys are:

> the evolving collection of individuals who may or may not have close per-
> sonal connections to the [care] recipient or to one another, but who provide
> care including help with activities of daily living (ADLs) and instrumental
> activities of daily living (IADLs), socio-emotional care, skilled health care,
> monitoring, and advocacy.
>
> *(Kemp et al., 2013, p. 18)*

The overall goal was to learn how to support informal care (unpaid care by family and friends) and care convoys in assisted living in ways that promote residents' abilities to age in place with optimal resident and caregiver (both paid and unpaid) quality of life.

An in-depth consideration of the study's design and methods appears elsewhere (see Kemp et al., 2017). Briefly, data collection methods consisted of in-depth and informal interviews, participant observation, and review of assisted living community and resident records. We collected data in eight assisted living communities that varied by size, location, resident characteristics, ownership, and resources—variables research suggests likely influence care experiences. We followed a sample of residents and their informal and formal caregivers over a two-year period, attempting at least weekly contact with residents and twice-monthly contact with convoy members. Data collection was organized in two separate stand-alone waves, each involving four sites, studied for two years. Our sequential design, motivated by analytic considerations, enhanced cumulative knowledge building regarding variables of interest and allowed us to make informed adjustments regarding data collection and analysis procedures over the five-year period. Here, we describe the data analysis for a recently published paper (Kemp et al., 2018), which generated a theory of how care network members navigate the care landscape.

Unlike most studies on families, social relationships, and care, ours endeavored to study entire networks rather than individuals or dyads (but see Bengtson, Biblarz, & Roberts, 2002; Connidis & Kemp, 2008). We aimed to recruit residents' complete care networks, including multiple informal members. Adult children were the most common informal caregiver, but grandchildren, siblings, extended family, and friends also participated. Formal caregivers included assisted living administrators and staff and external care workers, such as hospice personnel, physicians, and home health professionals.

During Wave 1, from 2013 to 2015, we collected longitudinal data on 28 residents and their entire care networks. We conducted formal interviews, digitally recorded and transcribed, with 28 residents and 114 caregivers. Data collection also included participant observation, including ongoing informal interviewing and resident record review. We logged 2,225 observation hours in 809 visits to study sites; observations and informal conversations were recorded in fieldnotes. Begun in 2016, Wave 2 was incomplete when this chapter was written; these data are not included here. We anticipate a final sample of 50 residents and 225 formal and informal caregivers across the eight diverse settings (see Kemp et al., 2017). Collecting and making sense of these data requires time, patience, and a systematic and rigorous, yet flexible approach, such as that offered by grounded theory methods.

Grounded Theory in Practice

Although there are numerous approaches to qualitative data collection and analysis, we have found that our research questions and topics are best suited to a grounded theory approach (Corbin & Strauss, 2015). We endeavor to develop knowledge cumulatively, and our most recent research builds upon our past work—much of which focused on understanding the processes of social and care relationships and networks. We also recognize the need to adopt research strategies that can be modified as needed to suit project needs and address our research goals.

Our approach to grounded theory highlights the interrelationship of data collection and analysis. These activities are performed simultaneously and iteratively and inform one another throughout the research process. Thus, our analysis began at the start of data collection.

As outlined, the Convoy Study was large, complex, and longitudinal, involving multiple data collection techniques at multiple sites and an evolving collection of participants and researchers. It called for procedures that simultaneously helped us organize and analyze vast amounts and sources of data. We started with *foundational* analytic strategies that provided the scaffolding for more advanced, *targeted* analysis. The targeted analysis addressed specific research questions, involved higher-level analysis, and generated conceptual models and theory.

Foundational Analytic Strategies

Foundational analytic activities were developed, refined, and carried out as part of the interplay of data collection and analysis. They included team meetings, ongoing data analysis and management (e.g., transcript and fieldnote review, data entry, and coding), development of site and resident/convoy profiles, and memoing. Our longitudinal study design required maintaining a large, dynamic research team (13 members on average), forming a *convoy of researchers* comprised of faculty, staff, and graduate students from diverse academic and social backgrounds. Although we had team transitions over the study course, we maintained a stable core at each site, enabling consistency in data quality and analysis (Kemp et al., 2017).

Team Meetings

Twice-monthly meetings with the entire research team led by Kemp, the principal investigator, provided an important forum for discussing data collection and analysis activities, including new lines of inquiry, fieldwork challenges, data gaps, sampling strategies, and discussions concerning similarities and differences across sites, residents, and time. Although agenda items varied, each meeting included site updates regarding research aims and ongoing analysis. We recorded team discussions in Microsoft Word documents, which became part of our qualitative database and subject to analysis.

Team meetings led to pivotal decisions throughout the study, especially early on. For example, initially, and as noted elsewhere (Kemp et al., 2017), we relied on residents to identify convoy members but discovered this approach led to the inclusion of individuals who contributed little, if anything, to care and the exclusion of active contributors. Based on ongoing dialogue and considerations of care convoys and relationships, we amended our definition of convoy members to be those we identified through our data as ongoing or periodic participants in resident support over the two years. We deemed it necessary to: "capture instances where networks were dense, but now are not (and why);" investigate "differences based on the assisted living community's connection to larger surrounding community;" "note people" who normatively would be expected "to be in a convoy" (e.g., children), "but who were not active convoy participants;" and "capture (and examine) positive and not-so-positive relationships" (meeting notes, October 16, 2014).

Ongoing Data Analysis and Management

Throughout the study we shared fieldnotes and interview transcripts, noting theoretical, methodological, and operational implications in memos (see the section on "Memoing") and team discussions. These practices allowed informed adjustments in the field and helped guide analysis. For instance, in Wave 2 we instituted a fieldnote template that included a table with a drop-down menu to track residents' health and convoy transitions, key foci of analysis. We stored all data and study files on a secure password-protected shared drive maintained by Georgia State University and only accessible to active team members. Files could be accessed by all, but only edited by one researcher at a time.

We used multiple databases and programs to store, manage, and analyze data (Kemp et al., 2017). IBM SPSS21 databases recorded site features (e.g., size, ownership, fees) and participants' social, demographic, and health characteristics. We maintained four SPSS databases for (a) sites, (b) residents, (c) informal caregivers, and (d) formal caregivers. These data helped characterize sites and participants, individually and in the aggregate, and aided in identifying and interpreting similarities and differences across sites and participants, discovered through qualitative analysis. For example, aggregate facility data regarding residents' functional status and staffing levels helped explain variations in convoy structure and function.

Although we retained paper files of interview transcripts and fieldnotes (created in Word) in three-ring binders for each site, we housed digital qualitative data in NVivo10 software, later NVivo11, for subsequent coding and analyses. We created and maintained separate NVivo projects for each of the eight research sites and for meeting notes. The site projects varied based on resident census, but each contained between 16 to 52 interviews and 87 to 371 fieldnotes. These projects could have been merged, but the smaller project files were easier to manage and less prone to instability. The team coded data directly in NVivo.

Coding is an essential activity in qualitative analysis and a way to categorize data (Maxwell & Chmiel, 2014). At the study's outset, as recommended by Lofland, Snow, Anderson, and Lofland (2006, p. 205), the team developed a set of basic, yet comprehensive, "folk/setting-specific" codes guided by observations in the field, research aims, and existing theory and research. These codes allowed us to tag, sort, and organize large chunks of data for higher-level analysis. We applied these broad codes to relevant words and phrases identified through line-by-line coding.

Given the volume of data, folk/setting-specific coding facilitated sorting the data into large, yet manageable, segments of broad categories captured by using 14 "parent" nodes, with varying numbers of "child" nodes (these terms represent NVivo's code hierarchy and terminology). For instance, and shown in Figure 11.1, the higher-order parent node "care needs and activities" was associated with eight child nodes delineating types of care, such as "medical" and "socioemotional." Nodes also captured multi-level factors (e.g., resident/caregiver, facility, cultural, community) expected to influence care processes, interactions, transitions, experiences, and outcomes. We created name codes for residents and staff in each setting, allowing easy retrieval and review of data associated with these residents and their convoys. For flexibility, we also designated a "to be coded" code for data that needed future coding, possibly with a new or refined code, which required group discussion before coding.

Team members received NVivo training, which consisted of an introduction to the program and coding features and culminated in homework assignments used to compare coders by using NVivo's coding comparison function with the goal of achieving near perfect inter-coder reliability (see Figure 11.2). We had ongoing discussions in team meetings and smaller groups, all recorded in notes, to establish the utility of codes and advance code definitions, and we also kept a Word document on our shared drive with current codes and definitions. Joy, our project manager, observed in a memo,

> I think it has been effective for the team to meet and talk about coding. The graduate assistants who have participated more in these conversations code more quickly than those who do not, and seemed to have gained analytical skills based on insights they offer individually and in team meetings.
>
> *(October 4, 2017)*

Our strategy for documenting and analyzing residents' convoy and health changes evolved over the study. In both waves we documented these changes in fieldnotes. In Wave 1 we recorded these data in a Microsoft Access database, a strategy we abandoned for a more nimble, manageable, and straightforward

SEE FIGURE 11.1   at eResource—NVivo Codes.

SEE FIGURE 11.2   at eResource—Inter-Coder Comparison.

SEE FIGURE 11.3 at eResource—Convoy Contacts and Health Convoy Changes.

Microsoft Excel database in Wave 2 (see Figure 11.3). Reflecting on our decision, Joy explained:

> We do not have enough participants to require such a complex database. Because the reporting tools are not as fluid as what we need to meet our needs, we end up doing most reporting in Excel, exporting data from Access.
> *(November 5, 2015)*

Convoy and health changes also were recorded in both waves through profile writing, which was a central component of our analytic strategy.

Profiles

We developed profiles for all eight sites and all 50 resident/convoys, which allowed in-depth, systematic study of individuals, networks, and settings and also facilitated constant comparison, an essential grounded theory activity (Strauss & Corbin, 1998). We created profile templates informed by the Convoys of Care Model (Kemp et al., 2013), our research aims and questions, and observations in the field. Site profiles described each setting, documenting size, location, history, ownership, staffing levels, care culture, policies, and practices and indicating local and wider community factors influencing care experiences and convoys.

Resident profiles contained details about: personal and health history; care needs; daily life; health transitions; convoy size, composition, activities, collaboration, and transitions; key factors; outcomes; and lessons learned. Profiles also included convoy tables (see Table 11.1), which identified members and their relationships, and diagrams representing residents' self-care activities and care contributions and connections of their informal and formal convoy members. We modified the diagrams to represent health and convoy changes over time. Initially, for example, Alice provided some self-care and her convoy was comprised mostly of staff and family (Figure 11.4). As she declined, her self-care decreased and the number and types of care providers expanded (Figure 11.5). Additionally, as data collection and analysis proceeded, we augmented resident profiles with examples from interview, fieldnotes, and record review data, including passages from resident or caregiver interviews that spoke to the care network and attitudes about receiving and giving care. In Wave 1, we made these additions retrospectively, often during coding. During Wave 2, which is ongoing, we are prospectively enhancing profiles, a technique that is less laborious and strengthens the connection between data collection and analysis. These profiles provide fundamental material for more targeted analyses.

TABLE 11.1 Resident/Convoy Profile Table: "Mr. Story's" Informal Convoy

Name	Relationship	Proximity to resident	Contact type	Contact frequency	Resident outcomes
Janet	Daughter	(15 miles) 25 minute drive	Phone In-person	Daily At least once per week	Calls Janet his "quarterback." He feels very supported.
Tim	Son-in-law	(15 miles) 25 minute drive	Phone In-person	At least weekly At least monthly	Calls Tim "the best son-in-law in Georgia" and feels very supported.
Justine	Granddaughter	School (80 miles) 90 minute drive Home (15 miles) 25 minute drive	Phone In-person	Occasionally At least monthly	Grandparenthood is very important. He enjoys time with grandchildren.

SEE FIGURE 11.4 at eResource—Alice's Convoy Summer 2013.

SEE FIGURE 11.5 at eResource—Alice's Convoy Winter 2014.

Memoing

Memoing is an important tool used by qualitative researchers that provides an ongoing way for team members to document and share thoughts on methods and analysis (Strauss & Corbin, 1998). We recorded "operational" memos to track problems and successes, procedural changes, and issues regarding relationships with participants. We used "theoretical" notes containing ideas about sampling and insights, observations, interpretations, and questions about the data to reflect on the analysis process and facilitate learning more about a topic's salience. For instance, after a conversation with a resident's daughter about the role church members played in informing her about her father's activity, our project manager reflected, "This shows the importance of informal caregivers supporting one another, as well as residents. I wonder if we see stronger support in convoys where there is involvement in a church or other organized religious or community group" (November 4, 2015). And, after a field visit Mary mused, "It will be interesting to see if Jan's son takes her to the neurologist. This is definitely an example of a convoy with no externally provided health care. This arrangement may not be in the resident's best interest" (March 4, 2015).

Most memoing activities were built into our procedures and researcher initiated in that individuals recorded their thoughts as they collected and analyzed data. Fieldnotes contained the heading "MEMO" at the end of the document allowing researchers to share ideas about ongoing processes and emerging insights. As part of each fieldnote, these memos were coded within NVivo under the parent node, "Research" with child nodes "operational" and "theoretical."

Early fieldnote memos largely concerned theoretical sampling, fitting into the setting, researcher-participant relationships, and reflections on the effectiveness of data collection procedures but also contained insights into sampling and data interpretation. Our reflections grew in sophistication and complexity as our knowledge and understanding increased. For example, in the first months of data collection while seeking maximum variation (Patton, 2015) based on resident and family characteristics, Molly noted in one memo, "Although Jenna tends to repeat herself, I think she would be an excellent resident participant. A care worker indicated that her family is somewhat dysfunctional and her primary caregiver is an aunt by marriage" (January 5, 2014). Memos also contained reflections on patterns and connections with existing literature. Candace noted after a Garden House visit (October 12, 2014), "Frank brings to mind some of the women in Mary's book, *Surviving Dependence* (Ball & Whittington, 1995) in terms of his ability to get people to do things for him. It is very interesting that his daughter disapproves. . . "

Alongside memoing within fieldnotes, located within the NVivo project files, each researcher created a personal memo in a Word document housed on our shared computer drive, located outside NVivo. In these additional memos, researchers recorded ongoing thoughts on data collection and analysis, including their feelings, connections between data and the literature, and avenues for further exploration. Personal memos will be moved into NVivo when data collection ends.

Researchers routinely added to their personal memo documents during NVivo coding sessions, and memoing was discussed informally and during team meetings. Meeting notes (January 20, 2016) recorded the following:

> Liz shared some thoughts she has been memoing about. She was coding Andrea's fieldnotes and she had a note about what is expected of males versus females when it comes to caregiving. She also discussed that there are contradicting stories at times between a resident and a caregiver. We seem to get multiple perspectives on things that happen that do not always align. Such reflections encouraged researcher discussions.

Candace encouraged the team to examine contradictory accounts within the data, including participant accounts. We embraced the notion that not all information would align, which in and of itself, was a key study contribution (Kemp et al., 2017). Some data were clearly conflicting; others were more nuanced. Candace hypothesized, for instance:

> The different views Catherine and Alice gave me about Jack [resident] emphasize the value and potential challenge of including multiple viewpoints. At first, their versions seemed in conflict, but upon reflection, it is possible they were addressing different dimensions of his well-being. Catherine is more apt to talk to him about his health care and conditions—his care needs, including the help he receives and his meds. . . . In contrast, not that Alice is unaware of his health and care, her interactions are more about keeping him mentally stimulated and socially engaged.
>
> *(April 30, 2015)*

Memos guided cumulative knowledge building by informing and advancing questioning of participants, settings, and data. As analysis progressed, we sharpened our focus on key patterns and concepts we were identifying. Memoing, for both foundational and targeted analysis, was key throughout the research process.

Targeted Analytic Strategies

The foundational analytic strategies described previously provided systematic methods to organize vast amounts of data, thereby setting the stage for higher-level analyses. Many of our targeted analytic activities were ongoing while writing this chapter and form the basis of publications in preparation. Throughout the project we maintained an "Analysis and Working Documents" folder to house all analytic files (e.g., reports and analysis charts in Word) organized by topic; within topics, subfolders contained analysis pertaining to each research site.

Ongoing analysis involved all researchers and was discussed in biweekly team meetings and recorded in Word as team meeting notes. The research team also organized into smaller teams that conducted more targeted analysis based on our research aims and ongoing analysis. Each team was led by different senior investigators and included Candace, the principal investigator. We maintained a Word document with the table, "Convoy Analysis Planning and Dissemination" to record targeted analysis. Columns included: analysis focus, analysis activities and goals, progress toward goals, and team leads and supports. We organized this information by analysis stage: (a) presented at conferences and manuscript in process; (b) to be presented, analysis needs advancing, and manuscript preparation; and (c) preliminary thinking phase.

For present purposes, we offer an in-depth description of one targeted analysis using Wave 1 data that we report in an article we refer to as the *patterns paper* (Kemp et al., 2018). Briefly, our aims of that analysis were to learn how residents' care convoys are structured and function and how and why they vary. Through this targeted analysis, we developed a typology of residents' care convoys and developed a conceptual model and a core process we labeled "maneuvering together, apart, and at odds." The model outlines various ways and factors that influence how residents and care network members negotiated care in assisted living across time. Next, we describe how we arrived at these conclusions.

Grounded Theory Coding

Our coding activities drew on our basic codes (described previously) and accompanying NVivo node reports most germane to understanding care network patterns. We ran node reports for "convoy properties," "influential factors," and "care activities, needs, and interactions," to access data describing the structure, function, and sources of variability of convoys, and examined resident/convoy profiles. Using these data, we followed the three-stage coding procedures outlined by Corbin and Strauss (2015), which involves open, axial, and selective coding. Through open coding, we inspected these data for concepts based on our questions about convoy patterns. Open coding can be accomplished multiple ways, including applying codes line by line and to a sentence, paragraph, or entire document (Strauss & Corbin, 1998). We used all of these units, but mostly coded sentences and paragraphs connected to individuals, convoys, and sites.

We applied initial codes to all data that provided insights into how convoys were structured (e.g., "primary informal caregiver" and "shared responsibility") and operated (e.g., "collaboration," "leadership," "consensus," "proactive," and "reactive"). Our coding was guided by sensitizing concepts from the literature, including our own past work, and by new patterns we observed in the data. For instance, both past work (Ball et al., 2005) and current data chronicle the existence of "primary" and "shared" roles among informal caregivers in support of assisted living residents. Using an inductive approach, we expanded these concepts and identified variations within these structures.

Early in our targeted analysis, we used Word to create analysis charts using the "Table" feature. Word permitted the flexibility to provide detailed information and insights beyond what was capable in the NVivo program. Our profiles informed the creation of charts and were fundamental to coding and analytic processes. The charts enabled us to compare and contrast convoys within and across study sites and over time and facilitated the identification of similarities and differences.

Each research site team was tasked with developing analysis charts focused on resident convoys from their respective sites. Our targeted coding and chart-making activities were based on "the use of questioning" (Strauss & Corbin, 1998, p. 89). In our first round of charts, we asked the data: How are residents involved in their own care and what are their needs? Who else is involved in residents' care? What do they do? How often, when, and where? Is there collaboration among caregivers? What, if any, changes have occurred to resident health and convoy structure and function?

Begun early in 2015, these charts evolved over time, building cumulatively on previous versions with our lines of questioning derived from data in previous charts. Tables 11.2 to 11.4 illustrate the progression of charts from early drafts focusing on the structure and function of each resident's informal and formal networks to a final version summarizing individual convoys. These initial charts provided a way of sorting convoys based on structure (primary informal caregiver and shared informal responsibilities) and function (what support was provided by whom and under what circumstances) and ultimately facilitated axial coding (Corbin & Strauss, 2015), through which we related initial and other categories to each other. In these more sophisticated charts (Table 11.5), we separated resident convoys according to the structure of their informal networks. At this stage, we asked the following questions of the data: What are the primary resident, informal caregiver, assisted living setting, and community factors that influence care experiences and outcomes? What, if any, convoy collaboration occurs? What are the outcomes for residents, informal caregivers, and the care setting? Based on these tables, we noticed the centrality of collaboration, communication, and consensus, the basis for our convoy typology.

The specific categories ("cohesive," "fragmented," and "discordant") associated with our typology (Kemp et al., 2018) were developed cumulatively and iteratively over a three-month period of reviewing analysis charts and profiles, memoing, and discussion. Over the years, our analytic discussions have taken place individually and collectively in conference rooms, offices, homes, and over meals, tea, and wine, during swims and hikes, and while traveling. Venue changes facilitated the creative process, but also broadened the time we spent on analysis. And, our extracurricular activities were essential distractions when analysis became overwhelming.

Among the many lessons learned, we can confidently say that rigorous analysis that does justice to the data cannot be done quickly or be forced, but also that clarity sometimes comes outside of the office. For instance, our typology labels were drafted on a notepad during a brainstorming session while two investigators, Candace and Mary, were traveling by car, discussed at great length, and applied to a sampling of the data.

During the ensuing full-team meeting, Candace presented the typology and analysis charts and asked researchers to evaluate whether the categories were universally compatible with the data and exhaustive. Through negative case analysis (Corbin & Strauss, 2015) we sought out cases that did not fit our theorizing. All Wave 1 convoys fit the typology, but we engaged in considerable discussion about the static nature of a typology, opting to conceptualize categories as fluid instead. For example, although most convoys were "cohesive," at times they contained elements associated with "fragmented" or "discordant" convoys. It was important to note these non-cohesive elements and understand how, why, and with what outcomes change happened. Thus, we refined our typology to account for the fluidity of categories.

TABLE 11.2 Resident Role and Informal Care Convoy Structure and Function

Res/AL	Resident role/need	Convoy structure	Children	Siblings	Other family	Non-kin
Ted	IADL specific/low (finances); HC management/high	Non-kin 1 primary caregiver			Brother-in-law occasional SEM	Friend (L) Regular/Universal IADL, SEM Friend's husband Occasional SEM
Debbie	IADL need moderate	Kin/non-kin Shared responsibility Imbalanced	Son (L); Daughter 1 (L); Daughter 2 (L) Regular SEM	Sister 1 (L) Regular/Universal IADL, SEM; Sister 2 (L) Occasional IADL, SEM		Boyfriend (L) Regular SEM Volunteer Occasional ADL

Note. ADL: activities of daily living; HC = health care; IADL = instrumental activities of daily living; L = local; SEM = socioemotional.

TABLE 11.3 Formal Care Convoy Structure, Function, Transitions, and Collaboration

Resident	ADL need	Facility ADL role	Facility IADL/HC role	External HC care in AL	External care HC, IADL	Convoy transition	Health transitions	Convoy collaboration
Ted	High	Bathing Dressing Mobility	Meds Laundry HC mgt	Intermittent PT, speech therapy Podiatrist Nurse Practitioner– primary	Nurse Practitioner– primary Podiatrist		Hospitalizations/ acute episodes	Good collaboration
Debbie	High	Bathing Dressing Toileting Oversight	Laundry HC mgt		Neurologist Primary care MD	Attempts to shift responsibility from siblings to children	Cognitive decline	Some collaboration; Poor communication and response from children

TABLE 11.4 Informal Convoy Structure, Function, Factors, and Outcomes for Primary and Shared Convoy Responsibilities

Resident / caregiver	Resident factors	Caregiver factors	Primary facility factors	Collaboration	Outcomes resident	Outcomes caregiver	Outcome facility
Primary informal caregiver							
Ted/ Friend	Alert, pleasing personality Able to self-advocate, long tenure, multiple chronic conditions	Friend loves Ted and committed to his care; Ted estranged from daughters	Quantity and quality of staff Provides needed ADL care Availability and coordination of onsite medical care Long relationship with Ted	Friend communicates with facility and Ted's daughters Facility communicates with daughters Facility communicates with medical caregivers	Feels loved and supported by friend Would like to have better connection to daughters Ted passed away after health crisis	Friend feels rewarded by her care Friend not burdened but frustrated with Ted's daughters	No burden
Shared informal caregiving							
Debbie/ Son Daughter 1 Daughter 2 Sister 1 Sister 2 Boyfriend	Dementia, young age, unable to communicate, high ADL needs, disruptive behaviors, Past family relationships, limited finances	Employment, children young and reluctant to assume greater role; all live far away Parents older with some impairments	Lack of appropriate activities for residents with dementia	Limited communication among caregivers Sisters trying to shift responsibility to children Sisters communicate with facility but children not responsive to requests	Often unhappy and needs unmet Discharged for disruptive behaviors	All feel burdened with care role and unhappy with resident outcomes	Unable to manage behaviors

TABLE 11.5 Convoy Typology

Resident	Informal leadership type/ division of responsibility (structure)	Resident care needs and informal roles (function)	Resident, informal, formal outcomes (adequacy/outcome)
Ted Cohesive Convoy	One primary person (friend) in charge; she has some support from her husband. Communication is good among caregivers.	Resident has moderate ADL need and minimal IADL need. He can toilet himself and participate in management and finances. His friend handles all IADL and provides socioemotional support and some management. Facility staff handle needed ADL care. Health Care received on site.	Resident's needs are met and feels supported; caregivers do not feel burdened. Ted wishes he could see his daughters more.
Debbie Discordant and Fragmented Convoy	Convoy is made up of 2 sisters, 3 children, and boyfriend. Convoy has no real leadership. Minimal communication and collaboration among family members and between the children and staff. No concerted effort. Some conflict exists among family. Children unresponsive to staff requests.	Debbie has Alzheimer's disease and virtually no role in her care. One sister manages financial affairs, with help from the other. The sisters and facility push Debbie's children to assume more responsibility with limited success. Her sisters, boyfriend, and son try to provide socioemotional support. Staff manage care and provide some socioemotional support. Her parents never visit.	Debbie is frequently bored and would like to see her family and boyfriend more. Her sisters find caring for her stressful because of work and health problems and Debbie's condition; the children are distressed about her condition and have limited time to help. Debbie is discharged because of behavior issues related to dementia; this outcome might have been avoided with a more cohesive convoy.

Identifying our typology based on Wave 1 data was accomplished during nearly three years of data collection and analysis. Yet, the overarching story line (LaRossa, 2005) required further analysis and an additional three months. By looking at similarities within and across convoys and noting the experiences of and language used by key convoy members, through selective coding (Corbin & Strauss, 2015) we refined and integrated our concepts into a conceptual framework organized around our core category, "maneuvering together, apart, and at odds" (Kemp et al., 2018). This category was central to all the concepts identified in our analysis and offers a theory explaining how convoys negotiate the assisted living terrain.

Evoking images of navigation found in our data, our core category linked subcategories in our explanatory scheme to characterize the dynamic and variable patterns and processes associated with residents' care in assisted living. Our analysis showed that the care landscape was marked by continuity and change, predictable and unpredictable, requiring convoy members to negotiate care in an ongoing way. Yet each resident, convoy member, and, by extension, entire convoy acted under variable circumstances with a range of outcomes for residents' quality of care and life and ability to age in place, and their caregivers' quality of life.

Diagraming

Diagraming relationships among categories, concepts, and contexts was a major part of the final stage of our selective coding analysis (Corbin & Strauss, 2015). While attempting to finalize the story line for this analysis and identify the relationship among concepts and categories and integrate our findings, Candace began sketching a conceptual model by hand on notepads, recycled paper, her office whiteboard, and even on napkins and envelopes. Figure 11.6 is an example of these early drawings, which were eventually refined using Word's drawing canvas and tools (Figure 11.7). Candace solicited feedback in team meetings that helped finalize the core category and conceptual model. Email correspondence from Molly to Candace (February 7, 2017) on a later version of the conceptual model offered the following observations:

> In contrast to Jen, the non-circular format of "Maneuvering Together, Apart, and at Odds" does not bother me. I agree with Jen that you need some element of time. What about pulling out "Resident Stability and Change" and making "Stability and Change" a stronger concept in your model? I think we saw stability and change in convoy members both formal and informal. We saw it in facility culture, etc. That might give you your time concept i.e., if you do not limit it to the one box and just to residents.

SEE FIGURE 11.6 at eResource—Early Diagraming.

SEE FIGURE 11.7 at eResource—Later Diagraming.

In addition to showing how collaboration occurs, this communication hints that multiple, sometimes competing viewpoints occur within research teams and, hence, can create challenges. Much like the contradictory accounts within our data, we felt that differences of opinion within the team reflected reality and embraced them as part of the research process. Regular meetings and ongoing communication, including listening, were important team-building exercises (Hall, Long, Bermbach, Jordan, & Patterson, 2005) throughout data collection and analysis. Our project manager memoed that investigators fostered an environment where all members felt "comfortable sharing their analytic and strategic ideas, which results in better results for everyone" (October 9, 2015). Ongoing group thought and collaboration were essential to developing an in-depth and complex understanding of themes and patterns that crosscut settings, participants, and convoys.

Final Reflections

In teaching qualitative analysis, Candace uses an illustration of a magician pulling a rabbit out of a hat to introduce the fallacy of themes emerging quickly and easily from the data. In the end, as this chapter and others show, qualitative analysis, when done well, is enormously laborious. There are no shortcuts or quick approaches to quality analysis. Our colleague Patrick Doyle noted in a personal communication, "You have to dive deep to see what's on the other side before you can really understand." We wholeheartedly agree and acknowledge that there are multiple ways to *dive deep*. We hope that by sharing our ways, others can learn from our experiences, adopt or modify what makes sense, and ultimately develop optimal strategies for conducting qualitative analysis tailored to specific projects.

KEY WORKS GUIDING OUR DATA ANALYSIS

Corbin, J., & Strauss, A. (2015). *Basics of qualitative research: Techniques and procedures for developing grounded theory* (4th ed.). Thousand Oaks, CA: Sage.

This latest version of Strauss and Corbin's seminal work is essential to how we conduct our research and analysis. The authors define grounded theory, situating it within the broader qualitative research landscape, and offer a step-by-step explanation of how data collection and analysis inform one another throughout the research process. The authors provide definitions, detailed examples, and key resources throughout the book, including those related to sampling, coding, memoing, and the development of theory grounded in the data.

Lofland, J., Snow, D., Anderson, L., & Lofland, L. H. (2006). *Analyzing social settings: A guide to qualitative observation and analysis* (4th ed.). Belmont, CA: Wadsworth.

> This classic text is invaluable to researchers conducting ethnographic research. The authors lead readers through the research process from beginning to end, encouraging self-reflection throughout. They outline steps from detailed accounts of gathering data to thinking about or "focusing" data to analysis and writing. They address important issues such as researcher access, potential bias, thinking about fact or fiction, and pragmatic considerations of how to manage and prepare data for analysis. They effectively use exemplary ethnographic research to illustrate key points. Their approach underscores the importance of thinking flexibly and reveals the hard work of qualitative analysis.

Acknowledgments

Work reported in this chapter was supported by the National Institute on Aging of the National Institutes of Health (NIH) (R01AG044368). Contents are the authors' responsibility and do not necessarily represent the views of the NIH. We are grateful to all those who participated in the study and to our convoy of researchers, including Joy Dillard, Elisabeth Burgess, Jennifer Craft Morgan, Patrick Doyle, Carole Hollingsworth, Elizabeth Avent, Victoria Helmly, Andrea Fitzroy, Russell Spornberger, and Debby Yoder.

References

Ball, M. M., Perkins, M. M., Whittington, F. J., Hollingsworth, C., King, S. V., & Combs, B. L. (2005). *Communities of care: Assisted living for African American elders.* Baltimore, MD: Johns Hopkins University Press.

Ball, M. M., & Whittington, F. J. (1995). *Surviving dependence: Voices of African American elders.* New York, NY: Routledge.

Bengtson, V. L., Biblarz, T. J., & Roberts, R. E. L. (2002). *How families still matter: A longitudinal study of youth in two generations.* New York, NY: Cambridge University Press.

Connidis, I. A., & Kemp, C. L. (2008). Negotiating actual and anticipated parental support: Multiple sibling voices in three-generation families. *Journal of Aging Studies, 22,* 229–238.

Corbin, J., & Strauss, A. (2015). *Basics of qualitative research: Techniques and procedures for developing grounded theory* (4th ed.). Thousand Oaks, CA: Sage.

Hall, W. A., Long, B., Bermbach, N., Jordan, S., & Patterson, K. (2005). Qualitative teamwork issues and strategies: Coordination through mutual adjustment. *Qualitative Health Research, 15,* 394–410.

Kemp, C. L., Ball, M. M., Morgan, J. C., Doyle, P. J., Burgess, E. O., Dillard, J. A., . . . Perkins, M. M. (2017). Exposing the backstage: Critical reflections on a longitudinal qualitative study of residents' care networks in assisted living. *Qualitative Health Research, 27,* 1190–1202.

Kemp, C. L., Ball, M. M., Morgan, J. C., Doyle, P. J., Burgess, E. O., & Perkins, M. M. (2018). Maneuvering together, apart, and at odds: Residents' care convoys in assisted living. *The Journals of Gerontology, Series B, 73,* e13–e23. doi:10.1093/geronb/gbx184

Kemp, C. L., Ball, M. M., & Perkins, M. M. (2013). Convoys of care: Theorizing intersections of formal and informal care. *Journal of Aging Studies, 27,* 15–29.

LaRossa, R. (2005). Grounded theory methods and qualitative family research. *Journal of Marriage and Family, 67,* 837–857.

Lofland, J., Snow, D., Anderson, L., & Lofland, L. H. (2006). *Analyzing social settings: A guide to qualitative observation and analysis* (4th ed.). Belmont, CA: Wadsworth.

Maxwell, J. A., & Chmiel, M. (2014). Notes towards a theory of qualitative data analysis. In U. Flick (Ed.), *The Sage handbook of qualitative data analysis* (pp. 21–34). Thousand Oaks, CA: Sage.

Patton, M. Q. (2015). *Qualitative methods and evaluation methods.* Thousand Oaks, CA: Sage.

Strauss, A., & Corbin, J. M. (1998). *Basics of qualitative research: Techniques and procedures for developing grounded theory* (2nd ed.). New York, NY: Sage.

12

USING FAMILY-LEVEL DATA IN RESEARCH ON WORK-RELATED TRAVEL

A Multi-Tonal Experience

Anisa Zvonkovic and Andrea Swenson

Based on innovative work by Daly (1996) and Galinsky (1999) on families and time, we were interested in how time operated in families with specific work demands. The journal article (Zvonkovic, Swenson, & Cornwell, 2017) upon which this chapter is based is from the Work-Related Travel: Families and Health study, a multi-method project studying how middle-class families experience time when one parent has frequent absences from the household due to work (requiring them to be away from the household overnight for at least 20 nights per year). This large-scale multi-method project generated qualitative data from multiple family members, some of which is the focus of our chapter. In the title, we chose the phrase "multi-tonal" because we wanted to give voice to multiple family members within the same family, privileging the tones used by children in the family, including what they said and the emotions they described.

A team of interviewers traveled to families' homes throughout the country to provide an orientation to the project, conduct interviews of all individuals in the household over the age of eight, gather survey information on the same family members, and demonstrate the use and completion of daily diary surveys on personal digital assistants. Data collection lasted from 2007 to 2011. Data were gathered with the family as the unit of analysis, with the goal of gaining an understanding of time from all family members (i.e., mothers, fathers, children). The article (Zvonkovic et al., 2017) is based on interviews from 43 families who had at least one child between the ages of 8 and 18 living at home (161 individuals: 75 children and 86 parents). Following a feminist social constructionist perspective and using grounded theory methodology, we identified three main themes about the experience of time in families: (a) "We have enough time AND we want more time," (b) "I'm lonely, I'm sad, I'm excited my parent's back," and (c) "Sprinting or chilling through time" (Zvonkovic et al., 2017, p. 990). Main findings from the study included understanding how children viewed their parents' ability to navigate work and family to arrange family time and the emotional consequences of work and family for children. Parents and children differed on their experiences of family time and spouses differed on how they constructed family time. Parents focused on structured activities making the experience of time rushed, while children focused on family time being calm with unstructured activities, especially the ability to talk with parents. Additionally, children expressed emotions regarding time with family, whereas parents downplayed their children's feelings by not acknowledging how they felt regarding time or by discounting their emotions (Zvonkovic et al., 2017).

The Beginning of the Story

Data analysis began in the fall of 2012 with a five-member research team lead by Zvonkovic, the principal investigator. Three individuals on the team (Zvonkovic et al., 2017) led work and trainings, while the remaining two graduate students assisted in the coding process. All research team members met regularly together and were trained on the basics of qualitative inquiry for three months prior to coding data. Training included reading published works on the principles of qualitative research and coding, as well as meetings to discuss readings and engagement in practice coding. All team members were also trained on the qualitative data analysis software program MAXQDA (version 11).

During this process, we read through paper copies of families' transcripts and generated face sheets for families. Face sheets are a tool that we used to reduce the data in order to have access to demographic information and what families said at a glance. This enabled us to later direct our attention to reading in detail the interview transcripts of each family member. We then used these face sheets to guide first impressions during the initial readings of the transcripts, while maintaining reference to the whole family. The construction of face sheets was adapted from the type of demographic interviews a researcher would have collected during a door-to-door demographic data collection design. We iteratively developed what would need to be included on the face sheets based on our study design (e.g., family role, work role, which parent was the traveler), other emerging categories related to our sample (e.g., how family dynamics changed in terms of emotion based on presence/absence from home), and information from structured questions in our interview guide. Our face sheets guided the research team members to focus on specific aspects of time with family. These sheets also included sections for parents and children, in order to have an encompassing snapshot of the family. Figure 12.1 is an example face sheet.

SEE FIGURE 12.1 at eResource—Example of a Face Sheet.

The face sheet started with identifying basic information about the family (identification number, who was the primary traveler, if they were married and for how long, and the number of children living with them). Boxes separated the information from parents (although we sampled to be inclusive of all family forms, all parents in the sample identified as heterosexual, husband and wife couples; the same-sex couples had no children and therefore were not included in the analyses in Zvonkovic et al., 2017). Due to varying numbers of children present in each family, the bottom of the sheet was left open to provide room for all children's responses to be recorded. Research team members were provided with one blank face sheet per family to complete while reading. While team members were reading the transcripts, they were instructed to write initial thoughts and what they deemed important information from the transcript regarding how time was experienced. Because the interview specifically asked about pace of time, rushed and calm time (following Galinsky's [1999] work) were also identified as guided responses for the face sheet. The research team then met to discuss the face sheets.

After completion of the face sheets, Zvonkovic, Swenson, and Cornwell engaged in initial coding by hand using printed transcripts (Charmaz, 2006) to establish a common coding scheme. This process also allowed space and time to prepare for questions that could emerge during coding by all members of the research team.

Initial Coding

One challenge associated with interviewing and conducting a family-level analysis was ensuring that the developed coding scheme did not privilege one voice within a family over another in the analysis. To avoid privileging one voice, initial coding was conducted by selecting one family (two adults and one child; the Crain family; pseudonyms are used throughout). The team was provided with paper copies of this family's three transcripts and instructed to conduct initial coding by reading and identifying the main concepts that were addressed in parts of sentences, full sentences, or several sentences of the transcripts. For example, in explaining why time in his family was calm, the dad, Colin said:

> Because, I mean, it's, to me, it's, it's just natural. It's not forced. So, the time that I have with them is just, you know, your typical time of, you know, going out and eat[ing] dinner or wrestling around on the carpet or, you know, playing games or whatever.

This segment was initially coded as "calm, natural family time." The team met to discuss our results of the initial coding process and any issues that emerged regarding process and what information should or should not be coded. For example, we decided after this meeting that we needed to include a code for the individual

members of the family who were mentioned in segments of text, because sometimes a parent might mention a lot of contact with only one child, and we thought
we might need to retain that information in case two children in a family had different perspectives on their parent's use of time. The advantage of using this approach
for initial coding was the ability to begin coding immediately (directed content
analysis; Hsieh & Shannon, 2005), although this approach is less flexible from the
outset. This practice is also efficient when there are multiple coders. From this meeting, a draft coding scheme was developed, which is discussed in detail next. Using
the previous example quotation, the draft coding scheme included codes of "family
time," "calm time," as well as the target individual of family. We called it a "draft"
because it was intended to be revised if it did not capture what was in the transcripts
or if it did not suit the analyses we were to pursue. Additionally, during the coding
process, each team member was asked to keep a list of notes and questions that they
thought of while coding. These memos were recorded by hand, discussed during the
team meetings, and used to revise and inform analysis if necessary. Memos that were
discussed were stored in a Microsoft Word file as part of the audit trail.

Draft Coding Scheme

The larger categories of the coding scheme remained consistent throughout the
coding and analytic process. A list of coding rules was created during team meetings. Each team member received copies of the coding rules and a list was kept
near each computer in the laboratory.

The first category was the "target individual," which represented who was
being discussed. Subcategories included discussing family in "general," "mothers," "fathers," "oldest child," "second oldest child," and so on, and "social network members" (including coworkers, extended family, friends). For example, if
the mother was talking about her relationship with her oldest child, it would be
coded "mother" and "oldest child;" if the mother was talking about the relationship between her husband and oldest child, it would be coded "husband" and
"oldest child." This subcategory scheme was developed in order to keep track
of who was being discussed throughout the family. As a result of this process,
we were able to use this category and subcategories when we entered them
into MAXQDA later in our process. This allowed us to quickly retrieve data in
MAXQDA regarding children discussing time with mothers, fathers, siblings,
and so forth.

The second category in the coding scheme was "domain." Subcategories were
"work," "school," "child activities," "family activities," "dyadic intimate relationships," "childcare" (separated into "older children childcare" and "younger children childcare"), "household labor," and "solitary." While coding, the interviewees
were explicit in mentioning different domains influenced by time. For example,
in the Schnacke family, Sacha, age 13, discussed her mother being gone: "Since
my dad is in college right now, he has a bunch of homework and so he's trying
to do that. Usually I'm the one who does the dishes, and gets all the chores done,

make sure everyone's in bed, do the laundry." This section of text was coded in the domain of "household labor."

While coding for both "child activities" and "family activities," we realized there were many examples and stories told about these activities, and so we examined the nature of these activities in depth. We devoted meeting time to discussing these activities in order to ascertain if there were different types of activities that related to how families experienced time in different ways. For example, we noted that parents and children would talk about some activities as sources of rush in the family time pace, whereas other events were discussed as calm times, or at least with fondness for how time unfolded during them. This impression about different types of activities and time provoked us to write memos and we considered in our team process what the different types of activities were and what they meant to family members. In this instance, questions regarding the importance of the number of activities families mentioned, if the type of activity mattered or if there was a difference in view of activities by parents and children were asked.

After group discussion and looking through existing coded materials, a coding subcategory of "structured" and "unstructured" activities was developed under "child activities" and under "family activities." The discussion lead to the development of a coding rule to indicate that "structured activities" were any activities in which control over the activity was external to the family; that the activity was organized outside of the family. For example, team soccer practice, youth group meetings, and church attendance were all considered "structured activities" in which the time commitments were outside the family's control. Examples of "unstructured activities" included playing games together, siblings watching a movie and the father coming into the room and joining. In each of these cases, the time in which each of these activities started and ended was inside of the family's control. For example, Samantha Schnacke, the mother of Sacha, described her time as rushed, because

> "I think just having three kids you're constantly coming and going. They're all active and in events and we're active in church. It just seems like there is always something on the calendar to do so we're always going from one activity to the next."

This segment was coded as "child activities, structured."

"Emotion" represented another coding category. Emotions were the feelings that individuals had about the time and activities. We originally noted emotions people mentioned as they described the pace and amount of time. These feelings included "feeling rushed" and "feeling calm." During coding, the experience of "stress" and "feeling hassled during time" were added as subcategories. For example, Saben Schnacke, age 15, and the son of Samantha, described time with his mother as "very calm . . . usually when I'm talking to her, she'll be on the computer. If we have something to tell her, then she'll listen. She can stop what she's doing, and pays attention to what we say." This segment of text was coded as "calm" and as "unstructured child activities."

Other coding categories were developed and coded in transcripts but not included in our final article (Zvonkovic et al., 2017). They included "routines" (adult routines and childcare routines), "travel schedule," and "travel status." These categories were included to examine if activities and emotions coincided with routines within the family's day-to-day experience or based on the unique experience of travel within the family. The results of these analyses, although fruitful for aiding analysis, did not prove to be germane to the narrative of the respondents and their experience of family time.

At this stage, we imported the transcripts into the MAXQDA software program and now coded the transcripts based on the aforementioned coding scheme, which had already been transferred into the MAXQDA code system window. All coding was completed in the principal investigator's laboratory space on one of two computers that had the MAXQDA program installed. Two separate MAXQDA projects were created, each with identical transcripts and coding scheme so that we could compare the two independently coded versions. A matrix was developed that displayed how the coding was assigned to two different team members amongst the five team members (essentially ensuring that different pairs of coders worked on different transcripts independently). The final results were two separate MAXQDA projects in which all transcripts were coded once. In addition to being responsible for part of the coding, two of the researchers, Swenson and Cornwell, were present in the laboratory during coding to address questions that came up during the coding process. All of these questions were recorded by the team members and addressed as a group during the regular team meetings. Examples of questions that were recorded included: What should you code when the child says mom listens to me? Does stress equate rushed time? When children discuss playing together, is that child activities or family activities?

When coding of all of the transcripts was completed, Swenson merged the coding (although MAXQDA has different functions available to aid in analysis, we merged coding manually to ensure closeness to the data). Merging was conducted to ensure all potential codes were captured and to identify areas in which there were disagreement over coding. We examined codes one-by-one and compared how segments of text were coded in each independent project. Any conflict in coding was recorded in a Word document, including instances in which (a) a segment of text was not coded by one team member, yet coded by the other team member and (b) when the same segment was coded with different code categories. The conflicts were brought forth to a team meeting and a series of rules developed with the team to guide the merging of codes. A list of the rules was kept in a shared Word document, outside of MAXQDA. Because of the multiple coders, it was important to allocate time to discuss the conflicts in coding and establish rules that all coders could review. An example of a merging rule would be the coding of play dates and whether or not play dates were "routines," "childcare," or "unstructured family activities." In discussion, we decided that if play dates were not a regular activity, they would be coded as "childcare." We also considered daycare and preschool as "childcare" and not "school" due to the difference structure and form of daycares and preschool from school.

The Middle: From Coding to Categories to Analysis and Theme Development

Once the initial coding was complete, the team met to revise coding categories. Using MAXQDA's "retrieved segments" function, all of the text coded as a particular response was retrieved, exported into a Word document, and distributed to the team, which was now reduced to three individuals: Zvonkovic, Swenson, and Cornwell. In order to facilitate differentiation between subcategories, one category was assessed at a time. Figure 12.2 is an example of the document for household labor.

During this process, we discussed the cohesion of the coding and worked to reach consensus on what was occurring within the code category. We retrieved all of the segments for a particular code and exported the results into a Word document. Each person was provided a paper copy of all the coded segments for the code category being discussed. Individuals read through the codes, making notes on the meaning of the code. After reading through the codes individually, the team meet to discuss notes and particular text segments to reach an agreement on the definition and inclusion or exclusion of segments of text. In addition to notes about the definition of code categories, memos were recorded in Word documents while reading and as from the meeting discussions. These memos were used to inform future steps and analysis. For example, one memo read, "Explore families whose perception matches versus those who did not?"

Following code refinement, analysis moved toward assessing the research question and the relationships between categories. As discussed in Zvonkovic et al. (2017), this particular analysis was part of data from a larger project on families' experiences of work-related travel. Using the research question as a guide and our memos from earlier stages, we developed a chart to assess children's expression of what they wished for each parent, their experience of time with each parent, their perceptions of their parents' experience of time, and their experience of time with siblings. Using the retrieval and activation functions in MAXQDA, we retrieved all emotion codes. These were exported into a Word document in which the retrieved data were organized into a Word chart.

SEE FIGURE 12.2 at eResource—Example of Exported Retrieved Segments.

SEE FIGURE 12.3 at eResource—Section of the Children's Experiences Chart.

Figure 12.3 presents a portion of this chart. The first column lists the person's pseudonym. Age was included to be conscious of potential age-related differences between participants (important when using information gathered from child respondents, as older children's interviews could be more nuanced than those from younger children). Family demographic information included information on the work demand central to the study—who traveled within the family and how many children were present in the household. The next column identified whether *both* parents traveled for work (as compared to just one parent traveling for work). We knew we wanted these details about each family to be easily accessible when reading over the data in case they made a difference for the family experience. In qualitative projects in which the sample would be more homogeneous, such information might not be needed. We developed this technique because we kept having to look up which parent traveled, how many siblings there were, and so forth, while we were reading over codes.

The information that followed in the chart included summaries and direct codes about how time was experienced in relation to particular interview questions. These questions (from Galinsky, 1999) were chosen to specifically elicit information about family time and pace. Questions included: "If you were granted one wish to change the way that your mother's work affected your life, would you wish that your mother would spend more time with you, your mother would be less tired by work, your mother would be less stressed by work, or your mother would make more money?" This question was asked for both mothers and fathers. Children were also asked how much time the felt they had with each parent and if they felt their time with their parent was very rushed, somewhat rushed, somewhat calm, or very calm. Next were summaries of each parent's responses to time being rushed or calm (parallel to the question children were asked). The final column was for families with siblings. All children with siblings 18 years or younger were asked about their siblings and time with specific siblings was summarized in this column.

Through the use of charts, data were viewable on a family level, accessing the multi-toned aspects of our data collection method. As the example in the next paragraph illustrates, we would use the charts, write memos about what was occurring (on the charts, on sticky notes, and in Word documents), and go back to the transcripts and family to view the context of what was said. The use of charts forefronted the iterative process of grounded theory methodology (LaRossa, 2005). They required us to examine the code categories and bring the pieces together to understand the overall theme of the data. Through the use of charts, we were able to examine the different stories woven throughout all families.

SEE FIGURE 12.4 at eResource—Example of Identifying Agreement Within the Children's Experiences Chart.

To illustrate this weaving, we use the example of matching perceptions of time. As indicated in the example memo presented earlier, we wanted to probe what was occurring in families when there was agreement or disagreement in the experience of family time. To start, we developed a chart that included the perception of time by each child who was interviewed. This chart also included basic demographic characteristics of the individual (age) and of the family (who traveled, number of children in the family, frequency of travel). Figure 12.4 is a snapshot of this chart.

During the interviews, we had children identify specific responses to how they felt time with parents was and we asked them to expand on their answer. The chart in Figure 12.4 provides information on the responses the child gave to specific questions. Reports were included for perception of time with their mother, what they wished for their mother, time with their father, and what they wished for their father. Because there were a few instances of mothers who reported being a stay-at-home parent, we included a column that indicated if the mother participated in outside the home paid employment. Parents were also asked to specify their own perception of family time (mother's perception of family time and father's perception of family time). The last six columns document how many nights a mother's or father's average trip was, the total number of trips per year, and the total number of nights per year the parent was absent from the home for work. This information was included to be conscious of how the intensity of the travel experience may vary by family.

We used different colors to identify patterns within these tables. The yellow boxes indicate matches on quantitative categorization of time between siblings and between parents; blue boxes indicate matches in perception of time as rushed or calm, but not the degree. The color coding of charts enabled us to easier identify patterns of agreement and disagreement within families.

In the chart in Figure 12.4, agreement between the different family members is circled. This chart allowed us to easily reference agreement within a family. We then used the previous chart to trigger us to go back to the transcripts and attempt to understand, for example, within the families who agreed on the perception of time, what were their sources and explanations provided about their perceptions of time. For example, from the chart, we could see that both children in the White family (Whitney and Wyatt) agreed that their time with their parents was somewhat calm. We could also see that the father agreed with the children, time was somewhat calm; however, the mother viewed family time as somewhat rushed.

The main purpose of charts in our data analysis was to spark deeper analysis and to organize vast quantities of data (Charmaz, 2006; Miles & Huberman, 1994).

SEE FIGURE 12.5 at eResource—The White Family's Responses With Memos.

SEE FIGURE 12.6 at eResource—Example of Summarized Information From Charts Related to the First Theme.

SEE FIGURE 12.7 at eResource—Example of Another Chart That Informed Analyses.

SEE FIGURE 12.8 at eResource—Example of Large Scope Memo That Aided in Final Stage Analyses.

Given how many transcripts we had, we needed more summary information than might be typical for a qualitative study, and we wanted to always be sure to keep multiple informants from families at the forefront of our minds (rather than basing our analysis on individuals), maintaining the multi-tonal aspect of the data. From the charts, we were able to break down the quantity of information into manageable pieces and interpret them from a family vantage point. Moreover, these pieces helped us put information together and reassess to develop a coherent story of how categories were connected. To follow the White family, we then looked to assess how each family member talked about time. Figure 12.5 shows the first chart, including the Whites. Using this chart to provide context of the family, we read through the transcripts again and memoed to provide a holistic view of the family.

Throughout this process, we would constantly break information down and bring it back together. Some examples follow that highlight how we would reduce and bring information back to the theme level. Figure 12.6 is an example of how we compiled information related to our first theme, children endorsing having enough time while simultaneously wanting more time.

The next example (Figure 12.7) is from an earlier draft of the paper in which there was a heavy analysis specific to the travel condition. This table broke the information down into the number of coded segments related to the pace of time for specific travel conditions (being at home, preparing for a trip, and being away).

The final example (Figure 12.8) is from our memos that were larger in scope and pertains to how the categories fit together with each other. As can be seen in the memos, this information is at a higher level of abstraction than previous examples. The resulting themes presented in Zvonkovic et al. (2017) were the product of the iterative process described and feedback from informal and formal review processes.

We refer readers to our published paper in which we describe the development of the themes (Zvonkovic et al., 2017). In terms of how we chose to present the themes, one point that is worth making is how we chose the families to quote. Recalling that we wanted children's voices to be the centerpiece (because they are often missing in family research), we purposefully tried to select families in which there was at least one child who was particularly vivid in descriptions and/or articulate about their perspectives on their family. We want to emphasize that we already had our theme and our story line by this point, so the selection of quotes did not influence those elements. We generally selected families based on the way a particular child expressed him/herself, then we looked in the transcripts to see if the parents also provided useful quotes. We did several reads of the quotes we had nominated for use to be sure that they did illustrate what we intended to say about the theme, rather than just being a good story, or even being a vivid counter-example. Lastly, we did a careful read-through to be sure that we were not quoting any particular family too much, trying as much as possible to spread the quotes across families.

Revisions and Publication: Variations on a Theme

The last steps in our data analysis could be characterized as occurring after we thought we were finished with analysis. This detail is important to include here because it illustrates the role of colleagues in the iterative process of analysis. A first draft of the resulting manuscript was presented at the 2013 National Council for Family Relations Theory Construction and Research Methodology (TCRM) preconference workshop. We started with a presentation of how travel intersects with children's perceptions of parental time and then discussed differences within time, focusing specifically on "calm time" in families. We ended with a section on siblings, focusing on how siblings' perspectives can be quite different from each other. Based on feedback from the conference, we continued with analysis, further examining sibling relationships, exploring the potential for seasonality in responses (i.e., summertime as compared to school-year), and household labor responsibilities. For example, one aspect of feedback was that the sibling relationship analysis was incomplete compared to the other analyses in the paper. This feedback led us to further examine sibling relationships at the family level, examining the characteristics and family dynamics of the families in which siblings shared perspectives and the families in which siblings did not share perspectives. We reviewed information related to travel experience within the families, age and gender of family members, and birth order of the siblings.

After incorporating feedback, we asked a colleague, Abbie Goldberg, to review the manuscript. Dr. Goldberg made suggestions to further our interpretations and include specificity in the methodology section of the manuscript (e.g., including examples of coding). Specifically, she suggested that we clarify the focus on children's experiences while using a family perspective, enhance the connection to feminist theory, and think about potential reviewer questions such as "I'm wondering about social class, status of jobs, etc." (A. Goldberg, personal communication, June 13, 2014). We incorporated this feedback and submitted to the *Journal of Marriage and Family* in November 2014.

The first submission resulted in a decision of revise and resubmit. Reviewers suggested reframing and reprioritizing our findings in conjunction with the specifics of our sample (e.g., our sample was a relatively high-earning, highly educated group). Additionally, they suggested focusing on the stories families told of time together and the emotional experience of time. They also commented on the balance of space devoted to the three themes. The themes were then revised to demonstrate the connections between them while highlighting the disconnection between the children's pace of time and parents' perceptions of pace.

We eliminated a section on differing sibling perspectives. In retrospect, analyzing sibling congruence and difference in perspective was important to our analytic process, but not as important to the overall story line. A similar process occurred in our initial careful analysis of work traveler schedule. These analytical efforts, which ultimately were not a part of any published paper, are important to report. They were necessary steps we went through when interviewing families and reading over the interviews. They were examples of being "too close to the data" and needing separation from the data to construct the story line. Also, by presenting at the TCRM workshop and sharing a draft with an esteemed qualitative scholar, we were able to distance ourselves from the data and consider carefully the story we were telling and how readers would experience it.

We submitted the paper again for review in July 2016. The changes in the manuscript related to analysis focused on finding balance between the three themes (in terms of the length of each theme's section) and how we presented them in the paper. The balance between the themes was difficult because of being too close to the data initially. It was very hard for us not to try to present many details about the work travel experience, and it was difficult for us to take the role of the reader and remember how the story we were trying to tell was about family time. With the passing of time between when we conducted the analysis and receiving feedback from the reviewers, however, we found it possible to overcome these difficulties and to make these changes requested.

One recurring comment from reviewers was to expand on the children's experience of emotion. This theme was briefly mentioned in the first submitted draft, but the reviewers thought it was a unique finding and encouraged its expansion. After the first set of reviews, we expanded and revised how we discussed children's emotion in the second submission. We received further feedback on the importance and interesting aspect of this finding and were once again encouraged to expand. Much of the analysis between the second and third revisions surrounded the intersection of children's emotional connection to time experienced. For the final revision, we focused the story mainly around the emotions experienced as a family, which allowed the themes to cohere more than they had in previous drafts. Because we knew that one strength of the paper was the depth of the information we had from children, expanding how we wrote about children's emotions capitalized on the methodological strength of the paper. The final version was submitted in August 2016.

Concluding Reflections

As we wrote this chapter, we are attuned to the fact that we had too much data and that the 2016 journal article took a very long time to write. If we count from when the first interviews for the project were conducted, it took nearly 10 years! The project generated other papers earlier, but this particular paper saw print in 2017.

Most of our data analytic work was necessitated by the fact that we had too much data: transcripts of 161 interviews are not recommended for qualitative work. However, data from 43 families certainly sounds more robust than data from 10 families, and we encountered no questions from reviewers about the sample size. We would be dismayed if our sample size somehow figured into some sort of metric for the future; indeed, one of the authors of this chapter has published on the issues with sample size in qualitative work (Roy, Zvonkovic, Goldberg, Sharp, & LaRossa, 2015; Sharp, Zvonkovic, Humble, & Radina, 2014). The various steps we took to reduce our data and to discover groups of families were necessary because of the volume of data. We needed a way to highlight certain families, and then we read in depth the transcripts from all families members within those groups. We hope the steps we took will be helpful to future investigators, because there was not much available to guide us.

Another component of our process had to do with the fact that we used multiple coders. (Our doctoral program had a research team requirement for doctoral students and we allowed this project to be a choice for students. This team was the only qualitative choice available that year.) At the same time as this qualitative analysis, the principal investigator was also leading another team focused on the quantitative data from the larger work travel family project. Managing a large team focused on different questions and methods from the same data set (seven total members involved in at least one of the two methods used in the larger project), with different foci had its own sets of challenges. Had the focus been solely on one aspect of the larger project and the research team been smaller, a more structured set of codes that could be easily taught and more easily reached agreement on may have resulted. However, that would have limited the experiences available to students for learning qualitative research and limited the principal investigator's larger project goal in understanding the family experience holistically. In the end, however, we felt the team was effective in getting to a point where data from families were organized, flagged, and relevant segments of their transcripts highlighted, to allow us to target deeper readings of the families.

We also acknowledge the vital role of presenting our preliminary findings, exposing drafts to reviewers, and the iterative nature of writing up the article. While reflecting on the project as a whole, we do not think we were changed in fundamental ways through this analysis; we did not have changes in our understandings of our own family time. This could be partly because we were interested in the topic from the start and we knew that each family member might experience family time in different ways. As work and family scholars, we reflexively consider our own work and family lives routinely (for better or for worse). Oddly, as a result of conducting interviews for this project, two of the three co-authors traveled in order to interview families, so we were experiencing work travel ourselves during the data collection phase. Our interest in family time could also be because of our family developmental trajectories that were also changing during the course of the project.

The most vivid lesson we have learned is that each member of a family has their own story of their experience in their family. Most family studies research does not obtain information from all household members. Even if it does, it rarely has such information in a qualitative format. Data are not typically analyzed as a family unit, so we must take with caution what is said about family phenomena. If our paper and this chapter helps future scholars to conceptualize from a family perspective and to carry out qualitative analyses in that way, then we will feel the efforts we undertook were fruitful.

KEY WORKS GUIDING OUR DATA ANALYSIS

Charmaz, K. (2006). *Constructing grounded theory: A practical guide through qualitative analysis*. Thousand Oaks, CA: Sage.

> This book provided background knowledge on how to engage with constructivist grounded theory. We used this book for building our own knowledge of qualitative methods and in our training of research team members new to qualitative research.

Hsieh, H. F., & Shannon, S. E. (2005). Three approaches to qualitative content analysis. *Qualitative Health Research, 15,* 1277–1288.

> This article reviews three different approaches for qualitative content analysis: conventional, directed, and summative. The authors outline the purpose for these different approaches and provide examples of them in action.

LaRossa, R. (2005). Grounded theory methods and qualitative family research. *Journal of Marriage and Family, 67,* 837–857.

> LaRossa's article provides an interpretation of grounded theory methods and the iterative process of data analysis. We benefitted from his "tinker toy" model and we used this paper for our training so that students could understand the multiple steps and the big picture of qualitative analysis.

References

Charmaz, K. (2006). *Constructing grounded theory: A practical guide through qualitative analysis.* Thousand Oaks, CA: Sage.

Daly, K. J. (1996). *Families and time: Keeping pace in a hurried culture.* Thousand Oaks, CA: Sage.

Galinsky, E. (1999). *Ask the children: What America's children really think about working parents.* New York, NY: Harper Collins.

Hsieh, H. F., & Shannon, S. E. (2005). Three approaches to qualitative content analysis. *Qualitative Health Research, 15,* 1277–1288.

LaRossa, R. (2005). Grounded theory methods and qualitative family research. *Journal of Marriage and Family, 67,* 837–857.

Miles, M. B., & Huberman, A. M. (1994). *Qualitative data analysis: An expanded sourcebook.* Thousand Oaks, CA: Sage.

Roy, K., Zvonkovic, A., Goldberg, A., Sharp, E., & LaRossa, R. (2015). Sampling richness and qualitative integrity: Challenges for research with families. *Journal of Marriage and Family, 77,* 243–260.

Sharp, E., Zvonkovic, A., Humble, A. M., & Radina, M. E. (2014). Cultivating the family studies terrain: A synthesis of qualitative conceptual articles. *Journal of Family Theory & Review, 6,* 139–168.

Zvonkovic, A. M., Swenson, A. V., & Cornwell, Z. (2017). Children's experiences of time when a parent travels for work. *Journal of Marriage and Family, 79,* 983–1000.

13

AN ETHNOGRAPHIC ANALYSIS OF LATINO GAY YOUTH'S PATHS TO HOMELESSNESS

H. Daniel Castellanos

This chapter examines chief processes, strategies, and tools for analyzing qualitative data for an ethnographic study of the relationship between sexual orientation and housing instability among Latino young gay and bisexual (LYGB) men in New York City (Castellanos, 2016). Concrete examples illustrate how the analytical process was embodied in material practices in which textual sources were manipulated and textual analysis generated in a systematic iterative process.

The disproportionate impact of homelessness among lesbian, gay, bisexual, and transgender (LGBT) youth (Ray, 2006), the scarce qualitative research, and the sensitivity of the subject demanded an exploratory and flexible methodology. A central aim was to examine the role of family conflict related to sexual orientation in creating housing instability among LYGB men. I relied primarily on ethnographic methods to study social interactions and settings (Agar, 1996), and on grounded theory approach for guiding the data analysis (Charmaz & Belgrave, 2012; Corbin & Strauss, 1996).

Fieldwork was conducted for 18 months at a community-based organization (CBO) serving LGBT homeless youth and in social venues frequented by LGBT youth. Data came from three main sources: (a) research articles, (b) fieldwork (50 pages of fieldnotes and jottings from informal interviews with youth and staff), (c) recorded single semi-structured interviews with 14 LYGB men (368 pages of transcripts), and (d) multiple semi-structured interviews with five service providers (130 pages of transcripts).

I identified three main pathways to homelessness (see Castellanos, 2016). First, some youth became homeless after systemization in foster care or group homes resulting from family abuse and neglect. In the second pathway, youth became homeless due to severe family conflict rooted in cultural and religious views on sexual orientation, masculinity, and gender performance. The third and most common pathway occurred when sexual orientation was layered on top of pre-existing family conflict, creating *pressure cookers* that ended in the youth being kicked out or leaving home. Each pathway had concrete implications for future housing stability. Youth with fewer experiences of systemization and more stable family situations held richer social networks, stronger human capital, and more negative views on homelessness. They were also more likely to transition out of homelessness faster. Regardless of their pathway, most youth found a supportive and accepting environment in homeless networks that sometimes was hard to abandon.

The project embraced the dialogic nature of ethnography (Campbell & Lassiter, 2014; Tedlock, 1987) by maintaining concurrent comparisons between previous research findings (e.g., Lock & Steiner, 1999; Prendergast, Dunne, & Telford, 2002), the participants' understandings of their experiences, and my interpretations. Additionally, I used a flexible approach when selecting the analytical strategy or tool most appropriate to the analytical phase. In particular, I borrowed from inductive strategies of grounded theory (Charmaz & Belgrave, 2012) for developing analytical categories and domain and componential analysis (Spradley, 2016) to generate plausible causal pathways to homelessness.

Due to previous familiarity with ATLAS.ti, a computer-assisted qualitative data analysiS (CAQDAS) software program, I chose it to support the different analysis stages in a systematized, visible, and documented manner (Fielding & Lee, 2002). A variety of CAQDAS programs exist, including NVivo, ATLAS.ti, QDA Miner, and MAXQDA. These programs are especially suited for implementing strategies associated with grounded theory projects through extensive and systematic data management capabilities and strong semantic and visual analytical tools.

Data analysis was not a linear process but an iterative one that contextualized, decontextualized, and recontextualized past research findings, transcripts, and fieldnotes. Each iteration involved research material practices (e.g., coding) that produced material objects—new textual materials that can be communicated, replicated, verified, and contested (Denzin & Lincoln, 2000; Konopásek, 2007). Albeit more complex, arduous, and time consuming, these iterations resulted in a more rigorous, comprehensive, and detailed analysis.

This chapter's first section discusses data analysis as a process of data reduction and generation through concurrent comparison. The following section examines some data analysis methods, strategies, and related tools used to develop a conceptual framework of homelessness pathways among LYGB men. I end the chapter with some reflections about the process of analyzing qualitative data in flexible and multifaceted methodologies such as ethnography.

The Concurrency of Data Collection and Analysis

Data collection and analysis consisted of overlapping, iterative, and increasingly focused steps. Analysis of the literature, fieldnotes, and transcripts of semi-structured interviews guided later theoretical sampling, suggested additional questions, and outlined issues for triangulation and member checking. Conversely, the new data collected suggested additional, albeit more narrowly focused, analytical tasks and literature reviews. Within this approach, fieldnotes were both a data collection and an analytical tool (Bernard, 1998). Similarly, informal interviews and semi-structured interviews became increasingly responsive to the analytical needs of the project. Finally, rapid literature reviews were embedded within data analysis to explore themes and concepts.

Utilizing Fieldnotes as Primary Data and as an Analytical Tool

I conducted approximately 400 hours of fieldwork over a period of 18 months. Fieldnotes described my observations at public venues and participation in service delivery as well as notes from the informal interviews with youth and staff described earlier. The fieldwork products consisted of several small notebooks filled with handwritten notes. After typing and editing them in Microsoft Word, the resulting 24 single-spaced page document was added to ATLAS.ti for analysis.

Early in the project, fieldnotes were more descriptive in nature. Later, they became more analytical, resembling analytical memos and narrowing the boundaries between data collection and analysis. Table 13.1 shows two fragments of fieldnotes, one from the first month of fieldwork and another six months later.

Given that fieldnote taking is in itself a process of identifying, describing, and/or categorizing the phenomena observed, I skipped standard grounded theory coding when analyzing fieldnotes. Instead, I identified their importance to the research questions and coded overarching central themes. The result was a series of codes and analytical memos within ATLAS.ti. Table 13.2 shows a fragment of a memo after coding the fieldnotes.

Sometimes, early analysis of fieldnotes guided later data collection. For instance, fieldnotes and institutional reports revealed early on that a high percentage of clients served were African Americans as compared to Hispanics, the focus of this study. This information was used for tailoring later informal and semi-structured interviews with staff. The following are the fieldnotes from an informal interview with an HIV Counselor during fieldwork.

I ASKED S: How is that AA [African Americans] account for the largest percentage at the Center? According to S, who is half Mexican and half AA, most AA come from out of state (is the data kept somewhere?). He also reported that most Hispanics come from in-state (where?). He reported that young black men might be more transient. "Because they think it's easier to be homeless *and gay* in NYC, lots of AA come from the South, mostly from poor neighborhoods." Check migration patterns in the literature.

TABLE 13.1 Fragment of a Fieldnote

Fragment of an early fieldnote:

Space: [CBO] reaching out capacity; what happens when someone is waiting to come inside? Some people are requested to leave. No more than 20 clients at a time. Not allowed to hang out, clients must go to a group. How is that managed? It was decided that [staff's name] will take care of it by asking people to leave. However, last week it was said that it's better to get someone else to ask rather than a facilitator because it can change the dynamics of the group.

Fragment of later fieldnote:

Traffic control involves a variety of tasks geared to maintain an appropriate degree of flow of clients in the services areas. It includes allowing or restricting access to the site based on regulations and sanctions. [. . .] But traffic control seems fluid and subjective. A staff described to me how she had to develop a "feel for when the space is crowded." As she explained it, "how crowded the place is depends on how many people but also on who the people are."

TABLE 13.2 Fragment of a Memo and Related Memos

MEMO: family conflict: relation between sexual orientation and perceived gay lifestyle (Super, 2010–02–10 17:53:38)

[Related] Memos: ["being stuck" because of "gay lifestyle"] [conflict with parents over gay lifestyle] [Distinction between conflict over sexual orientation and sexual behavior] [. . .]

Type: Theory

[. . .]

Parents and their children might understand home conflict differently, often conflating issues of sexual orientation with gay-related lifestyle or previous behavioral issues. The actual event leading to the youth to leave home or the parent to kick him/her out might be confusing to both parties. [Staff] makes also a distinction between knowing that the child is gay versus assuming. In some cases, parents seem to know (according to the kids) but there is no overt conflict about their sexuality.

The concurrent and iterative analysis of fieldnotes and gathering of new data further allowed me to then conduct more focused semi-structured interviews. For instance, key themes from fieldnotes on the relation between gender performance and family conflict were later explored in subsequent interviews with the same or different people through informal or semi-structured interviews, providing me with a deeper understanding on the underlying social and cultural norms fueling parental reactions to disclosure of sexual orientation.

Interviewing as Data Collection Responsive to Analytical Needs

Ethnography makes it possible to conduct both informal and semi-structured interviews over long periods of time (Marcus, 1998), providing ample opportunities for theoretical sampling (Coyne, 1997) and triangulation and member checking (Golafshani, 2003; Leech & Onwuegbuzie, 2008). Therefore, analytical needs at the time of the interviews determined the interview script, type of interview, and time span between them. Over the course of the 18 months, I engaged clients and staff in numerous informal interviews. I also conducted single semi-structured interviews with 14 youth between October 2008 and February 2010, and multiple semi-structured interviews with five staff between May 2009 and February 2010.

For youth, the flexible interview guide consisted of open-ended questions on a variety of issues including family relations, gender and sexual orientation experiences, and housing instability. However, the final set of questions ultimately depended on the participant's specific personal history and the analytical needs of the project. For instance, after interviewing 13 youths, I asked a young man his opinion about other youth's reports of discrimination. I said:

> I have done some interviews with other youth. I want you to think about something that I've been told: "If you are not good looking, if you have a hard time with interpersonal communicating with people or interacting with people, you are too aggressive, or if you are too dark, you're going to have a hard time getting a place."

Rather than merely descriptive questions, I asked staff higher-order questions on a variety of issues to obtain their professional assessment of chief sources of family conflict and cultural factors shaping reactions to homosexuality. Conducting multiple interviews with staff over a long period of time allowed for triangulating and member checking/obtaining feedback on my analytical interpretations (see the following more detailed explanations). In contrast, because youth were interviewed only once, findings were later discussed with new interviewees.

The interviews were transcribed and added to ATLAS.ti in the original language (English or Spanish). On average, transcripts were 32 pages double-spaced for single interviews with youth and 26 pages for multiple interviews with staff. I created a one-page template for summarizing each youth interview and recording my general observations on the interview. This information was pasted into an ATLAS.ti memo, which was attached to the interview transcript (primary document). Although these summaries were often jotted notes, they were, in fact, one of the first analytical steps of summarizing and categorizing salient data. Table 13.3 shows an excerpt of an interview summary.

Interview summaries *held* the interview as a whole whereas coding *lifted* its parts into analytical categories. By going back to these summaries, I was able to test the typologies I was creating against the complete story of the youth. For instance, I compared generalizations about types of family conflict with concrete descriptions of conflict events to ensure that key elements of their life stories were present in these categories. Importantly, this tension between the particular experiences of the interviewees and conceptual typologies was, and should be, present throughout the data analysis process.

TABLE 13.3 Fragment of an Interview Summary

LYGM2 Summary

Born in NYC, 21yrs old, grew up in NYC until 15–16 when he moved to Florida. Finished HS and came back to NYC.

Homelessness:

Ran away at 18; before coming back to NYC, for four to five months; slept in park for a couple of weeks; moved in with friends; living in shelters for last two years; has stayed in many different shelters for long periods of time; doesn't like [CBO] because of early curfew; therefore prefers [another CBO]; kicked out by aunt because of lacking a job.

[. . .] Employment:

While running away, worked for church where he stayed. Worked later at video store. Unemployed but starting a new job at a porn store.

[. . .] Friendships and relationships:

Has several friendship networks that he taps into for support; short-term relationships with other guys at shelters; very active sexual life; stories of peer conflict (no physical)

[. . .] Comments:

LYGM2 seems to enjoy his time off from the expected responsibilities of education and employment in order to explore his sexuality and his connections with gay culture; he defines himself as "sexual;" his background and social networks are emotionally and instrumentally supportive. During the interview, he seemed comfortable but somewhat bored. He got excited when talking about his sexual life in NYC and his mischievousness.

Interviews played an additional role in the analytical process through triangulation and member checking (Golafshani, 2003; Leech & Onwuegbuzie, 2008). Early interviews with youth focused primarily on their experiences. In contrast, later interviews included questions seeking youth's perspectives on identified themes and, equally important, their reactions to my analytical interpretations. The following is an exchange with a youth on the connection between retention in services and compliance with requirements.

DANIEL: Some of the people I interviewed actually said the opposite to what you just said, that one of the reasons why they don't like [organization X] is because they treat you like a child and like in the army. You're telling me something else.

LYGM12: Okay, the reason why people don't like [organization X] is because if you're not working, you have to go to this little program that they have. They say you're supposed to do it. You have the option of doing it or not. [But] people have realized this because many people do not go.

Embedding Literature Reviews Within Data Analysis

Prior to data collection I conducted an integrative literature review, using 26 articles, to increase my understanding of homelessness specifically among gay male youth. Unlike systematic reviews, integrative reviews allow the inclusion of a variety of methodologies, empirical, and theoretical reports, and a variety of research questions (Whittemore & Knafl, 2005). They provide a broader and deeper analysis of a phenomenon and serve a broad range of purposes (e.g., intervention development, evidence analysis, concept review).

Simultaneously, I conducted a rapid review of the peer-reviewed (i.e., journal articles) and gray literature (e.g., institutional reports, policy reports) on explanations of youth homelessness regardless of sexual orientation. Aimed to obtain reliable but prompt information on a particular issue, rapid reviews focus on a few policy or practice questions, use broader search strategies, target reviews, and restrict the amount of gray literature (Grant & Booth, 2009). Equally important, I utilized rapid reviews to explore additional themes and concepts depending on the data analysis needs. The rapid reviews supported the analytical process by expanding, corroborating, or contradicting findings; furthering the understanding of a concept; or placing my analyses within a larger literature. These literature reviews often trailed the analytical process and, therefore, increased my level of confidence on the provisional conceptual explanations being developed.

The following is a quote from an interview with a staff that created the need for an additional literature review. In this exchange, I described three potential sources of conflict derived from the literature and the analysis: sexual orientation, behavioral disorders, and general family conflict. The program manager's response was:

> I think there is a lot of merit to that. If we look at where they're coming from, systemically, the vast majority of them are coming from homes that were unstable long before anyone knew of their orientation, or their gender identity. That right there is a big strike against them. They're coming from an unstable environment, family of a lower socioeconomic status, family members who might have been abusive or drug addicted or alcoholics, etc.

The analysis of this and similar quotes suggested the need for a longer-term perspective on family conflict. A rapid review of the literature led me to Cumulative Risk Theories and Risk Amplification Models (Nesmith, 2006; Whitbeck, Hoyt, & Yoder, 1999). In turn, these models led to a deeper examination of associated codes and the temporal relation of events (e.g., family abuse, truancy, family drug use), which resulted in the creation in Word of a homeless risk table along major categories of family disruption and conflict. Table 13.4 shows the final version of risk distribution along different dimensions.

In combination with the analysis of youth's narratives, the literature on family dynamics suggested that the conflict leading to homelessness was not a discrete moment in family life. Instead, family conflict accumulated over time and amplified the new conflict over sexual orientation, conflating, for instance, histories of truancy with engagement in gay subcultures.

TABLE 13.4 Family Disruptions and Conflicts

Family disruption, conflict	Total youth
Separation from one or both biological parents before first homeless episode	12
Severe home abuse or neglect	5
Ongoing family conflict (pre-coming out)	7
Involvement of foster care or Administration for Children's Services	7
Early home exit	5
Severe and primordial conflict over sexual orientation	3
Family conflict over gay-related lifestyle (explicitly or not)	7

Data Analysis Methods, Strategies, and Tools

Selection of data analysis methods, strategies, and tools was dependent on the stage of the study. Grounded theory was the overall approach for data analysis, and I therefore used the constant comparison method (Whittemore & Knafl, 2005) and its coding types (open, axial, and selective) to develop categories, patterns, themes, and variations. However, although providing a general framework for coding, grounded theory literature lacked good descriptions of the actual coding process—the how. Other authors of qualitative analysis provide better theoretical support and guidance to what open, axial, and focused coding entail, albeit under different names. During axial coding, Domain Analysis (Spradley, 2016) was utilized for developing categories and their relational networks. Finally, during selective coding, strategies from Componential Analysis (Spradley, 2016) helped develop the specific dimensions of particular pathways to homelessness. These strategies included discerning common and unusual patterns, clustering, outlining relations and intervening factors, and cataloguing intra and inter-group characteristics. The utilization of these strategies and associated tools resulted in summaries, code families (an ATLAS.ti term), memos, evidence tables, diagrams, and writing of findings.

Open Coding

Being the only coder and wanting full flexibility, I did not create a formal codebook before or after the open coding. New codes could be created at any time, and older ones were sometimes modified. Over time, the frequency and need for changes to the codes decreased. Overall, open coding consisted of three steps: fragmenting the interview transcripts and fieldnotes (referred to as Primary Documents in ATLAS.ti) into quotations; assigning each quotation one or more labels (codes); and memoing relevant insights about the process. In general, I fragmented the text into quotations based on semantic cohesion instead of syntax or length. In other words, fragments did not follow grammatical rules but instead fragmentation kept words together when they conveyed a particular meaning even if cutting across sentences.

Because quotations can, and often do, convey different meanings, most quotations were assigned more than one code. Some codes were a simple group of nouns such as family composition or employment history. However, as suggested in grounded theory (Charmaz & Belgrave, 2012), most codes utilized a syntactic construction (e.g., gerunds, action verbs, prepositions) that conveyed an analytical function (e.g., descriptive, process, relational, or social interaction). Table 13.5 provides some examples of codes based on their analytical function.

In some instances, I also created an analytical memo to capture the potential uses of a code, its scope, or limitations. Figure 13.1 presents the code "Accepting sexual orientation but not effeminacy" in the code manager, with a memo detailing its meaning and use (lower box), two quotations associated with the code (floating window), and the primary document with the quotation linked to the code (background window).

The creation of memos was particularly important for coding complex narratives or themes in need of further examination such as youth's descriptions of confusing social interactions with parents regarding sexual orientation. Figure 13.2 provides an example of quotations and the use of some of the previously mentioned codes.

Open coding took slightly different forms and functions throughout the project. After interviewing the first three youths, I open coded the transcripts in a flexible manner without major consideration to a potentially similar code. However, I chose not to use the constant comparison method with these first three interviews so that I had the maximum freedom to assign codes based on a flexible interpretation of each quotation. The result of the first code parsing was a significantly large number of codes (2250). Although the prospect of managing such an incredible number of codes sounds terrifying, it felt liberating to be able to make all kinds of associations without having to worry about fitting a quotation into

TABLE 13.5 Examples of Codes Based on Analytical Function

Analytical function	Code examples
Descriptive codes	"Family composition," "Employment history"
Process codes	"Migrating to NYC," "Returning home"
Relational codes	"Accepting sexual orientation but not effeminacy," "Layering sexual orientation on top of family conflict"
Social interaction codes	"Kicked out for being gay," "Staying with older man"

SEE FIGURE 13.1   at eResource—Screenshot of a Code With a Memo and Quotations.

SEE FIGURE 13.2   at eResource—Screenshot of a Coded Interview Transcript.

SEE FIGURE 13.3   at eResource—Screenshot of the Code Manager.

a pre-defined code. The process was also helpful later during axial coding, when I started reducing the codes into categories, because I had already a considerable number of nuances (dimensions) for these categories coded.

Next, I reviewed the code manager function (Figure 13.3 presents a screenshot of the code manager) to identify potentially similar codes, a process more in line with the constant comparison method. A printout of the codes and their groundedness (number of quotations associated) allowed me to compare the codes more carefully and then split, merge, or eliminate codes. For example, the initial overarching code "Concealing one's sexual orientation" was split depending whether it was concealed from the father or the mother. The split helped me examine the more positive reactions of mothers to disclosure as well as the youth's explanations for concealing information from fathers.

Although I paid more attention to existing codes when coding new interviews, I still used open coding for all of the interview transcripts, regardless of when the interviews had been conducted. The ability to create additional codes ensured that potential new themes were not ignored and nuances of meaning were captured. The presence of a new code signified the presence of data not previously captured in previous data collection and, therefore, deserving of particular scrutiny. After the codes became more stable, the coding process resembled much more a coding process that utilizes a codebook. In fact, grouping dimensions or nuances into a higher conceptual category constituted the beginning of the axial coding process.

Axial Coding

Although codes of higher order were identified early in the analysis, the bulk of axial coding occurred after conducting half of the interviews. I relied primarily on the strategies of Domain Analysis (Spradley, 2016) to identify higher order, overarching categories (i.e., domains or typologies), including constructing a taxonomy of subcategories (i.e., dimensions or components), fully defining these subcategories, and linking related categories. At the practical level, I used ATLAS. ti's CODES/EDIT FAMILY function for linking codes to create code families (a set of linked codes) and super codes (relational query combining codes). A code family retrieves all the quotations associated with the codes in the family. In contrast, a super code only retrieves those quotations that meet the conditions of a search expression built with operators such as AND, OR, NOT (e.g., all quotations coded with both code "Family conflict" AND "Disclosing sexual orientation").

Over time, the 2250 codes became a more stable list of 269 code families and 25 super codes, as fewer modifications were necessary and fewer codes added

SEE FIGURE 13.4 at eResource—Screenshot of the Code Family Manager.

(saturation). Because code families and super codes are not specifically attached to a particular quotation but work as a dynamic query of codes, they constituted powerful tools for developing categories and their dimensions, a central step in data analysis. Figure 13.4 provides a screenshot of the code family manager.

Extracting quotations across interviews using the ATLAS.ti managers for code families and super codes can facilitate axial coding, but I also often corroborated the appropriateness of the resulting categories by assessing whether these categories could be confirmed in the context of the transcripts and whether additional nuances had been overlooked. For instance, a youth described family support in these terms: "I still have a family support system that, you know, my father still helps me out. I'm not really on my own yet. He still helps me out, even though I'm not living with him." Within the larger context, helping out alluded to being able to visit his family and obtaining financial help. The result was linking the codes "Familial instrumental support" and "Familial emotional support" into a code family called "Family support system."

New interview transcripts, designed to elicit deeper insights, contained information that sometimes resulted in the modification of existing code families or super codes rather than the creation of new ones. To decide whether to create a new code or modify an existing one, I examined the code family's groundedness (number of quotations) and density (number of linked codes) through the ATLAS.ti code managers to determine the course of action. Over time the code families and super codes became more stable: (a) their distinction from other categories was easier to articulate (boundaries); (b) the components of the definition seemed sufficient and necessary (dimensions); and (c) they indicated how the components related to each other (relations).

In addition to creating code families and super codes, I generated a series of tables and diagrams displaying the relations between categories and analytical memos describing patterns, typologies, or dimensions. These tables and diagrams constituted the beginning of selective coding. Here, the use of grid-like instruments (Timmins & McCabe, 2005) was helpful for mapping relations between categories and dimensions across youths. I created evidence tables in Word and examined them in parallel with primary data analysis. For instance, Table 13.6 shows an excerpt of a table mapping out gay and non-gay related conflict.

Whereas open coding focused on single interviews, the reduction of codes into code families and super codes focused on comparisons between interviews to identify commonalities and differences. This move required a greater theoretical understanding of themes. Therefore, I utilized rapid literature reviews to examine relevant concepts and to compare the subjects' experiences with those youths in other settings.

TABLE 13.6 Examples of Evidence Table for Histories of Family Conflict and Homelessness

	Non-gay related conflict			Conflict over sexual orientation			
	Severe conflict	Kicked out	Run away	Out to parents	Supportive at time of disclosure	Kicked out	Left home
Agustin	No			Yes	No (parents)		Yes
Hector	No	Yes	Yes	Yes	Yes (parents)		Yes
Frank	Yes		Yes	Yes	No (grandmother)	Yes	Yes
Walter	Yes		Yes	Unspoken	No (mother)		Yes
Rafael	No			Yes	Yes (mother) No (father)	Yes	

In turn, findings from these literature reviews resulted in the creation or modification of analytical memos and tables.

Selective Coding

The final step of coding consisted of the analytical movement from descriptive and semantic to conceptual stories. The integration of concepts around core categories was done through selective coding—finding central, high-level categories that have analytical power to "pull the other categories together to form an explanatory whole" (Corbin & Strauss, 1996, p. 146). Unlike open and axial coding, selective coding started much later in the project after the major super families and super codes became more stable and rich with quotations and memos.

Word tables developed during axial coding were further advanced through the sparing use of componential analysis (Spradley, 2016). This type of analysis searches for attributes (subcomponents of meaning) associated with particular themes (domains) and outline the differences among the attributes. As seen in Table 13.6, I used this strategy to distinguishing among the different components of family conflict over sexual orientation (e.g., disclosure, source of conflict, and outcomes).

Network views (visual representations) of these relationships in ATLAS.ti helped establish relations between higher-order categories. Overall, I utilized network views only for major themes related to the central research questions (pathways to and the course of homelessness) and for a few major themes. Figure 13.5 represents a network view on the negative impact of perceived gay lifestyle on family conflict.

SEE FIGURE 13.5 at eResource—Screenshot of a Network View.

Although code families and super codes constituted theoretical categories, it was the creation of network views rich with codes, quotations, memos, research findings, and their inter-relations that provided the structure and content of theoretical findings. Furthermore, these visual representations allowed the texts to be readily accessible throughout the process. Clicking on an element in the network view displayed the actual quotations, primary documents, or memos. Having direct and rapid access to the actual quotation, for instance, served as a counterpoint to the theoretical developments, sometimes harmonically providing conceptual strength but sometimes dissonantly unsettling the theoretical arguments.

Memoing

The analytical material practices described previously (coding, categorizing, building explanatory models) generated a great level of textual data in the form of memos. In some cases, these memos included suggestions for reviewing a transcript, modifying code structures, or collecting new data. The systematic and iterative process described in this chapter also applies to memoing. Multiple rereadings and relistening of interviews throughout the project helped clarify early memos and resulted in new ones with deeper analytical insights.

ATLAS.ti provided great flexibility in the creation, manipulation, and categorizing of memos. Although all analytical objects in ATLAS.ti can include comments/notes, memos became more central as my analysis progressed from open coding to selective coding. Memos can be linked to specific quotations, codes, and other memos as well as embedded in network views. For instance, I utilized the "type" field to distinguish between memos that were summaries, commentaries, methodological issues, or theoretical insights to facilitate the retrieval and cataloguing. I also assigned memos a meaningful title related to the analysis in order to facilitate retrieval. Figure 13.6 shows a screenshot of a memo in the code manager with a linked quotation in an interview transcript.

Overall, I could distinguish three different stages for memoing, albeit not strictly sequential. At the beginning, memos were more descriptive, written directly in ATLAS.ti, and attached to quotations. Over time, they became more analytical. I wrote them in Word because of better editing capabilities but I uploaded them into ATLAS.ti, sometimes as a free memo but often connected to code families or network views. Finally, memos became longer, resembling theoretical insights explicating the experiences of the participants. Because these memos were more reliant on theoretical concepts than on particular quotations, code families, or network views, I wrote them in Word but did not upload them to ATLAS.ti. These memos were in fact proto-essays on particular research questions.

SEE FIGURE 13.6 at eResource—Screenshot of a Memo With a Linked Quotation.

Reflections

My previous experiences with qualitative analysis (Padilla et al., 2008) had included more defined and structured parameters, including formalized research questions, interviewing scripts, and codebooks. Given the flexible approach in this project, I found myself hesitating about the relevance of the interview questions to the overall progress of the project. I questioned whether to devote resources to member checking and triangulation, conduct additional tinkering with coding, or explore additional leads. Because I used a variety of methods and strategies, I also worried about selecting the appropriate analytical strategies to increase the plausibility of the arguments.

Deciding when to move from one stage of data analysis to the next constituted an additional challenge. Given that data collection, data analysis, and literature reviews were conducted simultaneously, the concurrent and iterative process felt overwhelmingly repetitive, chaotic, and onerous. I often wanted to push forward but I was afraid that by moving too fast through the analytical stages, I might overlook key outliers or underdeveloped themes. The ongoing and systematic documentation of the data analysis process, particularly through memoing, provided some solace to these concerns. In addition, I felt that the limitations of a particular strategy or tool were addressed through the use of a different one, increasing my confidence in the thoroughness of the analysis. Although the hesitation and uncertainty did not completely vanish, I felt more confident by ensuring tasks were implemented systematically and developing explicit criteria for advancing to the next stage.

KEY WORKS GUIDING MY DATA ANALYSIS

Charmaz, K., & Belgrave, L. (2012). Qualitative interviewing and grounded theory analysis. In J. F. Gubrium, J. A. Holstein, A. B. Marvasti, & K. D. McKinney (Eds.), *The Sage handbook of interview research: The complexity of the craft* (2nd ed., pp. 347–366). Thousand Oaks, CA: Sage.

This chapter illustrates how a grounded theory approach shapes the interviewing process as well as the data analysis. In doing so, the authors emphasize the flexibility of the data collection and analysis strategies and the inductive and iterative nature of grounded theory. In particular, they provided me with guidance for developing interview scripts that would elicit participants' own understanding of their experiences and for implementing theoretical sampling in order to address the data collection needs of the data analysis. Overall, this chapter made more concrete to me the praxis involved in adopting a grounded theory approach.

Leech, N. L., & Onwuegbuzie, A. J. (2008). Qualitative data analysis: A compendium of techniques and a framework for selection for school psychology research and beyond. *School Psychology Quarterly, 23,* 587–604.

This article provides an overview of the 18 most common methods used for qualitative data analysis, from word count to domain analysis to semiotics, including the philosophical or theoretical underpinnings of each method and strategy. In addition to providing me with core practical tasks, this article validated the utilization of multiple and diverse strategies during qualitative analysis.

Konopásek, Z. (2007). Making thinking visible with Atlas.ti: Computer assisted qualitative analysis as textual practices. *Historical Social Research/Historische Sozialforschung,* Supplement, 276–298.

This paper makes a critique of data analysis understood as "mental processes and conceptual work" (abstract). The author proposes understanding it instead as a material praxis, a set of material practices that are visible and traceable. Through a concrete discussion of grounded theory methodology and the utilization of ATLAS.ti, the author provided me with a deeper understanding of the material practices and products constituting the process of data analysis.

References

Agar, M. H. (1996). *The professional stranger: An informal introduction to ethnography* (2nd ed.). San Diego: CA: Academic Press.

Bernard, H. R. (Ed.). (1998). *Handbook of methods in cultural anthropology.* Walnut Creek, CA: AltaMira Press.

Campbell, E., & Lassiter, L. E. (2014). *Doing ethnography today: Theories, methods, exercises.* Chichester, West Sussex, Malen, MA: Wiley-Blackwell.

Castellanos, H. D. (2016). The role of institutional placement, family conflict, and homosexuality in homelessness pathways among Latino LGBT youth in New York City. *Journal of Homosexuality, 63,* 601–632.

Charmaz, K., & Belgrave, L. L. (2012). Qualitative interviewing and grounded theory analysis. In J. F. Gubrium, J. A. Holstein, A. B. Marvasti, & K. D. McKinney (Eds.), *The Sage handbook of interview research: The complexity of the craft* (2nd ed., pp. 347–366). Thousand Oaks, CA: Sage.

Corbin, J., & Strauss, A. (1996). *Basics of qualitative research: Techniques and procedures for developing grounded theory* (2nd ed.). Thousand Oaks, CA: Sage.

Coyne, I. T. (1997). Sampling in qualitative research: Purposeful and theoretical sampling; merging or clear boundaries? *Journal of Advanced Nursing, 26,* 623–630.

Denzin, N. K., & Lincoln, Y. S. (Eds.). (2000). *Handbook of qualitative research* (2nd ed.). Thousand Oaks, CA: Sage.

Fielding, N. G., & Lee, R. M. (2002). New patterns in the adoption and use of qualitative software. *Field Methods, 14*, 197–216.

Golafshani, N. (2003). Understanding reliability and validity in qualitative research. *The Qualitative Report, 8*, 597–607.

Grant, M. J., & Booth, A. (2009). A typology of reviews: An analysis of 14 review types and associated methodologies. *Health Information & Libraries Journal, 26*, 91–108.

Konopásek, Z. (2007). Making thinking visible with Atlas.ti: Computer assisted qualitative analysis as textual practices. *Historical Social Research/Historische Sozialforschung* (suppl), 276–298.

Leech, N. L., & Onwuegbuzie, A. J. (2008). Qualitative data analysis: A compendium of techniques and a framework for selection for school psychology research and beyond. *School Psychology Quarterly, 23*, 587–604.

Lock, J., & Steiner, H. (1999). Gay, lesbian, and bisexual youth risks for emotional, physical, and social problems: Results from a community-based survey. *Journal of the American Academy of Child & Adolescent Psychiatry, 38*, 297–304.

Marcus, G. E. (1998). *Ethnography through thick and thin.* Princeton, NJ: Princeton University Press.

Nesmith, A. (2006). Predictors of running away from family foster care. *Child Welfare, 85*, 585–609.

Padilla, M., Castellanos, D., Guilamo-Ramos, V., Reyes, A. M., Marte, L. E. S., & Soriano, M. A. (2008). Stigma, social inequality, and HIV risk disclosure among Dominican male sex workers. *Social Science & Medicine, 67*, 380–388.

Prendergast, S., Dunne, G. A., & Telford, D. (2002). A light at the end of the tunnel? Experiences of leaving home for two contrasting groups of young lesbian, gay and bisexual people. *Youth & Policy, 75*, 42–61.

Ray, N. (2006). *Lesbian, gay, bisexual and transgender youth: An epidemic of homelessness.* Retrieved from National Gay and Lesbian Task Force Policy Institute and the National Coalition for the Homeless http://www.thetaskforce.org/lgbt-youth-an-epidemic-of-homelessness/

Spradley, J. P. (2016). *The ethnographic interview* (Reissue ed.). Long Grove, IL: Waveland Press.

Tedlock, D. (1987). Questions concerning dialogical anthropology. *Journal of Anthropological Research, 43*, 325–337.

Timmins, F., & McCabe, C. (2005). How to conduct an effective literature search. *Nursing Standard, 20*(11), 41–47.

Whitbeck, L. B., Hoyt, D. R., & Yoder, K. A. (1999). A risk-amplification model of victimization and depressive symptoms among runaway and homeless adolescents. *American Journal of Community Psychology, 27*, 273–296.

Whittemore, R., & Knafl, K. (2005). The integrative review: Updated methodology. *Journal of Advanced Nursing, 52*, 546–553.

SECTION II
Dialogues

14

DIALOGUE ABOUT ARTS-BASED RESEARCH

*Gwen Katheryn Healey, Evonne Miller, and
Marcus B. Weaver-Hightower*

How did you first encounter arts-based approaches to analysis? What drew you to this approach?

GWEN: In the Inuit worldview, knowledge and understanding come from many sources. It comes via our relationships with the animal, human, and spirit worlds, and from the environment around us. Knowledge and understanding can be derived through dance, music, or the creation or making of something— from using our voices or making things with our hands. Although *arts-based approach* doesn't feel like what I am describing, I believe the theoretical underpinnings are the same—that there are a diversity of ways in which we can come to know and understand a phenomena including through art- and music-making. When I pause and reflect, I believe that growing up in an Inuit community and being immersed in Inuit epistemology have influenced my natural inclination toward arts-based methods.

MARCUS: I grew up in the Southern United States, a region very different from Gwen's Inuit community in climate and culture. The South is not revered for its artistic sensibilities, though it does have a literary tradition (Faulkner, Welty, O'Connor) that, as a teenager, I discovered accidentally in searching my parents books locked away in the attic. Rather than nudie magazines, my parents hid away literature! I did, though, come of age in a family with artistic sensibilities. My aunt was a artist, my mother a voracious reader, and my father a gregarious storyteller in the way only a local politician and businessman can be. My brother and I were fed a steady diet of comic books and science fiction movies. I missed all of these things as a young high school teacher and then graduate student, so arts-based research was a revelation to me, something that called to me before I even knew it existed. It was a means of reconnecting with parts of myself and my brain that I had let atrophy so that I could become a *serious scholar*. Once I began to read more about the research applications of poetry, comics, drama, and especially autoethnographic writing, there was no way I could stop.

EVONNE: My background and experience is very different from the two of you. I grew up on a farm, in rural New Zealand, with no exposure to the creative arts, expressive, or arts-based analysis. My PhD was in experimental social psychology, at a very traditional university with a focus on quantitative analysis, randomized control trials, and hard data. In fact, I vividly remember sharing this dismissive view of qualitative research in an undergraduate consumer behavior class. Later, we designed and implemented a small qualitative interview study. This first-hand experience of *doing* qualitative research was transformative. All of a sudden, I realized that my positivist psychology professors (who privileged quantitative research, experimental designs, and the scientific method over other forms of enquiry, epistemologies, methodologies, and methods) were wrong: there was significant value in qualitative research, which amplified the voice and lived experience of participants. I have been an advocate for qualitative research ever since, moving away from hard-core experimental psychology towards arts-based qualitative approaches. Yet, I only stumbled across research poetry five years ago, when I was reading an issue of *Qualitative Inquiry*. It immediately intrigued me. The honest emotion and portrayal of the lived experience was so heartfelt and engaging, truly enabling a reader to *feel* the research findings. I wondered if I could do that with my research data, and started experimenting with creating poems (or poem-like prose) from my interview transcripts. I loved this immersive creative process, and took great joy in crafting an emotive and engaging poem from interview data. As well as greatly enjoying the poem creation process, I realized that research poetry is a wonderfully creative, novel, and impactful way to engage the broader community with research findings.

How has the process of analyzing and thinking about your data been enhanced or hindered by approaching it from an arts-based perspective?

GWEN: I believe that it has enhanced the findings. Different research approaches can be more or less appropriate for different communities, cultural groups, and linguistic groups. Inuktitut, for example, is a language that is inherently action-oriented. Philosophical and theoretical concepts are presented in a tense of *doing*. Therefore, a research method that involves doing, crafting, or making things aligns well with how concepts and ideas would be conveyed by research participants who communicate in that language. Those ideas don't translate the same way in English if one doesn't understand the nature of the interpretation that is required. Therefore, I think the use of diverse methodologies can help us, as researchers, collect better, more accurate information, which help us to understand the phenomena under study.

MARCUS: Gwen, your way of putting it is perfect. Once you have been a maker, you think like a maker, in languages (even if the words are in English) that only a maker can understand. It gives me voices for conveying ideas that I can't say in words. I don't think I would use arts-based approaches if I thought they hindered my analysis; indeed, I still go back to academic prose frequently when that's the best approach. I save arts-based methods for when they have something to contribute; those methods are not appropriate for every situation, just as academic prose isn't appropriate for every situation.

EVONNE: Engaging with research poetry has really enriched my analysis, as the poem creation process forces me to consciously think deeply and slowly about each word, each sentence, the structure, and the overall core narrative. In poetry, less is more. Each word is chosen deliberately, with thought. It is a different and slower way of approaching data and the world. Of course, as both of you remind us, arts-based approaches are not always appropriate for every research project. Yet, having arts-based methods, ways of thinking and approaching a problem in our research toolkit has made me a better, more reflective, and thoughtful researcher.

What have been the challenges to you in framing your scholarly work in this way? In particular, how has the choice of an unconventional way of analyzing and presenting your work been received by others (e.g., mentors, colleagues, reviewers, editors)?

GWEN: My greatest challenge has been to explain this approach in mainstream academia. Researchers who don't work in this paradigm or don't understand it, don't approve of it. This makes publishing and peer review a difficult process. I just keep trying, keep writing, keep talking—that is all we can do. Never give up.

MARCUS: Gwen, your experience seems very familiar, perhaps to all of us. I always feel sheepish, almost silly, when I tell people that I work with comics or that my articles are about my own experiences. Thankfully, an ever increasing number of people tell me they think it sounds *cool*. Perhaps they are just being kind, but I find an ever-expanding number of people actually doing this work now, as well. The family of arts-based researchers, particularly in my field of education, has grown by leaps and bounds over the past 20 years. You're right, too, that publishing and peer review continue to be problematic. The venues for arts-based research, though more numerous than years past, are still pretty limited. Good editors seek out reviewers with the appropriate expertise, but it's still common to run into reviewers that have no idea what to make of arts-based research. For my work in comics, too, the peer review process has been challenging because it's difficult to make revisions to art without significant time investments; you can't just add or delete a panel here or there without screwing up the entire layout. And academic journals don't know fundamental things that a comic artist must be told, like how big the artwork should be to fit the page. But at least my comics work is printed on the page; I feel for those artist-researchers whose work is ephemeral, like drama or music, for academia still doesn't know how to assess or credit performative work.

EVONNE: Like both of you, I think that the most challenging part of doing non-traditional arts-based research is fear about what others might think and say. This is particularly true for me, coming from a quantitative psychology background. Thus, I think it is really important to believe in the value and impact of your work. Right from the beginning, I was concerned that my poems were not good enough and that I did not know enough about poetry to write a poem! So, I consciously took steps to improve my skills. As well as reading poetry, I reached out to a renowned poet at our institution who kindly met with me and was keen to collaborate on a found poetry project. Her enthusiasm and positive feedback on the poems I crafted gave me the confidence to keep experimenting. Additionally, the reactions of audience members (from exhibitions and conferences) keeps me inspired. I find that people respond, in a very real way, to the shared human experience in a poem. Of course, publishing and peer review is not an easy process. But it never is, regardless of whether you are using arts-based methods or not. I am consciously pragmatic, using research poetry more in exhibitions and conference presentations than publications. Overall, however, I have found reviewers and editors generally receptive to this more unconventional way of analyzing and presenting work.

What advice would you give others who are interested in conducting arts-based research?

EVONNE: In terms of first steps for novices, I would recommend two steps. First, actively engage with the literature in this space (a good starting resource is Leavy, 2009). Second, *dive in* and start experimenting with research poetry. Take an old interview transcript, and try to compose a research poem by rearranging the words in poetic form. For me, the poem creation process was immediately challenging, enjoyable, and addictive.

Reference

Leavy, P. (2009). *Method meets art: Arts-based research practice*. New York, NY: Guilford Press.

Recommended Reading

Wilson, S. (2008). *Research is ceremony: Indigenous research methods*. Halifax, NS: Fernwood.

15

DIALOGUE ABOUT REFLEXIVITY

Katherine R. Allen, Bethany L. Letiecq, Karen A. Roberto, Paul C. Rosenblatt, and Elizabeth Wieling

How did you handle your social location and/or personal experience with the subject of the study? How did you handle being too close or too far away from the subject matter? Why did you choose to approach it in this way?

KATHERINE: Our study of older women with gynecological cancer was inspired by my personal experience of my own mother's diagnosis and death from ovarian cancer at age 75. Her cancer experience was always in the forefront of the study and was actually the catalyst that led Karen to suggest I pursue it. My mother's cancer experience provided a vivid touchstone that alerted me to the fact that the women I interviewed each had a unique and powerful story to tell, and my primary role was to listen well—from the head and from the heart. My insider's knowledge about gynecological cancer in a family context helped to sensitize me to the fact there would be many aspects of the women's stories that would be surprising. Indeed, my own mother had gone from being a very vigorous woman who was still working full time until the day she entered the hospital to her death just a few weeks later and this transformation was a reminder that I needed to keep the women's stories in the forefront and not *lead* the interviews with too many predetermined questions. Thus, I entered the field with a deep insider's knowledge of the experience, but I also bracketed it so that the focus would be on the women's experiences and not my own.

KAREN: I have always been drawn to understanding how older women manage chronic health conditions in every day, plus the opportunity to continue to work with Katherine, made pursing this research project a natural fit for me both professionally and personally. Although I had assumed a leading role in the Appalachian Cancer Community Network (ACCN), to engage in a study of cancer survivorship among older women was a new opportunity for me to extend my research agenda. The ACCN promoted, facilitated, and engaged in excellent cancer prevention programs and research within rural communities; yet, I often felt that the voices of older cancer survivors were not sought out or were overlooked. This project gave me an opportunity to learn from the experiences of the older women interviewed as well as to *push* an aging agenda within a larger network of research and practice.

LIZ: While intimacy in couple relationships is an integral topic in my work as a couple and family therapist, conducting a research study on intimacy was a new adventure. I had the privilege of embarking on this study with a dear colleague with whom I felt comfortable being vulnerable (even when it meant being emotionally exposed). Throughout the process I was humbled by the range of experiences that women, in particular, shared about a romantic loved one—accounts that were both heart-wrenching and inspirational. I was in my 30s at the time and also in an impossibly difficult romantic relationship. I resonated with some of the stories, feared others, and understood that there were certain paths that I wanted to try to avoid. Paul and I were committed to debriefing our understanding of the experiences that were shared and also made time to talk about the areas that touched us personally. This is a critical part of interrogating ourselves and attempting to uphold personal and professional integrity.

BETHANY: I really resonate with all of your reflections here. Conducting in-depth interviews across languages and cultures and with highly vulnerable and marginalized women (in this case, undocumented Central American mothers residing in an immigrant enclave in Northern Virginia) added complexity to my process as an interviewer. I found myself reliant on and trusting in my interpreter, Marlene (who became a co-interviewer) to help us gain entry, build mutuality and trust, and foster a safe space with the study participant. Over the course of the study, Marlene and I became very close and learned each other's style. With a glance, Marlene could signal to me that I could ask certain questions or should refrain from delving too deeply and risking disconnection. We were a team, and we had to navigate our locations together. For example, Marlene was younger than most study participants and was deferential and respectful. As an *older* woman in my late 40s, a mother, and an outsider, I could probe about relational intimacies or other sensitive topics and Marlene could shift to *my interpreter* as cover for her positionality so she would not be viewed as discourteous. We often jockeyed our positions as necessary to keep moving through an interview. This process was not always purposeful, but we've since talked about how valuable it was to our success in securing interviews and moving through often difficult subject matter (e.g., victimization, trauma exposures, fear, loss). Marlene and I also spent time debriefing post-interviews about not only what we experienced during the interviews, but also how stories related to our own histories of trauma and loss. Marlene was instrumental in helping me better understand the nuances at play during the interview or where I may have overstepped or misunderstood a part of the conversation. During those debriefs, we supported each other as we unpacked what we were hearing and witnessing—often incredible traumas, hardships, and injustices that were heart-wrenching. This work was/is humbling and I am constantly reminded of my privilege, the strength, courage, and resilience of the women who opened their homes and hearts to us, and our common humanity.

PAUL: One thing Katherine's paragraph stimulates me to say is that most of the qualitative research I have done has been about topics that were deeply important to me and/or to my collaborators. So I have lots of experience with bracketing my self issues in order to focus on the voices of the people interviewed and to respect and understand their realities. And I echo what Liz wrote. I could only do the study because Liz and I have collaborated for years, trust each other, and are on the same page about many things, so it was for me a safe, easy, and intellectually stimulating collaboration in which to handle my social location and self issues. Like Karen wrote about working with Katherine, I welcomed working with Liz and included in that was trusting her processes with herself and with me at relating to our personal connections with the issue and handling those connections optimally. And what Bethany wrote stimulates me to say that for me the issues of being too close or too far from the topic are entangled in gender and age. I think we only could achieve the quality of interviews we achieved because we differ in gender and age. Our differences were crucial, I think, particularly in our shared interviewing.

KATHERINE: I completely agree with the reflections and insights shared by all of you. And what I think is remarkable is that all of us are engaged in collaborative work, joining forces with others who bring both shared and distinct expertise to the research project, making it all the more valuable. For Karen and me, our shared passion in studying family relationships in later life, and particularly through the lens of older women, brought a synergy of intellectual curiosity and friendship that was so empowering. Karen's insider's knowledge and expertise in working with the ACCN on cancer research and programming freed me up to focus intensely with the women I interviewed.

What responsibility does the researcher have to the data, reader, etc. When it comes to identifying or not identifying his/her social location?

BETHANY: In our case, I think it is essential to identify social location variables. Using a community-based participatory research approach in partnership with our advisory board members (*Amigas de la Comunidad*), we attempt to foster community engagement and leadership across all aspects of the project because we acknowledge that our positionality (vis-à-vis nationality, ethnicity, race, social class, educational access, legal status, opportunity structure, etc.) may not be aligned with the interests or experiences or *truths* of the participants or readers. By essentializing social location variables, we are searching for new meanings, shared meanings—we are hoping to facilitate voices that have yet to be heard in many family science circles—and working to reconceptualize knowings from different vantage points. This process necessitates critical consciousness raising, reflexivity, and cultural humility. Moreover, by exposing my social location and my lack of knowledge about another's experiences, I am trying to humble myself to the community I wish to serve, to foster vulnerability, and shift power such that the study participant is owner of her story . . . the community is owner of their data and how it is disseminated and who benefits most pointedly.

LIZ: Bethany, I resonate deeply with your reflections regarding social location. One of the responsibilities I often ponder is how to navigate the multiple identities I hold and the identities that others might place on me, regardless of whether or not I see myself that way. For example, I identify as an economically privileged multiethnic woman of color. I was born in the United States and raised in Brazil. I hold a feminist, critical, postmodern position as a social scientist. Much of my work in the United States involves addressing social justice and mental health disparities, particularly for immigrant and refugee populations affected by traumatic stress. I have observed that the communities I work with tend to either over- or under-identify with me as a member of their own group (e.g., Latina, immigrant) leading to important ethical implications throughout the research process and ongoing community engagement efforts. The project I worked with Paul on intimacy in couple relationships did not evoke as many of these overt emic/etic issues for me, but I know they are always at play and indeed it takes skill and humility to navigate the intersectionalities.

KATHERINE: Claiming my subjective position is an essential part of the feminist research process I have practiced over many decades. Just as Bethany and Liz describe, I feel a tremendous responsibility to grapple with how my positions of privilege structure what I am able to *see* and *hear* when interviewing, observing, or analyzing others' experiences. At the same time, staying open and raw to the ways I am vulnerable and disempowered help me to listen for strength, resilience, and new insights even in circumstances that can be demoralizing or distressing to those who have let me into their lives. One of the silent mantras that I repeat to myself as I'm interviewing others is, "what is something about my own life that I would be ashamed or upset if my participant knew?" This serves as a reminder not to make too many presumptions about the experiences of others, but to stay open to the fact that if I'm open, transparent, and *empty* of presumption, I might just be able to bear witness to the experiences they share with me. So, I am always willing to reveal my social locations and intersections in personal and professional settings, and typically write about my life, but it is not always necessary or warranted to do so. All that is necessary might just be the *willingness* to share, if asked or if the situation calls for it. Getting out of my own way has been a hard lesson to learn, and sometimes this means just staying raw, transparent, and ready, but still not making it *about me*. My work has been highly influenced by feminist ethnographers in the late 20th century. For example, Susan Krieger's (1991) essay, "The vulnerability of a writer" in her brilliant book, *Social Science & the Self*, deconstructs the traditional scientific belief that the self is a "contaminant," and she reveals through excruciatingly honest, even painful, prose how powerful it can be to bring one's "self" out of hiding and into our autobiographical and scientific work. Although, as I have experienced, such revelations can make others squirm, they can also open new doors of understanding and insight.

PAUL: When Liz and I were processing each interview, analyzing our interview material, and writing we often addressed our social location issues as they related to our interviewing, our interviewees, and the material people had provided to us. There were issues of gender constantly in play, and there were also issues of sexual orientation, race, culture, privilege, and generation to explore. And yet I agree with what Liz wrote that social location issues were not as intrinsic to this study as it usually is in her research and mine. I think partly it is that with the exception of gender not many interviewees talked about their social location or addressed ours. The interviews focused on a key intimate relationship in their lives, and I think that focus often took them out of the larger society in which social location is so important. That was so even for interviewees who talked about a cross-cultural or interracial relationship. I also think that we had hopes of reaching an audience in social psychology in which issues of researcher social location are often not written about, and that limited how much we addressed social location in what we wrote.

KAREN: The response of each of you is a powerful reminder of the importance of recognizing social location as a two-way street in the research process. The information the women shared with Katherine about their experience with cancer provided the context for every aspect of their lives. As I read through the transcripts and discussed the interviews with Katherine, it was clear that even though I grew up in a hierarchical, blue collar family, I was sheltered from many of the hardships and challenges the women faced throughout their lives. Today, I sit in a position of privilege; my life is nothing like most of the women interviewed. This tension between *who they are* and *who we are* influences not just the interview process, but all aspects of the research process.

In what ways does revealing our social location create both truth and vulnerability?

PAUL: Liz and I are not fans of the word *truth*, because *truths* seem to us to be so relative, depending on social position, language use, the limitations of knowing, social context, and much else. As we said in our chapter, we worked hard to be clear with each other about our social location(s) regarding knowing and not knowing in intimate relationships. That was important in all phases of the research, helping us to know how our experiences might stimulate or make trouble in conceptualizing, interviewing, analyzing the data, and writing. I would say there was vulnerability in doing that self-disclosure, that we could not have done much of it without a lot of mutual trust. We did not reveal our social location to people we interviewed or to readers of the book we wrote, though I imagine it was easy for them to assume we had our own relationships to the topic. I believe our decision not to reveal our social location to interviewees and readers was not about truth or vulnerability, but about how much we wanted interviewee voices to carry the narrative. But then if we were working on a different topic, we might do things very differently.

KATHERINE: I have conducted qualitative interview studies for four decades, and one insight I have over these many years is that my revelations to participants about my own experiences are not all that important to their willingness and ability to share their stories with me. Rather, I have found that participants are more interested in telling their own stories, and my job is to listen, and to use my own experience as a way to anticipate the kinds of questions and probes that will enable their own deep storytelling. It does help, however, to gain access to a community and to the details of a person's life story, if I have been sensitized through lived experience to the issues I'm asking participants to talk with me about (e.g., loss of a loved one, family caregiving, health crisis, lesbian motherhood, divorce), but once in the field, the details of my own experiences of loss, change, trauma, and the like must fade in order to make room for me to bear witness to another's perceptions and experiences about what has happened to them. One of the lessons I have learned from the aftermath of my own son's death as a young man is that there are no predictably *right* words that someone else can say to me that might be helpful in the moment, and so, my own social location, in that moment, as a bereaved parent, especially if I am interviewing someone who has suffered a great loss as well, is to put my own identity and experiences aside and pay attention to them. In conducting data analysis, I journal fiercely throughout the process, because my own emotional reactions are a constant intrusion on reading through transcripts and sorting through data. Ultimately, sharing the products of data analysis—with my co-analysts, with live audiences, and throughout the publication process—are some of the best *checks* on imposing my own narrow slice of understanding onto the topics I study.

LIZ: Paul captured our sentiments about truth statements in social science research and how we approached sharing our social location with participants on the intimacy project. I concur with Katherine about participants mostly being interested in sharing their stories, with less interest in how we might present ourselves. This leads me to reflect on another dimension related to action-based social justice research. I have experienced underrepresented and vulnerable communities become increasingly sophisticated in screening potential collaborators and holding scholars accountable for their work. It is impossible for me to completely disentangle the expectations I bring to the table versus what I perceive the communities I work with to expect from me, but I believe it is critical to be explicit about one's motivations for conducting research with vulnerable populations, even when it means a commitment to a longer engagement process upfront to enhance the likelihood of shared expectations for how research outcomes might further their own interests.

BETHANY: As I read through your responses, I have been pushed to think about my social location versus (and) my connection to the topic of study. In conducting interviews and analyzing data, I agree with Paul and Liz about the importance of being critically conscious and reflexive about my social location and my ability to bracket my experiences and grow understanding, particularly around difference. How I am perceived by others, how I perceive others, and how my social location may help or hinder trust-building are all part of the dance or the art of the interview. I find myself working hard to negotiate those spaces to build authentic human connections across social locations. As Liz notes, particularly in social justice work, we must hold ourselves accountable (as communities increasingly hold us accountable) to these critical and just processes so we do not replicate color/gender/class-blind, decontextualized, or misaligned research practices that do more harm than good.

Yet, as I read Katherine's words, I realized that I hold a belief that my connection and my own experience to a topic of interest (e.g., trauma, loss, resilience) can be transcendent. As Katherine shared, I too bring my history of trauma and loss into our interviews—not verbally, not by retelling my story—but by connecting to the topic and opening up to vulnerability while bearing witness to and taking in another's telling of their story sans judgment, and feeling my way through probes with sensitivity, compassion, and empathy. As with Katherine's process, I hope that our collaborative data analyses and dissemination processes have resulted in deeper understanding, in this case, of undocumented immigrant women's lived experiences.

A few references that have been helpful to my thinking are Pollner's (1991) call for radical reflexivity and Tervalon and Murray-Garcia's (1998) piece on cultural humility. I also appreciate and have been challenged in a good way by Smith's (2012) work on decolonizing methodologies.

KATHERINE: One responsibility I surmise that we all share is that our own social locations must be in service to the people we are working with and whose lives we are studying. I agree that our motivations for doing research must be examined and held up to scrutiny. For me, a core part of this examination process occurs through writing—including reflexive memos about issues that arise during interviewing, and through the publication process of subjecting my interpretations to the scrutiny of peers, who are often much harder to convince than those whose experiences I'm actually describing. What keeps me going, though, is that the research I do must *matter*—not just to myself, but also to be in service to the people whose experiences I'm trying to shed new light on. Conducting research that matters is another feminist principle that has infused my work for decades.

KAREN: I really do not have much more to offer. Your comments resonate with me and my view of who I am as a researcher and my responsibility to others when I take on that role. As each of you have commented in one way or another, it is the voices of interviewees that are of utmost importance and need to be clearly and accurately heard throughout the process of interviewing, analyzing, and disseminating our findings. As I tell my students, of course I like the accolades that go along with publishing our research findings and advancing the study of aging, but it is when, after giving a public lecture, an old woman comes up to me and asks, "How did you know my story?" that I know that my research does indeed make a difference. And, that is what it is all about!

References

Krieger, S. (1991). *Social science & the self: Personal essays on an art form.* New Brunswick, NJ: Rutgers University Press.

Pollner, M. (1991). Left of ethnometholology: The rise and decline of radical reflexivity. *American Sociological Review, 56,* 370–380.

Smith, L. T. (2012). *Decolonizing methodologies: Research and indigenous peoples* (2nd ed.). New York, NY: Zed Books.

Tervalon, M., & Murray-Garcia, J. (1998). Cultural humility versus cultural competence: A critical distinction in defining physician training outcomes in multicultural education. *Journal of Health Care for the Poor and Underserved, 9*(2), 117–125.

16

DIALOGUE ABOUT QUALITATIVE DATA ANALYSIS SOFTWARE

Tyler Jamison, Candace L. Kemp, Katherine E. Speirs, Andrea Swenson, and Colleen K. Vesely

Does using a CAQDAS (computer-assisted qualitative data analysis) software program influence how you carry out your qualitative analysis (for example, if you did your qualitative analysis for other studies without CAQDAS software before, do you notice a change in what you are doing now?)? In what ways has it changed or not changed, and why do you think that is?

CANDACE: I had not yet been introduced to qualitative software when I worked on my first qualitative research project, which involved participant observation and 10 formal interviews. The coding process was similar in terms of reviewing the data and assigning and organizing codes, but I did all of it by hand on hard copies of fieldnotes and transcripts using different colored highlighters to assign/indicate codes and paper folders for each coding category. Since that time, my research has evolved to larger projects and team research and I have used various iterations of QSR NVivo (previously NUD*IST). The software has not changed the underlying coding concepts and analysis, but facilitates collaboration and more sophisticated analysis than by hand in terms of allowing quick searches of simultaneous instances of multiple codes (e.g. caregiving, communication, and health decline) or searching on participant types (e.g., widowed women) or specific research sites.

TYLER: I have always used qualitative coding software for open coding, so unlike you, Candace, I can't make a before-and-after comparison. I do think that using coding software allows me to be a bit more flexible in my approach to coding. I can easily recode a section or change the name of a code without going back through all of the previous transcripts and carrying out the change. This gives me the freedom to get it wrong the first time, which puts me at ease about coding. The other way that software changes the research process for me is in terms of writing. Having easy access to all of the quotes under one theme allows me to add lots of rich data examples into my manuscripts without returning to the raw data. This is an aspect of convenience that changes the narrative quality of my publications.

COLLEEN: Like you, Tyler, I have always used some sort of CAQDAS program, particularly for open coding. Over time as my knowledge and understanding of qualitative methods, and specifically formal coding, have increased I have gained a better sense of and greater comfort in how to use these tools in ways that work best for various research projects and me/my way of thinking and organizing. In particular, I have gained comfort in moving back and forth between paper and pencil strategies and using CAQDAS software. When possible I prefer to open code in ATLAS.ti, for reasons like the one you noted, Tyler, being able to change the names of codes as analyses evolve is really helpful. In addition, I have no counterfactual, but it seems my persistence with keeping a detailed codebook is likely better when using a CAQDAS program as it is so easy to update right as I am coding.

KATE: Colleen, your last point really resonates with me. I don't think I would be nearly as good about keeping a detailed and up-to-date codebook if I had to do it in a separate document. Even being able to write code definitions in a CAQDAS program, I find that sometimes I neglect to update them as my thinking about the codes changes. I also appreciate how easy CAQDAS programs make it to pull together all of the quotes associated with one code. Having always used CAQDAS software, I can't imagine having to do this by hand or using index cards laid out on a table or the floor. I think my analysis is more rigorous because I can easily pull together all of the quotes associated with one code and make sure they are all describing the same idea or phenomena. I do this multiple times and continue to do it as I write up my findings. I think I might be more likely to go with my first idea or understanding of the data if this were not so easy to do using a CAQDAS program.

TYLER: Colleen and Kate, I think your discussion about keeping a detailed codebook is a great one—and it relates to the issue of working on teams as well. When multiple people are creating codes, it is necessary for them to define them carefully so that others can come through and use the code as it was intended. CAQDAS programs make that process much easier.

KATE: Tyler, I have found the same thing, a CAQDAS program makes it easier to keep track of codes as a team. Though I find it's also necessary, at least in the beginning, to talk in person or on the phone about the codes to make sure everyone is on the same page.

ANDREA: I agree with Kate and Tyler, that CAQDAS is useful with teams. I would add that the use of CAQDAS software programs is also helpful with large quantities of data. In examining differences between projects in which CAQDAS software was used versus not, I think the use related to the volume of data (but not depth of analysis) and the number of individuals involved in the analysis.

What is it like to use a CAQDAS program with multiple team members?

CANDACE: It is difficult for me to imagine how it would be possible to organize and manage large data sets collected and analyzed by multiple team members, including students, who may not be part of the study for the entire duration, without computer-assisted qualitative data analysis software. Everyone is able to work on the project simultaneously and frequently, remotely. The coder comparison feature allows us to understand how consistently coders are applying codes, which is essential in teamwork. And, multiple team members are also able to simultaneously enter and code data.

COLLEEN: Unlike Candace, it is working in larger teams that has somewhat precluded an extensive use of ATLAS.ti for me. Specifically, as I worked on a project with another faculty member (a Mac user) and a couple of graduate students a few years back, we discovered that despite the Mac version of ATLAS.ti being released, the Mac and PC versions didn't *talk* well to each other. Specifically, we could not use the copy bundle feature across the Mac and PC versions of ATLAS.ti. My graduate student still checks in with IT support at ATLAS.ti every so often to understand if this feature has been fixed, and to my knowledge it still has not been fixed. As a result we used ATLAS.ti to store and manage the qualitative data for the entire project. For open coding, we were able to borrow a PC from our college for students to use, and conduct open coding in ATLAS.ti for the project this way. However, as we moved into axial coding our coding in teams moved back to paper. Candace, have you run into any issues using Macs and PCs with NVivo? Or have you had any issues during particular phases of formal coding?

CANDACE: The [in]compatibility issue between Mac and PC version of NVivo is one of the reasons that I and other faculty have resisted switching to Mac over the years. All of our team members use PCs and we have avoided any potential pitfalls. As we move to axial coding, we typically switch over to paper too and ultimately create analysis charts populated with data and diagrams in Microsoft Word. This move is not so much a software limitation, but a preference and possibly a user limitation that speaks to the next set of questions.

COLLEEN: That makes sense, Candace, especially in terms of user limitations—or project limitations. In some of the community-based participatory research (CBPR) work in which I am involved, as we work with community members to conduct coding, using a CAQDAS program becomes particularly cumbersome due to resources, as well as the flow of group coding meetings. We often open code using paper and pencil, and then as time consuming as it might be, we enter these open codes into ATLAS.ti to help with organizing codes for axial coding. We then conduct axial coding with community members by using analysis charts in Microsoft's Excel program. As I reflect, it seems that my preference is to use CAQDAS software for open coding but depending on project circumstances this does not always look the same.

KATE: I have used Dedoose which is an online CAQDAS program for analysis with groups. It gets around the Mac/PC compatibility issues and allows for real time sharing. Everyone logs in to the same project and can see each other's codes and coding. It's also relatively inexpensive, which makes it easier to work with students. However, I think there are some limitations in terms of the interface and exporting codes to Word documents for work outside of the CAQDAS program.

TYLER: I think all of these comments speak to the challenges of conducting qualitative research in groups. Coding alone is tricky because it is easy to get entrenched in the data and lose perspective about the narrative you're creating. However, working in groups poses practical challenges like computer compatibility and other struggles with how to get everyone on the same page during coding (literally and figuratively). I have worked with teams in Dedoose and I never felt we got to a good place with group coding. The limitations of the software (as Kate pointed out) paired with the lack of norms for coding in teams made meetings long and arduous. This seems to be an area where qualitative researchers might benefit from sharing resources about best practices for coding in groups. I can imagine that successful qualitative teams could articulate their processes in a way that might benefit others.

KATE: Yes! It would be great to hear more about how people do qualitative analysis in teams. This is something that I'm also working to figure out, especially for groups of three or more. It's a shame that there usually isn't room in journal articles to describe this process in detail.

ANDREA: CAQDAS software worked well for our team and the project goals. We had two laptops set up in the project laboratory that students would do coding on for the project using MAXQDA software. While this limited flexibility in terms of when and where students could code, this ensured that there were at least two people present that could discuss questions that emerged during the coding process.

What are your thoughts on all the features available in your program (what parts of your program did you use, what didn't you use, and why)?

CANDACE: I confess to not using NVivo to its fullest capacity and am working on learning more about the program, particularly its ability to facilitate analysis of network data. To date, I have mostly used the program to store, organize, and code the data. When it comes to analysis, the teams I have led or worked on mostly use node searches and queries to search on specific topics, participants, and research sites.

TYLER: Candace, my use of NVivo is nearly identical to you. I wonder sometimes if I am missing out on important features of the software, but it seems to work better for me to code and organize the data using NVivo and then step back and do the higher-order thinking through writing and modeling on paper. That said, I have recently started using MAXQDA to analyze a mixed methods dataset. Now that I have more quantitative data to go along with interview transcripts, it may be beneficial for me to learn about other features of this software to make the best use of the information I have.

COLLEEN: As I reflect on what both of you have written, as someone who also does not use ATLAS.ti to its fullest capacity, it makes me think of the time it takes to keep up with all the features of CAQDAS software programs, and how this bumps up against other time pressures of the academy and research-oriented positions. I think back to when I was a graduate student and what a luxury it was the attend a training on ATLAS.ti—I often reflect on the discussions in this training in which using ATLAS.ti with a team of coders was discussed (this was not my reality at the time as I was dissertating), and tell myself that I need to go back to my notes or explore this more. But because of resource constraints (time and money for training) I tend to stick with the features I know.

KATE: I am also guilty of not taking advantage of all of the features that ATLAS.ti and Dedoose have to offer, and primarily use them for open and axial coding. I am quite sure that there are features that I don't even know exist but might find useful. Part of this is likely, as Colleen mentioned, the tradeoff between the time it takes to learn something new and just doing it the way you've always done it even if it might be less efficient. I wonder if part of it is also that for axial and selective coding some of this work and thinking happens when I'm away from my desk doing something else or talking to someone about the project and can then think through how to make sense of the data or am able to see the data in a new way. I think to some extent, for me, this work will never be done (or at least not exclusively done) while sitting in front of a computer using a CAQDAS program.

TYLER: Kate, I think you make a really important point about where, when, and how qualitative analysis really happens. When the researcher is the analytical tool, the work is happening all the time as we move through our day by having conversations with colleagues or chatting with our partners over dinner. For me, the most important analysis often happens while writing. I arrive at a tentative core concept or structure for the results and then I try to write it up with support from the data. I find out quickly where the gaps are and then I can return to the raw data (and the CAQDAS program) and regroup. So it's also true for me that I will never do all of my analysis at the computer, even if I fully mastered a software package.

ANDREA: In a similar vein, I do not use MAXQDA to the fullest extent. I agree with Kate and Tyler on the importance of the researcher. For me, the software is a tool and extent of use depends on the aim of the study and the analytic strategy of the researcher. There are plenty of useful features to explore and that can help provide insight into data. In the study discussed in this book, the software was mainly used as a means to organize data and to easily retrieve segments of transcripts for the researchers to analyze. I have used different functions within MAXQDA to visualize codes, which has been useful to see codes in individual transcripts in relation to codes in other family member transcripts.

People often don't talk about how they use their CAQDAS software programs in their research. Aside from the issue of space (e.g., journal articles with specific page limits), why do you think this is?

CANDACE: Aside from space, which is a very pragmatic issue, beyond mentioning use of a specific program, describing how it is used has not become part of the scientific reporting protocol. However, as qualitative software evolves, I think it would be very helpful to understand how researchers use it and under what circumstances.

TYLER: I agree with you, Candace, that we all tend to leave out details if we don't think reviewers will be looking for them. Space is too precious. However, I think the other piece is that I don't want to admit all of the ways I *didn't* use the software. Candace said she had to *confess* that she doesn't use NVivo fully, and I feel the same way. If I can avoid admitting that I only use qualitative software for organizing and basic coding, I do.

CANDACE: Well said, Tyler. If I think about it carefully, I believe that I share your underlying reason for not fully discussing how I use the software.

KATE: In addition to what the two of you have said, I am also very careful to say that I used ATLAS.ti (or whatever software program I used) to *organize* my data analysis because I want to be clear that the software did not do the analysis. I (or the team) did the analysis, the software just helped me keep track of it. I think how we use software for qualitative analysis is different from how it's used for quantitative analysis and although the structure of the software and how it organizes and stores codes and memos may impact our analysis I think it has less of an impact than quantitative software. So I probably avoid talking in detail about the software I used so as to avoid giving the impression (mainly for audiences not familiar with qualitative analysis) that the software in some way produced the themes that I am reporting.

COLLEEN: I agree with everything stated by all of you. And I just looked back at a few publications to recall how extensively I noted the use of ATLAS.ti in my work. It seems I tend to indicate my use of ATLAS.ti for managing the data, but do not discuss how I used ATLAS.ti through each phase of analysis. Even more than space, I tend to reflect what Kate stated in terms of not wanting to give the impression that the CAQDAS program actually produced the themes. However, this conversation is making me think that by including more details regarding the use of CAQDAS programs, we may help educate audiences who are less familiar with qualitative analyses with exactly how the analyses are done—with CAQDAS software being but one (potential) tool in the analysis process.

ANDREA: I think space is the primary reason there is not as much discussion of CAQDAS. With limited space available in a manuscript, we need to communicate clearly and effectively our analytic process. While we used the software, we did the analytic process rather than the software doing it for us. For example, we had a reviewer state they were unclear on how we used the software and asked us to clarify our role in the analysis. This resulted in a focus on the process and our role and put the software in the background, which was true to the analytic process.

17

DIALOGUE ABOUT DATA DISPLAY

H. Daniel Castellanos, Mary M. Ball, and
Anisa Zvonkovic

What kind of data displays (e.g., matrices, graphs, charts, networks, or maps) did you use in your study?

MARY: The aim of the research reported on in my chapter was to understand the structure and function of assisted living residents' care convoys and how and why they varied within and across homes and over time. Primarily we used two types of data displays in our analyses: (a) charts (i.e., Microsoft Word tables), and (b) diagrams. We used charts throughout analysis and on several analytic levels. Initial charts focused on individual residents and facilitated, for example, identification of network members and their care roles, changes over time, care outcomes, and influential factors. Building on initial charts, subsequent charts compared and contrasted convoys within and across homes. Diagrams allowed a more visual representation of the structure and function of individual convoys and their transitions.

DANIEL: Like you, Mary, I also used data displays over the course of the concurrent data collection and analysis exploring the relation between sexual orientation and homelessness among 14 young Latino gay and bisexual men in New York City. I relied on tables and matrices created in Word and the network views created in ATLAS.ti to further the axial and selective coding as well as the data collection. In particular, tables and matrices were used to visualize how categories related to each other. Networks views were used primarily during the last part of the analytical process to create explanatory narratives of specific areas of inquiry.

ANISA: It's interesting that you both used tables in Word (that I think you created from analysis) and that Mary's process was maybe more similar to ours in the use of charts and diagrams, outside of any qualitative software program. In our study, we used data displays at a few points in our analytic process: to help us to summarize data across families (with more than the typical number of families in the data set, we had about 100 families); and later, when we had themes, to get a quick understanding about the prevalence of elements within the themes. All of this was done outside of a software program.

MARY: Correct, this data display work was done without the qualitative software program. We used NVivo 11 to facilitate earlier analyses, primarily to code and then sort data related to our 28 focal residents/convoys and other relevant categories, such as care interactions. However, we then used Word to create diagrams and figures and likely underutilized the NVivo software.

DANIEL: It's interesting that we all decided not to use some of the features of the analytical software for data display. In my case, I realized that Word gave me more flexibility to display and manipulate the data than ATLAS.ti. Specifically, it was easier for me to move and create columns or split and combine tables to display the data in different ways, allowing me to explore connections between different categories.

Why have using matrices, graphs, maps, etc. been helpful in your research?

MARY: Because of the vast amount of qualitative data we collected across 28 focal residents and their care convoys across four assisted living settings and the complexity of the data, charts proved essential in understanding variation across residents and homes and identifying patterns in the structure and function of convoys. Ultimately charts facilitated deeper analysis with axial coding, identification of our core category, and the development of our pattern typology and conceptual model.

DANIEL: While my number of respondents was smaller than you, Mary and Anisa, tables were still also essential in understanding variations across respondents, including stories of coming out, family conflict, and home separation. For instance, I created a table with the distribution (presence) of family conflict categories developed during axial coding in the narratives of the respondents.

As the analysis became more complex, tables became less focused on distribution and sought to describe relations between categories. The relationships between these categories were better expressed through a matrix. For instance, I created a matrix with grouping types of family conflict (column subheaders) based on whether they were examples of non-gay related conflict or conflict over sexual orientation (column headers) for each respondent (row). In addition to mapping out the distribution of different types of conflict, this matrix helped me visualize the co-occurrence of different types of conflict.

Diagrams (using ATLAS.ti's "Network view" function) created in ATLAS. ti were mostly used during selective coding to create explanatory models that could shed light on the chief reasons for housing instability. ATLAS.ti networks are particularly useful for developing these explanations because in addition to helping establish connections between different categories, they provide ready access to memos and primary data (fragments of the interviews). For instance, I created a network view for family conflict related to gay lifestyle (a subcategory of family conflict related to sexual orientation) that included a collections of quotations, memos, and codes.

ANISA: Our study had a lot more respondents, nested within families. I think compared to your projects, our data were not as thick. But the challenge was always keeping all family members distinct while keeping the larger family as a unit of analysis, different from the types of projects you all have.

When I think beyond the paper on which my chapter is based and consider other papers and research projects, charts and other visual displays have been helpful in a few ways, in these different studies. In a paper published in the *Journal of Social and Personal Relationships*, we used pie charts in order to essentially derive typologies of individuals and, later, couples. The pie charts displayed how codes within categories were distributed within the interviews of each interviewee; then we compared the pie charts within couples. We thought it was very interesting that although the exact codes differed between partners within a couple, the distribution of categories did not. Therefore, we established that each member of the couple fell into the same typology, thereby demonstrating that our typology was a couple typology.

More generally, these tools have been helpful in summarizing large amounts of data, and then comparing and contrasting within families. My general method has been to gather interview data from members of the same family, and so graphs, charts, etc. have been helpful in order to summarize information.

MARY: In our study, focal residents were nested within care convoys (families and a variety of formal caregivers) and then within assisted living facilities and local communities. It is indeed a challenge to understand these various influences at different levels and we found ourselves designing and redesigning charts during the analytic process.

ANISA: I think that the analytic process of trying out one type of chart or one type of data display, then abandoning that and trying another, is worth discussing a bit more. Maybe because by the time an article is written, a coherent story line necessitates *sanitizing* that messy process. So it seem like readers are left with an impression that other scholars are *successful* in their original decisions about data reduction, etc. For us, we tried many different things. Each effort helped us get more familiar with our data, and helps us to consider whether the data reduction technique captured something important or something superficial. And then we tried again! Is that true for you all? There's also the interesting issue of working with a team and how to normalize this iterative process for them. I'm curious about the people on your team and how you worked with them.

MARY: I completely agree, Anisa. Trying and re-trying is definitely how we operate! Frequently, we design a chart and then discover as we are attempting to *put* the data in it, it just doesn't work the way we envisaged. In this iterative process sometimes the focus of analysis even changes as, like you say, we get more familiar with the data. As an example, in a current analysis to better understand communication within and across convoys, our initial charts examining types and modes of communication and influential factors led us to concentrate the analysis on communication surrounding health transitions. We then were able to utilize/combine previously developed charts that addressed health care delivery and heath transitions over time with initial communication charts. I might add also that sometimes it feels as if we develop analyses that never are fully used.

 We work with a large team that includes faculty members and students. Generally we take a divide and conquer approach and assign various analytic areas to smaller groups. Usually one person will design a preliminary chart and then the rest of the group will *try it out*. We typically meet as a group to discuss how the tactic is working, a process that often leads to a redesign.

DANIEL: I think that the process of creating chart, tables, matrices, and networks that we seem to be describing is not so different from the core processes/features of textual analysis, including reiterations, coherent story lines, deeper familiarity of the data, and data reduction, among other analytical processes. Similar to the development of higher order categories or analytical memos, each iteration of a matrix, for instance, provided me with a better understanding of the participants' narratives and the commonalities and differences among them. I would also add that sometimes I redesigned a matrix not necessarily to include or exclude data but to reorganize the data so that it highlighted a particular argument. For example, by organizing different types of family conflict (columns) along participant's age at first occurrence, the matrix created different temporal trajectories of family conflict and homelessness.

In their 2014 book, *Qualitative Data Analysis: A Methods Sourcebook* (3rd ed.), Miles, Huberman, and Saldaña state that *designing* a display (e.g., "deciding on the rows and columns of a matrix for a qualitative data and deciding which data, in which form, should be entered in the cells" – p. 13) *is an analytic activity.* What are your thoughts on this?

MARY: Although I have limited experience with using a matrix in these authors' sense in analysis of qualitative data, I would agree that the design of the display would require analysis, including when to use the technique and with what types of data. In our current research the matrix technique might be useful in examining data from additional homes and residents for fit with the existing pattern typology.

DANIEL: At the most basic level, tables in my research were used to examine the distribution of particular characteristics of the interview subjects or key life events in their lives. For instance, a table of types of family disruption and conflict allowed me to examine the most common reasons of conflict and disruption (e.g., separation from biological parent) versus less common ones (e.g., severe abuse and neglect). As the analysis grows in complexity, matrices were used to examine patterns, co-occurrences, and relations rather than frequencies. While the creation of a table is in itself a categorizing decision, a tabular table with frequencies is limited to help determine more complex and multivariate patterns. As you have said, Mary, matrices are useful for examining pattern typologies. The creation of matrices requires a greater analytical effort to determine the groups and subgroups of columns or rows.

ANISA: I agree with you both, and I bet others would as well. How we array data is an analytic decision. It seems like the challenge is justifying and explaining each decision along the way. Experienced qualitative researchers like you two have a sense of playing with different approaches and knowing what approach is yielding interesting information from which a story can emerge. I think that many elements of study design can be analytic activities. Deciding on rows and columns is analytic and I think that it's important that authors try out different ways of displaying rows and columns, displaying different elements. All of these data reduction techniques need to be considered as tentative ways of showing what the data tell us, and should never be a substitute for going back to individual cases and keeping attention on what participants say.

MARY: Anisa, I like the way you said "playing around with different approaches" because that is exactly what I find happens frequently. In a current analysis focusing on communication within convoys we have done just that, regularly going back to fieldnote and interview data related to individuals.

DANIEL: I could be wrong but I feel that we are all saying that these data displays helped us visualize and formulate relations between different categories along patterns, typologies, or co-occurrence. Like both of you, I spent some time designing and redesigning the visual displays. I agree, Anisa, that deciding on rows and columns is analytic. At the same time, I am not sure if I could pinpoint for each table why I would conclude that the table version was final. I guess that I checked that the table was honest to the data and that it told an overarching story, including gaps. I hope this makes sense.

Reference

Miles, M. B., Huberman, A. M., & Saldaña, J. (2014). *Qualitative data analysis: A methods sourcebook* (3rd ed.). Los Angeles, CA: Sage.

INDEX

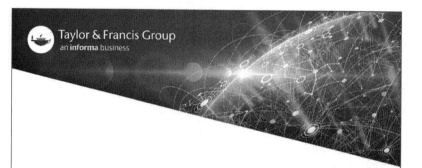